BODYBUILDING
NUTRITION

BODYBUILDING NUTRITION

Mandy Tanny

HarperPerennial
A Division of HarperCollinsPublishers

First HarperPerennial edition published 1991.

Library of Congress Cataloging-in-Publication Data

Tanny, Mandy.
    Bodybuilding nutrition / by Mandy Tanny.—1st ed.
        p.
    Includes index.
    ISBN 0-06-096497-9 (pbk.)
    1. Bodybuilders—Nutrition.   2. Cookery.   I. Title.
TX361.B64T36   1991
613.2—dc20   90-55817

    92 93 94 95 DT/RRD 10 9 8 7 6 5 4 3 2

CONTENTS

▼

FOREWORD

When you think of the health of our nation, it is clear that most of our health problems are not caused by the infectious diseases that used to plague us. The biggest threat to our health today is poor nutrition and lack of exercise. When we don't eat right or exercise enough, we lay the groundwork for heart disease, stroke, and diabetes—fatal disorders that have become epidemic. These present-day illnesses aren't going to be cured by drugs or vaccines. What it will take are preventive measures. That means direct involvement by you.

You have to take control of your life by eliminating such dangerous health habits as smoking, drinking, overeating, and lack of exercise. It's ridiculous to wait for a heart attack before learning good health habits. Although medicine in the United States has developed very technical and competent solutions to many health problems, the main thrust of any personal health program depends on what we put into our bodies. In other words, we are what we eat.

As the publisher of several major health and fitness magazines, I determined to cover the full spectrum of health-related subjects. Among the columns in my flagship magazine, *Muscle and Fitness,* is Mandy Tanny's Muscular Gourmet, which has been a big hit worldwide for nearly a decade. Mandy has taken all the facts of proper nutrition and blended them into gourmet meals fit for a king. Rather than a punishing, diet-type eating, she offers an underlying philosophy of pleasurable eating that complements any training program geared for maximum health and fitness. She tells you how to change your eating habits without taking the pleasure out of life. Her prandial blandishments are irresistible.

I have the utmost respect and admiration for Mandy Tanny and her work. I urge you to read this book, her second one on the subject dedicated to rewarding the workout experience with delectable repasts that will make a perfect body and perfect health a reality.

JOE WEIDER
Publisher and Editor,
Muscle and Fitness Magazine

— PART ONE —
NUTRITION PRIMER

Photo: Michele Mattei

— 1 —
PERFECT NUTRITION

Many people feel they are lucky to go through life in a state of average health. They think if they are not sick or dying, they are okay. They can't explain why they don't look the way they want to look, why they don't feel energetic all the time, and why they are not as strong as they would like to be. They just accept aches and pains, insomnia, allergies, digestive disorders, obesity, and even stress as normal. But the reason for this state of average health is average nourishment, a diet that does not produce a high level of health, only normal health.

For many years while we are young, we can eat any foods we like and show no real signs of illness, but the degeneration starts from within. Depending on our constitution and how well or how badly we have cared for our bodies, degeneration will manifest itself in the insidious form of those "normal afflictions" eventually leading to premature aging and disease, a condition we also accept as a "normal" part of life. This leads us to doctors, many of whom do not have a clear picture of how interacting nutrients work toward Perfect Nutrition and whose purpose now is to cure, not prevent. Because of the doctor's position, his or her job is to treat the medical symptom; the nutritional problem is yours.

What does this have to do with bodybuilding? Everything, because building our bodies can be done only at a level of high health with Perfect Nutrition. How can we build maximum muscle if we are semi-healthy? Muscle building is a luxury, something our bodies will save for last after it has taken all the nutrients it needs for other functions. If you don't fortify your body with the best, it won't reach its maximum potential, no matter how much work you put into it.

NUTRITION'S BEST-KEPT SECRET

Muscle building starts at the cellular level with optimum health. And that starts with Perfect Nutrition based on a balanced diet of natural foods of high biological quality. High biological quality has been given various definitions in the area of nutrition, but the dictionary defines it as "the science of life in relation to living organisms collectively." The word "living" is the key. All food in the beginning is alive and contains living enzymes within its cells until we apply heat to it by cooking it. Consider this: If we are going to regenerate, nourish, and build the living cells within our bodies, are we going to replenish them with devitalized cells from cooked food? Cooked food can sustain a level of life, but it won't optimally enhance it. Since we are in the business of building our bodies, simply sustaining it won't do.

By old standards good nutrition was judged by the biochemical condition of food, how many vitamins and minerals it contained. Newer standards include protein, fiber, fats, and cholesterol. But we have been overlooking something of vital and primary importance—the biological condition, the aliveness of the food and the premise for Perfect Nutrition. Let the food live and all other nutritional factors will remain intact and in balance naturally.

ENZYME POWER

All plant and animal foods consist of protein, vitamins, minerals, and living enzymes, all of which are made up of active molecules. It is a widely recognized fact that cooking destroys or reduces the vitamin and mineral content of most foods. What is little known is that this is linked with the destruction of living enzymes made up of these molecules. Enzyme destruction occurs when food is heated or cooked at a temperature of 118°F. The higher the heat and the longer the food is cooked, the greater the degree of destruction. These molecules become hindered and lose their microelectric potential. The enzymes necessary to rejuvenate living cells and digest nutrients are then deactivated. This greatly reduces the energy exchange among the other nutrients and nutrient disbursement becomes impaired.

Because cooking destroys the living nature of food, the body reacts to cooked food as a foreign substance. In self-defense, the immune system kicks in and the intestine must continually produce white blood cells to fight it off as long as cooked food is ingested, which in most cases is a lifetime. As a result, the rest of the body's defenses are less armed and more susceptible to illness, disease, aging, and chronic little conditions we accept as a matter of life. But that's not all. When we eat cooked food and denature the enzymes necessary for digestion, the body has to rev up and manufacture its own. The pancreatic hormones have to work harder, which in turn leads to all of the body's systems working on overload. Aside from continually not feeling or being in a state of high health, this mishmash of faulty mechanism is what ultimately hampers muscle building. The bottom line: The more you give your body in the way of Perfect Nutrition and the less you make it work to compensate for faulty nutrition, the more you will get out of your bodybuilding efforts for maximum gain.

THE PERMANENT WAY TO LOWER BODY FAT

Whether food is eaten cooked or raw also plays an important role in body fat composition. Cooked food overstimulates the pancreatic juices that make you want to eat more. That in turn overstimulates the glands and hormones that metabolize calories into fat. It throws your "appe-stat" off, so you eat without really knowing when to stop. And your body won't let you because it is trying to get all the nutrients it can from depleted food. It takes more cooked food than raw food to give your body what it needs. When food is eaten raw, less is needed because the body utilizes 100 percent of the available nutrients. And less is eaten, because raw food contains more fiber and bulk. Raw foods also see to it that your body receives a constant, long-lasting supply of glucose necessary to keep your blood sugar stable and hunger under control. If glucose enters the bloodstream too quickly, as it can with cooked food, your body cannot handle it all at once and converts it into excess fat. Soon your glucose level is down and your blood sugar is low again, and you are hungry for more cooked food. It is a vicious weight-gaining cycle where you are the loser. Quite simply, calories become more fattening when cooked, therefore raw foods are the answer to overall lower body fat and successful weight control.

ESSENTIALIZE YOUR DIET

Does all this mean you are supposed to eat only raw foods for the rest of your life? No, not at all. You don't have to jump into the fire to get warm, but you can dance around it. In the course of evolution we have adapted admirably to cooked foods, especially the protein foods. But we have also received miraculous benefits from raw foods, especially the carbohydrate foods. Ideally our diets should be comprised of both cooked and raw foods, divided equally at least, and under controlled conditions. This means you can't waste calories.

Your purpose is to build your body. Whether you want to gain muscle, lose fat, or just maintain your present condition, everything you eat must support that cause. It must be in proportion and it must be essential. Based on the government's recommended daily amount of nutrients and the proper ratios of protein, fats, and carbohydrates combined with our present standards of eating, it is impossible to have Perfect Nutrition and get all that we need every day from a largely cooked diet. This is bad news for the average person, and worse for the bodybuilder, because the bodybuilder's needs are even higher!

So here is what to do. Start by "essentializing" your diet. Eat all types of fresh fruits and vegetables, raw nuts, seeds, sprouted grains, unrefined or cold-pressed oils, eggs (see Muscle-Building Breakfast Drinks, page 134, for handling and heat treatment), aged cheeses made from raw or cultured milk, or any other dairy products you can obtain made from certified raw milk. These foods are of *excellent biological quality*. Next are the cooked essentials: meats, poultry, fish, eggs, whole grains, legumes, nuts, seeds, fruits, vegetables, and pasteurized milk products. These foods are of *good biological quality* because they are cooked, but are of *primary value* because they are directly from the natural animal or plant source, with no steps of destructive processing in between their natural source and your plate. Next are foods that have been cooked and processed, but made from foods of *good biological quality*. These include whole-grain breads, pastries, pastas, and cereals, and any cooked foods of *primary value* that have been further frozen, canned, packaged, or otherwise tampered with. These foods become of *fair biological quality* and of *secondary value*. With any luck they will have gone through no more than two steps of cooking or processing before they reach your plate. Last are the foods of *poor biological quality*. These include most foods in a can, bottle, or package that have gone through two or more steps of cooking or processing and have a long shelf life. This also includes foods that contain refined sugar, white flour, hydrogenated fats and oils, and any chemicals that promote better and longer storage and enhance the food unnaturally. Many prepared packaged, canned, and frozen foods, fast foods and "junk foods" fall into this category. They offer inferior ingredients, fat-inducing calories, and by the standards of Perfect Nutrition, are of very little value. Stay away from them.

THE BACKBONE OF NUTRITION

Perfect Nutrition begins at the cellular level with vital foods, and these vital foods are comprised of three constituents: protein, fats, and carbohydrates. Their purpose is to build cells and provide energy. It's a team effort. The extent and efficiency to which these functions are carried out depends on the presence, quality, and balance of proteins, fats, and carbohydrates. If any one of these factors is in default, all bodily functions, including muscle building, will be impaired.

PROTEIN—THE BLOCKBUSTER OF NUTRITION

New discoveries are constantly being made about protein, but one thing is certain—protein is becoming increasingly important in our diet. Protein is what builds and repairs cells and promotes life and growth. It is the very source of life. Fats, starches, and sugars all contain elements of carbon, hydrogen, and oxygen, but protein contains nitrogen as well, something humans can obtain only from protein. Keeping nitrogen in balance with adequate protein is an important muscle-building factor.

Protein is made up of approximately twenty-two to twenty-five known amino acids (AA). Each amino acid is a group of organic compounds that result from protein hydrolysis. Linked together, these amino acids create hundreds of configurations that go toward various functions of cell building. We now know that between eight and ten of these amino acids are essential amino acids (EAA), meaning they cannot be manufactured by the body and must be obtained through food. We say "approximately" because some amino acids are necessary for the synthesis of others and vice versa. Amino acids are the building blocks of protein. Their availability and structure is what determines the utilization and efficiency of protein for muscle-building purposes.

And when amino acid needs have been met, protein needs have been met. Animal protein contains all the amino acids in plentiful proportions. Plant proteins do not. They contain only limited proportions of some amino acids. For optimum protein utilization of foods, the amino acids in most foods must duplicate, or closely match, the same amount in protein required by the body. If they don't, protein utilization will be impaired or even stop. The foods supplying the most complete proteins and with the highest protein efficiency ratio (PER) in descending order are: eggs, milk and milk products, glandular meats, muscle meats, fish, fowl, brewer's yeast, wheat germ, soy products, nuts and seeds, legumes, grains, and fruits and vegetables.

With the least complete protein foods, such as plant foods, the EAA that is present in the lowest amount or absent altogether (also known as the "limiting amino acid") which determines the level at which all the other EAAs will be utilized. In other words, if a food contains 100 percent of a person's requirement for all but one of the eight EAAs, but only 10 percent of the remaining EAA, only 10 percent of the protein in that food will go toward tissue building. And you cannot make up for it at another meal unless the "limiting amino acid" containing meal is eaten within two hours. By eating meals consisting of only fruits, vegetables, grains, or legumes, you will greatly limit protein synthesis, hence muscle-building potential.

But that's not the worst of it. It is a fact that the protein value of foods decreases by as much as 80 percent when the food is cooked. Just what percentage depends on the degree to which the food is heated. It is also known that excess heat makes some amino acids unavailable by forming linkages that digestive enzymes cannot split. So theoretically, if you are getting only 10 percent of the available protein in a food because of the "limiting amino acid" factor, and the food is thoroughly heat-treated as well, you end up getting only 20 percent of the 10 percent of the protein. That amounts to a grand total of 2 percent of the available protein in that food going toward building your body. And don't forget that muscle is not the only thing your body needs protein for. If you are lucky at this point, you will end up with 1 percent of the protein your body needs for making muscle! Nothing can help you now, except the next meal. It is a grim scenario, but it does happen. The point is, do not exclude protein from animal sources from your diet if you want to build and maintain high-quality muscle. Follow the guidelines set down for the high biological quality of foods, using the premise that less cooking is better.

Always try to precede your protein meal with fresh fruit or vegetables. It has been found that when something raw is eaten before something cooked, such as "salad first," the digestive enzymes, in a limited capacity, treat the cooked food as raw food, freeing its protein and nutrients better for utilization. And the more a protein meal is accompanied by a raw (as opposed to cooked) carbohydrate food, the easier it will be on the digestive system, saving it for the hard job of breaking down the protein and sorting out the amino acids. Some fat in protein food is necessary, too, otherwise the body will burn up valuable amino acids for energy instead of using them to build muscle. If protein is eaten lean, then it should be accompanied by some high carbohydrate food to supply the energy, thus sparing the amino acids.

Our daily food intake should consist of a minimum of 20 percent protein of high biological quality. (Variances of protein amounts depending on bodybuilding needs will be discussed in Chapter 3.) The more protein foods you can include from the essential "raw" list, the better. So many diets today hype the high-carbohydrate low-protein (as low as 10 percent) theory. There is no good reason for this other than fear of fats and high-energy claims. If you are following the program for Perfect Nutrition, there is no need to do this, nor should you do this. We have no problem getting energy from starches and sugars, but we do have a real problem getting first-rate protein. What most people don't realize, however, is that unused protein can also be converted to energy and is one of the primary functions of amino acids. One gram of protein will yield four calories, about the same as starches and sugars. If an amino acid is not needed for muscle building, it goes through a process of deaminization, in which the body converts it into glucose and glycogen. It is then stored in the liver to be used as energy. It is stored as fat only when the diet is too high in calories and not enough energy is expended. Because of all the factors effecting the utilization of protein, it is always better to "CYA" (cover your aminos) and have too much protein than too little. Although regarded as an expensive source of fuel, amino acids can be relied on as a form of energy insurance.

THE CARBOHYDRATE EXPLOSION

Carbohydrates are the body's explosives. They provide energy for every function of the body in the form of blood sugar or glucose. Insulin and other pancreatic hormones convert this blood sugar into glycogen, which is stored in the liver. Liver glycogen is then converted back into glucose when blood-sugar levels are low and energy is needed. Carbohydrates are your fuel to train and leave the amino acids free to work at building muscle. If the carbohydrate intake is not high enough to supply blood sugar immediately to the bloodstream, or the glycogen level is too low for a certain energy demand, the body will utilize its fat stores for fuel. If the diet is too low in protein, or the body is too low in fat, the body will then burn muscle tissue for fuel, causing muscle loss, fatigue, weakness, and the inability to train with full power. Those are the mechanics of carbohydrates and the chain of events that can lead to an imbalance of them.

The wrong kind of carbohydrates can cause any one of these processes to malfunction. The body reacts to simple carbohydrate or refined sugar by overproducing insulin, which will rapidly convert blood sugar into glycogen. This sudden loss of blood sugar will then cause moodiness, depression, lethargy, shakiness, loss of strength and coordination, ineffective muscle contractions, and false hunger for more refined carbohydrate to replenish the supply and perpetuate this ugly cycle.

Yes, there is a big difference between the wrong and right kind of carbohydrates. Complex carbohydrates are the right kind. They include starches such as grains, legumes, nuts, seeds, and vegetables. Fruit is also a complex carbohydrate, high in starchy fiber, but also high in the naturally occurring sugars of fructose and glucose. Because of these characteristics, fruit might be considered, if you will, a "simplex" carbohydrate, containing both slow-burning starch and fast-burning sugar, making it an excellent source of carbohydrate. Another simple sugar is lactose, naturally occurring in milk products. All of the foods mentioned, including fruit and milk, are natural foods that contain many vital nutrients, protein, and/or fiber, and you need them in your diet to stay healthy. The standard diet should be comprised of about 60 percent of these healthy carbohydrates. (Variances of carbohydrate amounts depending on bodybuilding needs will be discussed in Chapter 3.) Of this 60 percent, at least half the caloric value of your carbohydrate foods should be of *excellent biological quality,* which means they should be natural and uncooked. If you are dieting to lose fat, about three quarters of the caloric value of your carbohydrate foods should be uncooked.

On the other end of the spectrum are simple carbohydrates, which are the refined sugars of sucrose, fructose, and dextrose. They are found in empty calorie foods like candy, cakes, pies, soft drinks, syrups, and table sugar. These carbohydrates, because of their source and degree of refinement, are a poor excuse for carbohydrates and are really bad for you. Avoid them.

BEWARE OF "SKELETON POWDER"

Refined sugar is more harmful to human health than once thought, and there is more and more evidence to back this up. White sugar, better deemed "skeleton powder," is a highly refined substance, devoid of any nutrients. Instead, it robs the body of its own nutrients and gives nothing back, causing a variety of ills stemming from nutritional deficiencies. It weakens the body's defenses and leads to degenerative diseases including diabetes, heart disease, and obesity. Sugar also plays a big role in raising blood cholesterol by lowering the ratio of HDL (good cholesterol) and raising the circulating triglycerides in the bloodstream. Also remember that nobody eats just plain sugar. It is always *in* something to make it taste good, and it is usually in high-fat foods, so you get plenty of saturated fat as well to aggravate cholesterol. In fact, many people are addicted to the deadly sugar-fat combination and don't even know it. It is an acquired taste that is hard to break, and that is a major cause of health problems in our country. The bottom line is that sugar causes stress on the body. It puts a demand on the pancreas and adrenal system, which will eventually break down from overuse and abuse, and in the long run cause the body to deteriorate more rapidly. In the short run, you get low blood sugar. The symptoms of low blood sugar cause the pancreas to react with an overproduction of hormones, among them adrenaline. The immediate result is anxiety, tension, irritability, depression—all very stressful. It causes not only physical problems, but mental and emotional problems that can have profound and detrimental effects on your life. In light of the fact that the average American consumes 100 pounds of sugar a year, this is a serious matter.

You don't need the refined sugar of simple carbohydrates to get the energy you need. Instead, the complex carbohydrates provide all the carbohydrate you need in natural, unrefined foods. And even here there is a difference in quality. Although breads, pizzas, and pastas are complex carbohydrates, they also contain a lot of nutrient-depleted starch, because they have been processed, cooked, and largely stripped of their vitality. Your first aim should always be to get the most nutrients for your calories essentially, that is from the complex carbohydrate foods that come directly from their natural source with a minimum of cooking and processing, or none at all. The more unrefined the complex carbohydrates, the better they work to keep your blood sugar up in the right amount with a nice steady flow. That is the way nature intended it to be.

THE INCREDIBLE BULK

One of the best by-products of carbohydrates is fiber. It is a common belief that fiber is just another word for bran, but this is not so. Unfortunately, the word "fiber" is a crude catchall for something that is comprised of many elements, so it is necessary to establish what they are and what they do.

They are actually a half dozen known types of food fiber and all are found almost exclusively in plant foods. The first three types are cellulose, hemicelluloses, and lignins, and are insoluble fibers. They are coarse and chewy and cannot dissolve in water. They hasten food through the digestive tract, promoting regularity, and help eliminate problems such as obesity, diverticulosis, constipation, and colon cancer. Insoluble fibers are found primarily in whole grains and foods made with whole grains. They are also found in lesser degrees in fresh fruits, vegetables, and legumes. The last three types are gums, mucilages, and pectin and are soluble fibers. They dissolve in water and are relatively undetectable, but their impact is powerful on the body's metabolism of fats and sugars. They are positively associated with reducing the risk of cardiovascular disease and diabetes, and more subtly, obesity. Soluble fibers are found primarily in fresh fruits, vegetables, legumes, and more recently in oat bran. Oat bran is rich in a gum called beta-glucan, again a soluble fiber associated with reducing the risk of heart disease.

Oat bran has merit in its effect for lowering cholesterol, but so do fresh fruits and vegetables. And they are naturally unprocessed, which means they contain all the vitamins, minerals, and enzymes they are meant to. But manufacturers cannot package, market, and sell you fresh produce, so they sell oat bran. Brans and bran products are an excellent source of fiber, but there is no need to overdose on them when there are many other important fibers found in natural foods as well. The key to getting enough healthy fiber in your diet is to get a well-rounded selection of foods containing both insoluble and soluble fibers. And yes, cooking does break down fibers so it is important to eat them as uncooked and unprocessed as possible to ensure that you are getting all the fiber as well as the available nutrients in food. Fiber itself does not have nutrients; the nutrients are in the foods that contain the fiber, so they go hand in hand. Eat whole grains along with the brans (raw is better) to get their immediate laxative effects, and eat fresh fruits and vegetables (and oat bran if you will) for the long range cholesterol-lowering effects. Combined, all fibers will add to the total picture of good health.

Fiber is a big factor in keeping body weight under control. Body fat comes mainly from the fats we eat—not from the carbohydrates. It takes eight times more energy for the body to burn carbohydrates as it does to burn fat. Carbohydrates have to go through more metabolic steps than fats to be stored as fat in the body. This constitutes a greater heat loss that stimulates the burning up of more calories, thus the burning of more body fat. Compared to simple carbohydrate foods that are low or lacking in fiber, complex carbohydrate foods are slow-burning, efficient sources of fuel that keep your blood sugar stable and control hunger. And because of their high fiber content, unrefined carbohydrate foods contain more bulk, so you eat less to get full. Finally, as they sweep through your digestive system, they take with them excess calories that would otherwise stay there and metabolize into fat. So once again, the more natural and unrefined complex carbohydrates replace refined and fatty foods, the trimmer and healthier you will be.

How much fiber you should get each day is quite simple. Forget about counting grams of fiber. That could do you more harm than good, because it is the quality of the diet that counts. Just remember that some combination of fiber is found in all complex carbohydrates. If a good portion of your diet is carbohydrate and includes fresh fruits, vegetables, whole grains, seeds, and legumes, you will get enough fiber naturally.

FEAR OF FATS

Carbohydrates are the kindling for our energy fires but fats are the log. Fats, or lipids, are the most reliable source of energy in our diets. One gram of dietary fat supplies nine calories, which is 2.25 times more energy than protein or carbohydrates. Fats curb hunger and give you the long-lasting, steady-burning fuel to train with real strength and endurance. Fat supports cellular structure, insulates and protects internal organs, transports the fat soluble vitamins A, D, E, and K, and is necessary to carry out numerous metabolic functions.

There are two types of fatty acids, saturated and unsaturated. Our bodies need both types to function properly, totaling 15 to 20 percent of our daily food intake. About one third of that should come from saturated fat and two thirds from unsaturated fat, both polyunsaturated and monounsaturated fats equally. However, the higher the diet is in protein, the higher the ratio will be of saturated fat—perhaps 50/50.

The fats in all foods make up not just one, but all types and combinations of fatty acids, both saturated and unsaturated. However, there are three types of unsaturated fatty acids that are "essential" because they can be obtained only from specific foods. They are linoleic, linolenic, and arachidonic acids, and along with other functions, play a role in the breakdown and passage of cholesterol.

Saturated fats, or fats that are solid at room temperature, are found primarily in meat and milk and dairy products. Polyunsaturated and monounsaturated fats, also known to lower cholesterol, are usually liquid at room temperature, and are derived from the oils of vegetables, nuts, and seeds. Fish oils are also high in unsaturated fats.

All these fats in their natural state are healthy and good. It is what we do to them that is bad. High heat and hydrogenation (a process that hardens a liquid oil, altering its molecular bonds with a combination of heat and chemical purification) is extremely detrimental to our health and is linked to cancer and arterial damage. Saturated fats, lately regarded as harmful, are no more harmful than unsaturated fats that have been hydrogenated, such as margarine. And saturated fats become saturated in the harmful sense only when they have been exposed to high heat, which destroys their own beneficial "fat neutralizing" enzymes, particularly lipase. Our fears of fats are not ungrounded, however. Our problem is that we generally don't eat animal foods high in saturated fats in an uncooked state. And more and more, we are eating plant foods high in unsaturated fats cooked as well. The solution is to eliminate processed foods from our diet, especially those with a high fat and calorie content. Prepare foods of *primary value* with the least amount of heat destruction as possible, and include in your diet a good portion of your foods from the category of *excellent biological quality*. Since overall dietary requirements of fat are comparatively low to protein and carbohydrate requirements, and since all natural foods supply varying and correct amounts of both saturated and unsaturated fats with most of their beneficial properties intact, getting the right amount of the right kind of fats can be remedied automatically with Perfect Nutrition.

Vegetable oils are another problem. Touted as healthful because they are polyunsaturated, they're really in a neutral category and offer healthful benefits only if they are cold-pressed and unrefined. But most are not because they don't last on the grocer's shelves. It is a process that is rarely used. If they are not cold-pressed but are labeled as "expeller pressed" instead, they still have less value. It is a process that requires 160°F of heat but does not use harmful chemicals. If they are not labeled at all and are clear and extremely liquid, then they are totally refined. You are better off going back to "expeller pressed" if cold-pressed is not available. When you do use oils, use them sparingly, as they are a highly concentrated source of calories (about 125 calories per tablespoon). Count on getting most of your fatty acids from the natural sources of raw vegetables, nuts, and seeds.

THE CASE WITH CHOLESTEROL

Cholesterol is a natural, pearly-like fat-related substance that has no nutritional value and no calories. It is a normal component of body tissues that is needed as an outer protector to nerve and cell membranes. It is necessary in the conversion of sunlight to vitamin D, and is needed to produce bile salts that aid in the digestion of fats. Cholesterol is also essential in producing sex and adrenal hormones, thus playing an important role in the production of natural steroid hormones.

Cholesterol is found primarily in the fats of animal foods like meat, eggs, and milk. That you know. But as a rule, only 20 to 30 percent of cholesterol actually comes from your diet, no matter what you eat. The remainder of the body's cholesterol is supplied by the liver. However, what you eat, the quality of the cholesterol food as well as the quality of other foods, determines whether your body is going to use it wisely or not.

To begin with, don't confuse dietary cholesterol with blood cholesterol. Although they are biologically the same substance, they do not necessarily affect each other adversely. It has not been scientifically proven that dietary cholesterol causes harmful cholesterol buildup in the arteries. It has been proven only that by lowering cholesterol intake (which coincidentally means cutting out foods you should not be eating anyway for other health reasons), you can lower your blood cholesterol to a degree. Blood cholesterol levels can be affected by many factors, however, which can be as temporary as what you ate for breakfast. If your cholesterol is high, it does not necessarily mean you are a candidate for a heart attack, particularly if your overall lifestyle looks favorable. Conversely, 60 percent of heart disease patients do not have high cholesterol counts.

But high blood cholesterol is not a favorable sign either. It could very well indicate cholesterol buildup in the arteries, in which case you would have to look at your overall lifestyle: your dietary habits, your amount of body fat, your level of physical activity, stress, alcohol, smoking, etc. You obviously know the answers and if you have been neglecting to attend to any of these things, then you should address them immediately.

There is another factor that even the most informed people don't know about: Everyone metabolizes cholesterol a little differently. In a healthy individual, a cholesterol overload will cause the liver to compensate by cutting back its own production of cholesterol. Conversely, if too little cholesterol is consumed, the liver may compensate by over-producing it for you. This does not mean your liver's own production of cholesterol is going to cause your arteries to clog, but it can temporarily affect your system and throw your metabolic processes off (as well as give you a scare). In other words, too little dietary cholesterol is not good either because your body needs a certain amount of it to function properly (between 250 and 300 mg. per day) and it is going to get it one way or the other.

Yet another matter comes to light involving high blood cholesterol. Although total blood cholesterol should ideally be under 200 mg. per deciliter of blood, the ratio of HDLs (high-density lipoproteins or "good cholesterol") to LDLs (low-density lipoproteins or "bad cholesterol") ultimately determines the risk of heart disease. The higher the ratio of HDLs to LDLs, the lower the risk of heart disease. In some cases, there can be high blood cholesterol and high levels of HDLs, which would lower the risk, but high cholesterol usually indicates a high amount of LDLs. Some simple blood tests can tell you this.

All that has been said about cholesterol may make it sound bad, and this too has become an issue of much controversy. True, high levels of blood cholesterol are associated with dangerous plaque that builds up on the arterial walls, but dietary cholesterol is not necessarily the cause. The real culprit is saturated fats in which cholesterol happens to be present in high amounts. Saturated fats are found most abundantly in meat and dairy products, so you can't cut them out of your diet.

Although cutting down on these would be wise for the average person, the answer is not that simple.

And this is where we go wrong—trying to cure a lifetime of adulterated diets and complicated eating patterns with one solution: cut out fats and the foods that contain them. Unfortunately we start off by blaming the basics, which are of course meat, eggs, and milk. But it is not these foods that are harmful, again it is what we do to them. In themselves, these are natural foods that contain many essential nutrients, protein, and fats (saturated and unsaturated) our bodies need every day. But add the combination of hydrogenated fats and oils, processed starches, and refined sugars to these natural foods and they become something else—foods that are the real nutritional villain in heart disease, as well as other degenerative diseases. In essence, if we had been predisposed to eating natural foods all of our lives, heart disease (and cholesterol) would not be the problem that it is today. So before you begin cutting natural foods out of your diet to combat cholesterol, start with the junk foods that have been harmfully denatured and devoid of nutrition.

This doesn't mean to start gobbling down steak and eggs for breakfast because they are natural foods. If you have arterial damage, that would be adding fuel to the fire. Nothing should be eaten in excess, even natural foods. So if you have a case with cholesterol, take these precautions:

- Eat plenty of fiber in the form of fresh fruits and vegetables, legumes, whole grains, and brans, particularly oat bran.

- Eat more fish, especially the oily kind that is high in Omega-3 fatty acids, an unsaturated fat that significantly lowers cholesterol and inhibits clotting that can lead to heart attacks.

- If you use vegetable oils, try to use the oils and the products that contain them that are higher in monounsaturated fats than polyunsaturated fats. Although both types of fats are beneficial in lowering total blood cholesterol, monounsaturated fats lower total blood cholesterol without lowering the HDLs. The best oils highest in the monounsaturated fats in order are olive, almond, rice bran, and sesame oil. Use the olive and sesame oils chiefly for cooking with heat. Canola oil is high in the monounsaturated and essential fatty acids, but allegedly contains a toxin that needs further study. The remaining oils—corn, safflower, sunflower, and peanut oil—are high in the polyunsaturated fats and are also fine to use. Also include the oils, as well as the products themselves, that contain the essential fatty acids. These are flax (linseed), pumpkin seed, soybean, and walnut oils. Stay away from oils that have been hydrogenated and partially hydrogenated (i.e., margarine), which in turn makes them more saturated—just what you are trying to avoid—and, of course, palm and coconut oils.

• Use skim or partially skim milk products whenever possible, and if you are a milk drinker, stay away from whole milk that has been homogenized (as most commercially sold milk is). Homogenization is a process of breaking up the fat molecules in milk, making it more palatable and storable. However, by making the size of the fat molecules smaller, it enables them to enter the bloodstream more readily, which leads to the inevitable clogging of the arteries. The solution? Drink only nonfat milk.

• Avoid refined sugar and anything made with it. Remember, sugar affects cholesterol. It causes reduced ratios of HDLs in the blood by lowering the body's ability to metabolize sugar with saturated fats properly, therefore raising its ability to produce the harmful type of cholesterol.

• Exercise. A carefully managed diet will lower LDLs but exercise will raise HDLs, further widening that critical gap in total cholesterol. Stay lean. Clearly the fatter you are, the higher your cholesterol will be. Exercise, compounded with diet, not only curbs obesity, but it increases lean body mass, something diet alone cannot do.

THE SODIUM FACTOR

Salt (sodium chloride) is a potent chemical that borders on harmful when its effects are analyzed in conjunction with the amount of it found in the average diet. But once again it becomes a factor where "the whole is more than the sum of its parts." You cannot point to sodium as the culprit in various health problems, such as hypertension, without looking at the total diet.

Salt alone does not cause high blood pressure, but cutting down or omitting salt from the diet will lower the blood pressure in people who already have hypertension. And by eliminating salt, you also eliminate the processed, fatty foods in which it is most abundant. We need only about 200 mg. of sodium per day to survive. We should get only about

2000 mg. per day. But the average person consumes between 4000 and 6000 mg. per day! In our diet, only 10 percent of that sodium is found naturally in foods; 15 percent comes from the salt shaker; the remaining 75 percent is in processed foods. If we eliminated just the processed foods, which we know are a major cause of health problems, we would lower our sodium intake to less than one half, about what we should get without even a conscious effort. So which one is the real enemy here—sodium or processed foods?

Sodium is a key bodybuilding mineral. A certain amount of it is necessary in retaining other minerals and establishing the electrolyte mineral (sodium, calcium, potassium, and magnesium) balance in the body. It works together in a big way with potassium in stimulating nerve impulses, and muscle contractions and expansion. About 2000 mg. of sodium (or the equivalent of one teaspoon of salt) per day is considered a moderate intake. However, if you are training hard and perspiring, you need an additional 1000 mg. of sodium per quart of fluid lost to maintain your electrolyte balance and achieve peak muscular performance. If you don't get it, you will feel it. Too much sodium can cause water retention, but a moderate amount will be quickly excreted through body fluids simply by cutting back on salt. Excessive water retention, however, may cause abnormal amounts of potassium to be lost in the urine, causing muscle weakness and inefficiency. An excess of salt can also interfere with the absorption and utilization of foods, particularly protein.

A natural amount of sodium is necessary and you cannot safely eliminate it from your diet (nor should you try) without eliminating an entire spectrum of basic and important foods in which it is naturally present. There are times, however, when sodium intake should be cut back as a measure of temporary water loss to enhance muscular definition (no less than the essential intake of 200 to 400 mg. of sodium is advised), during the premenstrual days, and of course to reduce the effects of high blood pressure. But if you are a normal healthy person with no health problems related to salt intake, and are getting a well-balanced, unprocessed diet with plenty of fresh fruits and vegetables, there is no reason to eliminate a moderate amount of salt from your diet. Just stay away from commercial table salt. Choose natural sea salt containing trace minerals or "vegetable salt," a blend of sea salt, yeast, and vegetable concentrates containing trace amounts of vitamins and minerals. The salt shaker then really becomes a matter of personal choice, and one that will do you no harm either way, provided you don't eliminate natural foods containing sodium.

Photo: Mike Neveux

— 2 —
SUPERNUTRIENTS

In bodybuilding and sports, nutritional supplements are replacing drugs in achieving greater anabolic (muscle-building) effects, aerobic energy, and metabolic efficiency. That is the goal behind a food supplementation program. All nutrients are important and you should count on getting them from a balanced diet of natural foods every day. Ideally, if you were following the plan for Perfect Nutrition and made no other demand on your body but to maintain it, this would not be a problem. But nutrient availability and utilization are not always ideal. Superhuman endeavors such as bodybuilding have superhuman requirements. For the bodybuilder who wants to build muscle size and strength, or who may be monitoring calories, nutrients will play a more significant role. Because greater stress is put on the body during strenuous activity or dieting, some nutrient requirements will be higher. And because reduced food intake often causes an imbalance of protein, fats, and carbohydrates, some nutrients will be needed in higher proportions. Therefore, if you are training hard and watching your caloric intake, taking food supplements would be a prudent move.

Each and every nutrient has a separate job to do and is important to our total health, but they all work synergistically with each other and should not be isolated. Instead they should be boosted, on a diet of natural foods and in the presence of all other nutrients. Supplements work best in conjunction with natural foods and should not be used arbitrarily as a crutch for an inadequate diet.

SUPER SUPPLEMENTS

Nutritional supplementation in the form of vitamins, minerals, amino acids, and co-factors is a very intricate and growing science. Since food supplement dosages are contingent on an individual's sex, size, health, diet, and level of activity, this book makes only basic recommendations and suggestions. You work your way up from there depending on your personal requirement. The best supplements to take are manufactured from natural sources, without the application of heat if possible. They should be pure and contain no salt, sugar, artificial coatings, binders, or fillers.

All vitamins are considered organic in that they contain elements of carbon, but not all vitamins are natural. Some are derived from synthetic sources as well. Natural vitamins are generally regarded as purer and better because they have been extracted from food sources with little disturbance to their molecular structure. Megadose and time-released vitamins, as a rule, come from synthetic sources, and therefore require more processing. However, many vitamins can be a mixture of both. Be moderate with your dosages because more isn't always better. Again, you don't want to overtax your digestive system when it is needed for other functions, especially protein synthesis. An overdose of vitamins can also result in a higher requirement of other vitamins that you may not be getting. Megadoses are recommended in times of extreme stress, illness, injury, or diagnosed deficiency. Moderate dosages are recommended for healthy stress—like endurance or weight training. Your best bet is to take vitamins in duplicate proportions to the body's requirement after assimilation and deficiency factors have been taken into account. A good daily multivitamin will provide this.

The best mineral supplements are chelated with amino acids. Alone, they are inorganic and not easily assimilated, but this process renders them organic by bonding them to amino acid molecules. This gives them a better chance of being assimilated and makes them more absorbable into the blood stream. Also, the presence of amino acids themselves helps because of their very active nature working in conjunction with other vitamins and minerals. Both major and trace minerals have important functions in the body. But because the body needs smaller amounts of trace minerals, they are easier to obtain than major minerals. One mineral tablet may do the trick with most trace minerals, whereas additional supplementation may be necessary for minerals such as calcium, magnesium, phosphorus, and iron where larger amounts are required, therefore increasing dietary and assimilation factors as well. Also diets that call for a decrease in dairy products require more calcium, magnesium, and phosphorus; meat reduction requires more iron.

All amino acid supplements should be free-form, preceded by an "L" on the label, and are best if they are of the highest "pharmaceutical grade." This means that they have been biochemically fermented without the use of heat and are in their purest biologically reactive, singular form, able to go right to work where you need them. "Food grade" amino acids, the type most often used in food supplements, do the same thing but with less efficiency. Peptide-bonded amino acids found in the "predigested" or hydrolyzed proteins of supplements and formulated drinks merely increase the PER of dietary protein and are even less effective. But bear in mind that brewer's yeast, though often overlooked with distaste, is a potent natural source of most of the amino acids as well as many other essential nutrients. On taking amino acids, choose a broad-based formula that includes lysine, methionine, phenylalanine, tryptophan, arginine, and ornithine. Based on potency, generally you should follow the manufacturer's directions for amounts, taking into account that if you are consuming a large quantity of your protein foods cooked, a portion of the amino acid value, as well as their enzyme vehicles, are destroyed. You may then want to take more than the recommended dosage.

Vitamins, minerals, and amino acids are also found in other kinds of food supplements, many of which are concentrated forms of natural foods. Among them are brewer's yeast, fish liver oils, wheat germ oil and wheat germ, lecithin, bran, and kelp. These are excellent supplements and including any of them in your diet on a regular basis would be wise. Others such as desiccated liver and raw glandulars have a fair degree of value, but their sources are sometimes questionable. Protein powder supplements are usually regarded as a major supplement in the bodybuilder's diet. Egg white protein is superior to milk protein (caseinate), but most affordable protein supplements contain both. Try to obtain protein powders that are manufactured with the least amount of heat processing, contain at least 5 percent egg white protein and no additives, starches, sugars, fillers, or vegetable proteins. Vegetable or soy protein powders are biologically substandard to milk and egg white protein powders and should be a secondary choice. Otherwise a good bet is straight noninstant, nonfat dry milk. It is very economical, very pure, and very nutritious.

Vitamins

● Vitamin A, or *retinol,* is fat-soluble. Carotene, from plant sources, is converted in the body to vitamin A. Retinol is obtained from animal sources. Vitamin A is one of the antioxidants that combats free radical damage and degeneration and strengthens the immune system in fighting off cancer and heart disease. It is necessary for better vision, skin, hair, and membrane tissue and for the development of teeth and bones. The average adult's RDA of vitamin A is 1000 REs (retinol equivalents) —or 5000 IUs (international units)—per day, and it should be obtained from both plant and animal sources. (Vitamin A obtained from animal foods is worth three times more in retinol equivalents than vitamin A found in plant foods when measured in international units.) The most natural supplemental form of vitamin A is retinol from fish liver oils. Vitamin A is light sensitive and 15 to 35 percent of it is lost when food is cooked. The major sources of carotene are carrots, sweet potatoes, yams, pumpkins, winter squash, dandelion greens, turnip greens, red peppers, peas, spinach, kale, collard, cress, endive, broccoli, tomatoes, dried apricots, cantaloupe, mango, and papaya. The major food sources of retinol are liver, eggs, milk, and butter.

● All B-complex vitamins are water soluble. Excess is excreted through bodily fluids so they must be replenished daily. They work synergistically with each other and are more potent when taken together than separately.

Vitamin B–1, or *thiamin,* is important to the health and maintenance of the muscles and heart, and vital to the nervous system. It is essential in the metabolism of carbohydrates and it helps promote growth. The RDA of thiamin is 1.5 mg. It is easily and quickly destroyed by heat. More is lost in cooking vegetables than meat, and the less heat that is used the better. Cooking food in water readily leaches out the B-vitamins, so avoid this method whenever possible. The major food sources of thiamin are pork, wheat germ, bran, sunflower seeds, peas, fish, shellfish, soy products, nuts, and supplemental brewer's yeast.

Vitamin B–2, or *riboflavin,* is necessary for growth and cellular repair and aids in the synthesis of DNA. It functions with other substances in metabolizing proteins, fats, and carbohydrates. The RDA of riboflavin is 1.7 mg., although people who exercise heavily have been found to need more. It is fragile to sunlight and ultraviolet light. Most of it is retained when cooking meat, but 20 to 30 percent of it is lost in cooking vegetables when the liquid is discarded. The major food sources of riboflavin are liver, kidney, spinach, broccoli, milk, cheese, eggs, fish, and supplemental brewer's yeast.

Vitamin B–3, a group of B-complex vitamins known as *niacin,* improves circulation and a synthetic dosage of 100 mg. or more will cause a flush due to the dilation of blood vessels. It reduces blood cholesterol levels and assists in the breakdown and utilization of proteins, fats, and carbohydrates, and aids in weight reduction in its ability to elevate and stabilize blood sugar levels. It is necessary for the synthesis of sex hormones and in the formation of DNA. It is also important to the activity of the nervous system and helps relieve stiffness while increasing mobility of joints. The RDA of niacin is 16 mg., however niacin can be converted from tryptophan in the body at a rate of 60 mg. of tryptophan to make 1 mg. of niacin. It is very resistant to heat, light, and oxidation, but up to 50 percent of the niacin in vegetables may be lost when cooked in water. The major food sources of niacin are canned tuna, bran, liver, poultry, fish, veal, oysters, sardines, peanuts, and supplemental brewer's yeast.

Vitamin B–5, or *pantothenic acid,* increases the production of cortisone and other adrenal hormones to promote healthy skin and nerves and help the body withstand stress. It aids in the utilization of protein, fats, and carbohydrates, and in the synthesis of cholesterol, steroids (fat-soluble organic compounds), and fatty acids. It also protects against premature aging due to cellular damage caused by excessive radiation. The recommended daily allowance is 10 mg., though more is advised in times of stress. Up to 35 percent of pantothenic acid is lost in cooking meat, and up to 50 percent in just the milling of flour; further amounts are lost when food is cooked. The major food sources of pantothenic acid are heart, liver, kidney, egg yolks, legumes, whole grains, wheat germ, salmon, and supplemental brewer's yeast.

Vitamin B–6, or *pyridoxine,* is actually a group of six B-complex compounds. It is needed to synthesize hemoglobin and promote proper synthesis of anti-aging nucleic acids. It plays a role in regulating blood glucose levels. It helps assimilate protein and fat, and aids in the conversion of fatty acids and amino acids. It alleviates muscle spasms and leg cramps and sometimes numbness to extremities. It also works as a natural diuretic and is needed to convert tryptophan to niacin. The RDA of vitamin B–6 is 2.2 mg. It is fairly susceptible to heat destruction and vitamin B–6 losses in meat can reach up to 55 percent. Cooking destroys up to 30 percent in vegetables. Similar losses also occur in milk pasteurization. The major food sources of vitamin B–6 are liver, kidney, heart, tuna, poultry, spinach, broccoli, carrots, brussels sprouts, sweet potatoes, soy beans, bananas, dried apricots, peanuts, raisins, blackstrap molasses, and supplemental brewer's yeast.

Vitamin B–12, *cyanocobalamin,* is the only vitamin that contains essential mineral elements. It helps generate red blood cells, prevent anemia, and increase energy. It promotes growth in healthy nerve tissue and helps utilize protein, fats, and carbohydrates properly. It is essential to cell generation and to the synthesis of DNA. The RDA of vitamin B–12 is 3 mcg. (micrograms) but more is recommended since it is not easily absorbed in the intestines. The most natural supplemental form is cyanocobalamin or cobalamin concentrate. Vitamin B–12 is quite resistant to heat except when cooking in liquid is involved. The major food sources of vitamin B–12 are liver, kidney, meat, seafood, milk, cheese, and eggs.

Biotin is a vitamin B complex that as a coenzyme assists in the synthesis and oxidation of fatty acids, and in the metabolism of protein, fats, and carbohydrates. It also boosts the utilization of other B-vitamins. The RDA of biotin is 300 mcg. The major food sources of biotin are egg yolks, liver, milk, rice bran, whole grains, legumes, sardines, nuts, fruits, and supplemental brewer's yeast.

The vitamin B complex substances *choline* and *inositol* work together as a *lipotropic* (fat emulsifier) agent in mobilizing fats and emulsifying cholesterol. They also play an important role in the proper functioning of neurotransmitters. No RDAs have been established for choline and inositol, but the recommended daily amount is approximately 900 mg. of choline and 1000 mg. of inositol. Supplementation of the two can best be found in dietary lecithin, of which they are the chief component. The major food sources of choline and inositol are meat, organ meats, wheat germ, egg yolks, fish, soy beans, milk, nuts, fruits, leafy green vegetables, and supplemental brewer's yeast.

Folic acid is a group of compounds from the vitamin B complex that is essential to the formation of red blood cells, the division of body cells, and in the production of RNA and DNA (nucleic acids). It is also needed for the proper utilization of sugars and amino acids. The RDA of folic acid is .4 mg. Folic acid is extremely susceptible to light storage and heat and vegetables lose up to 85 percent of it when cooked in water. The major food sources of folic acid are organ meats, leafy green vegetables, root vegetables, asparagus, brussels sprouts, bran, wheat germ, whole grains, corn, legumes, milk, cantaloupe, oranges, avocados, filberts, almonds, cashews, and supplemental brewer's yeast.

Para-aminobenzoic acid (PABA) of the vitamin B complex can be synthesized in the intestine and acts in combination with folic acid in the breakdown and utilization of proteins, and in the formation of red blood cells. It contributes to healthy skin and hair pigmentation and is effectively used as a sunscreen in ointments. There is no RDA for PABA, although vitamin supplements usually provide 10 to 50 mg. The major food sources of PABA are liver, kidney, yogurt, whole grains, rice, wheat germ, bran, leafy green vegetables, molasses, and supplemental brewer's yeast.

There are three more compounds in the vitamin B complex that are not acknowledged as vitamins. They are B–13 *(orotic acid),* B–15 *(pangamic acid),* and B–17 *(laetrile).* Their nutritional value has been recognized, though not clearly defined. No RDAs have been established and they are not readily available in supplemental form. Except for pangamic acid, which can be obtained in rare beef, liver, brown rice, seeds, and supplemental brewer's yeast, these vitamins are not found in the usual food sources.

● Vitamin C, *ascorbic acid,* is a water-soluble vitamin and truly a miracle nutrient. It promotes cellular repair of skin, muscles, tendons, and ligaments, and strengthens teeth and bones. It also helps produce and maintain collagen and boosts the absorption of iron. It strengthens the immune system remarkably to help fight off infection and disease. It is also one of the antioxidants that works to combat cell destruction, a prelude to cancer and atherosclerosis. The RDA for vitamin C is 6 mg., but more is advised due to its healthful benefits and fragility to oxidation and heat. It dissipates very quickly in cut fruits and vegetables and up to 100 percent of vitamin C is lost in cooking and processing. Microwaving, however, seems to preserve more vitamin C than conventional cooking. The major food sources of vitamin C are bell peppers, guavas, kiwi, papayas, oranges, broccoli, cauliflower, cabbage, strawberries, cantaloupe, tomatoes, blackberries, cherries, brussels sprouts, kale, and potatoes. The natural form of food supplements are acerola cherries and rose hips, and are very potent in vitamin C.

● *Bioflavonoids* (vitamin P) are the natural companions to vitamin C and are found in many of the same foods, particularly citrus fruits. They aid in the absorption of vitamin C, and help strengthen capillaries and prevent bruising.

● Vitamin D is a fat-soluble vitamin that can be obtained through diet or synthesized from sunlight. It aids in the absorption and assimilation of calcium and phosphorus, and is essential for teeth and bone formation, especially during the period of growth. It is utilized best when taken with vitamin A. The recommended daily amount of vitamin D is 400 IUs. The major food sources of vitamin D are salmon, sardines, herring, vitamin D fortified milk products, egg yolks, organ meats, and the food supplement of fish liver oil, which contains both vitamins A and D.

● Vitamin E is a fat-soluble vitamin composed of eight compounds called *tocopherols*. It is necessary to the reproductive system and sexual potency. It helps supply oxygen, giving the body more stamina and endurance, and is one of the essential antioxidants that fight the effects of environmental pollutants and cellular aging due to free radical damage. It also helps prevent scar tissue formation from burns when applied externally as well as taken internally. The RDA for vitamin E is 10 IUs, though more is recommended in periods of hard training. In supplements, dry vitamin E is considered by some a more stable form than oil-based vitamin E. Either way, make sure it contains the all natural "D-mixed tocopherols." The major food sources of vitamin E are wheat germ, organ meats, eggs, soy beans, broccoli, brussels sprouts, leafy green vegetables, blackstrap molasses, unrefined vegetable oils, and wheat germ oil, a superior supplemental food high in the mixed tocopherols of vitamin E.

● Unsaturated Fatty Acids (vitamin F) are also the essential fatty acids —*linoleic, linolenic, arachidonic*. They help prevent cholesterol deposits in the arteries by burning saturated fats and act as an aid in weight reduction. They combine with proteins to form membranes that hold cells together and make calcium available to body tissues. They also promote adrenal and thyroid activity and the respiration of vital organs. They are essential in that they must be obtained through foods, however linolenic and arachidonic acid can be synthesized if linoleic acid is present. The recommended daily amount of the unsaturated fatty acids is about 10 percent of total caloric intake. Since they are destroyed by heating and oxidation of the oils in which they're found, this requirement can best be met with avocados, raw nuts and seeds, cold-pressed unrefined vegetable oils, and vitamin supplements.

● Vitamin K *(menadione)* is a fat-soluble vitamin that can be synthesized by natural intestinal bacteria. Its chief function is in the formation of prothrombin, needed for proper blood coagulation. The RDA for vitamin K is 500 mcg. The major food sources of vitamin K are egg yolks, unrefined vegetable oils, soy beans, cauliflower, yogurt, alfalfa, leafy green vegetables, kelp, and blackstrap molasses.

Major Minerals

● Calcium is a precious mineral that is without doubt the most significant in the body. It is critical to strong bones and teeth (especially with age) and it is essential to a number of enzyme systems, particularly nerve transmission and muscle contraction in both the heart and skeletal muscles. It helps calm nerves, relaxes muscle cramps, aids in muscular growth, and plays a vital role in regulating the heartbeat and lowering blood pressure. In addition it assists the body in the passage of nutrients in and out of the cell walls, in the utilization of iron, and in the process of blood clotting. The RDA of calcium is 800 mg. but heavy training and sweat losses require more. And since dietary calcium is absorbed at a rate of only 20 to 30 percent, supplementation is advised. Among the best calcium supplements are calcium carbonate, calcium gluconate, calcium lactate, and calcium pangamic. Bone meal and dolomite are least absorbable, therefore the least favorable. Your best bet is to take chewable calcium that, when mixed with saliva, is given a predigestive boost. To function properly, calcium must be accompanied by vitamins A, C, D, and magnesium and phosphorus. Calcium is fairly resistant to heat, but since its utilization depends on other nutrients that are sensitive to heat, raw natural sources are best. The major food sources of calcium are milk and milk products, canned fish with bones, shellfish, egg yolks, legumes (particularly soy beans), tofu, leafy green vegetables, artichokes, broccoli, cabbage, nuts, seeds, dried fruits, and blackstrap molasses.

● Phosphorus is important to skeletal development, tissue repair, muscular contraction, and nerve transmission. It plays a role in the utilization of proteins, fats, and carbohydrates, and is needed for energy and cell reproduction. The RDA for phosphorus is 800 mg. Its absorption depends on the presence of vitamin D and the balance of calcium, with a ratio of 2.5 parts calcium to 1 part phosphorus. Although nutritional requirements are the same for phosphorus and calcium, phosphorus is about two and a half times more absorbable than calcium. The natural supplemental form of phosphorus is bone meal and potassium phosphate. The major food sources of phosphorus are meat, poultry, fish, eggs, legumes, milk and milk products, whole grains, nuts, and blackstrap molasses.

● Magnesium is needed for calcium absorption and is an effective anti-stress mineral. It is important for nerve and muscle functioning and is a necessary element in converting blood sugar into energy. The RDA for magnesium is 350 m, and is recommended in proportion to calcium of 2 parts calcium to 1 part magnesium. The natural supplemental form of magnesium is dolomite and magnesium oxide. The major food sources of magnesium are seafood, whole grains, leafy green vegetables, nuts, and blackstrap molasses.

● Potassium is necessary to stimulate nerve impulses for muscle contraction. It assists in the conversion of glucose to glycogen and helps convert amino acids in the bloodstream into muscle protein. It is vitally important in regulating fluid balance in the body when sweat is lost, and prevents a loss of minerals that causes muscle weakness. It also assists in sending oxygen to the brain and regulating neuromuscular activity. The recommended daily amount of potassium is between 2000 and 4000 mg., but more is recommended during periods of heavy sweat losses. The highest dosage by law in a daily supplement is 99 mg. of potassium. The major food sources of potassium are meat, avocados, bananas, oranges, nectarines, papayas, yogurt, whole grains, vegetables, legumes, sunflower seeds, dried fruits, and blackstrap molasses.

Trace Minerals

● Zinc occurs in the body in comparatively large amounts to other trace elements. It helps in the production of insulin and plays a role in the maintenance of enzyme systems involved in digestion and metabolism. It is essential for protein synthesis and assists in the contractibility of muscles. Zinc may be required for the synthesis of DNA and has been found to be effective in healing wounds and normalizing functions of the reproductive organs and prostate gland. The RDA for zinc is 15 mg.

The major food sources of zinc are meat, organ meats, oysters, seafood, eggs, bran, wheat germ, soy beans, mushrooms, pumpkin seeds, sunflower seeds, and supplemental brewer's yeast.

● Iron is the trace mineral that is most abundant in the body. It is necessary for the production of hemoglobin in red blood cells, which transports oxygen throughout the body. It is also needed in the formation of myoglobin, which transports oxygen to the muscle cells to ensure proper muscular contraction. Iron increases resistance to disease and stress, prevents fatigue and iron-deficiency anemia, and aids in growth. The RDA for iron is 18 mg., but only about 8 percent of total iron intake is assimilated by the body. The presence of vitamin C can help boost the utilization of iron by as much as eight times. Supplemental iron, however, can destroy vitamin E and should be taken in the organically rendered forms of ferrous gluconate, ferrous fumarate, ferrous citrate, and ferrous peptonate to prevent this. There are two kinds of iron: heme iron, which is found in animal sources, and nonheme iron, which is found in plant sources. Heme iron is more potent, more absorbable, and helps boost the absorption of nonheme iron as well. The major food sources of iron are liver and organ meats, eggs, poultry, fish, clams, oysters, green leafy vegetables, legumes, asparagus, dried fruits, nuts, blackstrap molasses, and supplemental desiccated liver.

● Chromium plays a major bodybuilding role in the "glucose tolerance factor" (GTF). GTF assists insulin in the metabolism of protein into muscle from amino acids in the blood. It protects and enhances the cell life of protein. Chromium also aids in the regulation of glucose and in lipid fat metabolism—factors in diabetes and arteriosclerosis respectively. The average person does not get enough chromium and loses up to five times more during exercise, so a chromium supplement is recommended in the form of GTF-chromium (chromium polynicotinate containing niacin). At least .2 milligrams of chromium per day is recommended. The major food sources of chromium are organ meats, meat, chicken, shellfish, whole grains, potatoes, egg yolks, nuts, cheese, mushrooms, asparagus, and supplemental brewer's yeast.

● Copper is another trace mineral that is deficient in the average diet. It is required by the body to convert iron into hemoglobin. It is essential for the proper functioning of the central nervous system and for the utilization of vitamin C, and is a necessary nutrient in the Krebs cycle (a series of biochemical reactions that produce carbon dioxide and water from food and release energy). The recommended daily dosage of copper is 3 milligrams, although most people get less than half of that. Its absorption is boosted by calcium. The major food sources of copper are shellfish, liver, meat, green leafy vegetables, whole grains, nuts, and seeds.

● Selenium is the mineral member of the antioxidants. It is essential to the immune system in combating cancer and degenerative aging. It is also needed to assist the body's utilization of vitamin E. A selenium deficiency can lead to the destruction of muscle cells and weaken muscle performance. The recommended dosage of selenium is between 100 and 200 mcg. per day. However, high amounts of selenium can be toxic and should not exceed the recommended dosage. The major food sources of selenium are swordfish, wheat germ, bran, canned fish, nuts and seeds, liver, eggs, onions, tomatoes, and broccoli.

The remaining trace minerals are vital to the working mechanisms of the body and contribute to overall health. Although trace minerals occur in the body in minuscule amounts, many are just as important as major minerals. They are chlorine, cobalt, fluorine, iodine (RDA is 150 mcg.), manganese, molybdenum, nickel, silicon, sodium (see Chapter 1), strontium, sulfur, tin, and vanadium. Aside from a chelated mineral supplement, a good balanced diet containing meat, seafood, eggs, leafy green vegetables, whole grains, nuts, and seeds will adequately supply the body's requirement of trace minerals.

Essential Amino Acids

● *L-isoleucine, L-leucine,* and *L-valine* are a group that make up the branched-chain amino acids. Up to 90 percent of the dietary branched-chain amino acids go toward protein synthesis. As a supplement they promote muscle growth and tissue repair, and should be taken collectively. Leucine promotes the breakdown of fats within fat cells and intramuscularly, and as an insulin stimulator has a stabilizing effect on blood sugar. Valine has an appetite-suppressant factor and is useful for insomnia and calming muscular and mental upsets. The major food sources of these three amino acids are liver, beef, chicken, fish, soy products, milk, cottage cheese, eggs, brown rice, lima beans, chick-peas, lentils, mushrooms, corn, wheat, rye, almonds, cashews, Brazil nuts, peanuts, pumpkin seeds, sesame seeds, sunflower seeds, and supplemental brewer's yeast.

• *L-lysine* is a growth enhancer that improves the ratio of lean body mass to fat. It is necessary for tissue repair and elastin in the skin. It aids in the production of enzymes, hormones, and antibodies in the immune system. It helps utilize fatty acids needed for energy production and promotes better overall concentration. The major food sources of lysine are fish, chicken, beef, lamb, lima beans, milk, cheese, eggs, soy products, mung bean sprouts, and supplemental brewer's yeast. It is deficient in most grains.

• *L-methionine* is one of the sulfur-containing amino acids and that gives rise to cysteine and cystine, which act as detoxifying agents. Methionine itself is a powerful antioxidant and plays a role in the structure of collagen, cellular repair, and protein synthesis. It is a property of lecithin, which acts as a lipotropic agent. The major food sources of methionine are liver, beef, chicken, fish, pork, soy products, eggs, cottage cheese, sardines, yogurt, lentils, pumpkin seeds, sesame seeds, and supplemental brewer's yeast.

• *L-phenylalanine* promotes the body's natural pain-killing response to stress and injury by producing and activating endorphins, and is now widely used for this purpose therapeutically. It also acts as an appetite suppressant and a mood elevator when taken on an empty stomach. The major food sources of phenylalanine are beef, lamb, pork, fish, poultry, milk, cottage cheese, eggs, wheat, oats, peanuts, walnuts, pecans, and supplemental brewer's yeast.

• *L-threonine* converts to glucose for energy when carbohydrates are absent. It aids in digestion and acts as a lipotropic factor to blood fats. The major food sources of threonine are beef, lamb, veal, turkey, liver, fish, eggs, milk, cottage cheese, peanuts, walnuts, and supplemental brewer's yeast. It is deficient in most grains.

• *L-tryptophan* plays a key role in the release of growth hormones and in the production of serotonin, a neurotransmitter that induces sleep and relaxation. It is also used in the therapeutic treatment of depression, anxiety, and appetite control in the form of carbohydrate craving.

Tryptophan's effectiveness is enhanced by niacin in ratios of two parts tryptophan to one part niacin. The major food sources of tryptophan are cottage cheese, milk, meat, fish, turkey, bananas, dates, peanuts, and supplemental brewer's yeast.

• *L-arginine* is an essential amino acid during the growth period, and in some cases through adult life. It is synthesized from citrulline in a reaction involving aspartic and glutamic acids, and is a precursor of ornithine. Together they act in the detoxification of nitrogenous waste products, a process essential to amino acid metabolism. Arginine and ornithine, along with phenylalanine and other neurochemicals, are required for the synthesis and release of human growth hormone (HGH) from the pituitary gland. Arginine stimulates the production of ornithine and vice versa, and together they provide energy, help metabolize stored body fat, aid in the immune response favoring cellular repair, and produce hormones that build muscle. When taken as a supplement on an empty stomach at bedtime, they have a significant anabolic effect. The major food sources of arginine are all protein-rich foods, peanuts, cashews, pecans, almonds, corn, gelatin, carob, brown rice, oats, sunflower seeds, sesame seeds, peas, wheat, raisins, eggs, and supplemental brewer's yeast. It is also found in a free state in garlic and ginseng.

• *L-histidine* is another amino acid that is essential during the growth period. It is necessary for the maintenance of the myelin sheaths, the principal component of nerve fibers, and plays a key role in the treatment of arthritis. It is a source of the derivative "histamine," an important neurotransmitter. The major food sources of histidine are beef, lamb, pork, veal, poultry, milk, cheese, eggs, wheat, peanuts, walnuts, and supplemental brewer's yeast.

Nonessential Amino Acids

• *L-cysteine* and *L-cystine* are two more of the sulfur-containing amino acids. Cystine is a form of cysteine and one can be converted to the other as needed by the body. Cysteine has the ability to maintain elasticity and texture in the skin by slowing abnormal cross linkages in collagen. Cystine plays a role in forming the proteins found in hair, keratin, insulin, and digestive enzymes.

• *L-glutamine* and *L-glutamic* acid are both important to brain functions. Glutamine is the dominant amino acid in serum and cerebrospinal fluid, and acts as a detoxifier of ammonia-containing waste cells in the brain that affect the central nervous system. Glutamic acid is a derivative of glutamine, and it has the characteristic of converting from glutamine when needed along with glucose as fuel for brain cells. It can also be synthesized as a nitrogen source to and from other nonessential amino acids.

• *L-alanine* functions in the metabolism of tryptophan and as a stabilizer of blood glucose over prolonged periods of hunger when amino acids break down resulting in muscle loss. It also has a cholesterol-reducing effect when combined with arginine and glycine.

• *L-aspartic* acid plays an essential role in the metabolic processes of the liver and brain. It is chiefly glycogenic in that it is active in the process of transamination and deaminization of amino acids in the liver. It also plays a role in the detoxification of ammonia, which improves stamina and endurance. It is plentiful in plant foods, especially sprouted seeds.

• *L-carnitine* has been established to be an essential element to the metabolism of fat. It reduces triglycerides by transferring fatty acids in the body across the membranes of the mitochondria where they can be utilized as a source of energy. It is not found in vegetable proteins, only in muscle and organ meats.

• *L-glycine* is necessary for the biosynthesis of nucleic acids as well as bile acids. It also has glycogenic properties and is used in the treatment of hypoglycemia. Glycine becomes readily available for synthesis of other nonessential amino acids in the body, and is utilized in liver detoxification as well. Glycine supplementation along with arginine improves nitrogen retention in the muscles, and along with ornithine repairs and heals connective and damaged tissue.

• *L-proline* is one of the main components of collagen. It is readily transformed into hydroxyproline, which is incorporated into the structure of tendons and ligaments. Vitamin C supplementation makes proline more effective.

• *L-serine* has glycogenic properties and takes part in the biosynthesis of pyrimidine, purine, creatine, and porphyrin, substances needed for energy transfer in the body. It is also needed to form cystine. It is involved in skin metabolism and, topically used, contains natural moisturizing properties.

• *L-taurine* is a sulfur-containing amino acid derivative that is synthesized from methionine and cysteine. It functions as a neurotransmitter and has been shown to stimulate the production of growth hormone in large amounts. It helps maintain the correct composition of bile and the solubility of cholesterol. It plays a key role in sparing the loss of calcium and potassium, and has a stabilizing influence on blood sugar level, similar to that of insulin. It is deficient in diets consisting of vegetable proteins.

• *L-tyrosine* is derived from phenylalanine in the body and is effective in increasing brain levels of neurotransmitters. It is involved in the production of melanin (pigment) and is a precursor to the hormones adrenaline and thyroxin, and a deficiency results in low-thyroid symptoms.

Nutritional Cofactors

This selection of substances has been derived or biochemically isolated from nutritional sources and produces significant ergogenic effects on muscle size, strength, and performance when taken as supplements to a well augmented program of vitamins, minerals, and amino acids. They do this chiefly by aiding the enzyme structures necessary in synthesizing nutrients and/or natural hormones.

• Inosine *(hypoxanthine riboside)* is a nucleic acid derivative. Nucleic acids occur naturally in brewer's yeast. Inosine is used effectively to stimulate and utilize the body's production of ATP (adenisotriphosphate), which helps oxygenate deprived muscle tissue, giving the body strength and energy during a workout to train harder and longer. As a supplement, it is purest in crystalline form, and most significant when taken just prior to training.

• Ferulic acid is a molecule of Gamma Oryzonal, an extract of rice bran oil and a member of the plant sterols. Cycloartenol is also a molecule of

Gamma Oryzonal. Together the two molecules possess antioxidant, hypothalamic, fat-mobilizing, and anabolic effects. However, by enzymatically separating the two molecules from Gamma Oryzonal, their effect becomes up to thirty times more intensified. The result is FRAC, the trademark name for a superior product that contains biologically active trans-ferulic acid.

• Coenzyme B–12, or *Dibencozide,* is the biologically active form of vitamin B–12 (which often gets wasted in the gastrointestinal tract), and the only form found in cellular storage sites. When taken as a sublingual tablet rather than being ingested, it becomes up to twelve times more efficient as an activator of protein metabolism. It also produces rapid cell regeneration and faster recovery. It is best taken in dosages of at least 3000 mcg. and is most effective when taken with folic acid.

• Coenzyme Q–10 *(ubiquinone)* is considered to be one of the missing links in the body's food-to-energy chain. It assists the mitochondria in cell metabolism to produce heat and has been shown to be effective in promoting better strength and energy during physical performance. It is boosted by Vitamin E.

• Siberian ginseng (a root known as eleutherococcus) and smilax officinalis (from the sarsaparilla herb) are the two most widely accepted plant extracts that offer ergogenic properties. They've long been considered to increase stamina, strength, and endurance, and to some degree they aid the body in its own production of testosterone naturally, without harmful side effects.

Photo: Mike Neveux

— 3 —
THE DYNAMICS OF DIET

Training is your vehicle to strength, endurance, and the ultimate physique, but nutrition is your fuel. You are not going to go the distance without it. You have learned the principles of Perfect Nutrition and the functions of Supernutrients. Now with the application of this knowledge, learn how the Dynamics of Diet can lead you to your goals.

THE MUSCLE DIET

When you are training for peaks, power, performance, or simply the body you want, it is muscle that you are after. Whether you want to increase the size of muscles, change their shape, or improve their ability for athletic performance, this can be accomplished only by changes within the muscle fibers—changes that result in some degree of growth. Muscular growth is the necessary and inevitable result of all physical endeavors. Call it what you will, but any form of muscular development is bodybuilding, and that requires the right proportions of protein, fats, and carbohydrates in your diet.

The body's protein needs are actually higher than most standard recommendations and certainly higher than most people suspect. And the bodybuilder's needs are greater yet. Not only does the body need more protein to grow, but it needs more protein to maintain the muscle mass that is acquired. The National Research Council's RDA for the average adult is .42 grams of protein per pound of body weight. That allows for only about 10 percent of the diet to consist of protein. This would be almost adequate if the rest of the diet were perfectly compensated for in fats and carbohydrates, all amino acid requirements were being met, and the protein was 100 percent assimilated. But this is rarely the case. And bodybuilders have an even greater need above and beyond dietary problems. They have a body to build and maintain as well. A body with more muscle needs more protein. Recent studies have shown that athletes require between 1 and 1.5 grams of protein per pound of body weight, indicating that they need up to 35 percent protein from their diet and possibly more at times. That amounts to about three times as much protein as the average person for the athlete wanting to build and maintain muscle size and strength. This can be accomplished optimally in three ways: increasing the biological quality of dietary protein (see Chapter 1), nutrient supplementation (see Chapter 2), and increasing protein quantity. This does not mean increasing calories over what is needed for expenditure, but increasing the proportion of protein in the diet while keeping it in practicable balance with fats and carbohydrates. This will insure that energy demands are being met by the correct supplies of fats and carbohydrates, while leaving protein utilization for maximum muscle growth unhampered.

It takes more intricate processes and enzyme and absorption factoring for the body to convert protein into muscle than it does to convert carbohydrate into energy. If protein isn't readily available or properly broken down into amino acids ready to go to work, protein synthesis will pass right by the opportunity to build muscle and improve performance from a hard-earned workout. Instead it may even burn up muscle tissue if energy is needed. Remember, excess amino acids are stored in the liver and can be relied on for a reserve of energy. If ever in question, except when an energy explosion for a peak performance is required, it is better for a bodybuilder or athlete in training to be on the protein side of a dietary error.

The following guidelines are meant to help bodybuilders and athletes at all levels to build and retain muscle size and strength, increase energy, and maintain or reduce body fat while in training with optimum results.

Maximum Muscle-Building Range

(for the heavy anaerobic activity of bodybuilding, weightlifting, and powerlifting)

30 to 40 percent protein
30 to 40 percent carbohydrate
10 to 20 percent fat

The high end of the range is ideal for maximum muscle gain, strength, and power.

Muscle Maintaining/Defining Range

(for heavy anaerobic or cross-training activity)

> 60 to 70 percent protein
> 20 to 30 percent carbohydrate
> 5 to 10 percent fat

This is ideal as a temporary measure to acquire muscular definition by decreasing calories or increasing energy expenditure without losing muscle mass. However, training for more than three days on a regimen of low carbohydrates and low fats can deplete glycogen stores and burn up muscle at an expenditure rate of less than 500 calories per pound. Therefore, on the fourth day, increase the carbohydrate intake to at least equal the protein intake to replenish glycogen. Continue this three-day-on/one-day-off carbohydrate depletion/loading cycle until you have lost your desired amount of body fat. If your goal is to achieve peak muscularity, strength, and endurance for an event, you should plan on competing on a second consecutive carbohydrate-loading day (three days on/two days off) at the end of a cycle for best results. As you close in on your goal, you may need to decrease (or increase) your carbohydrates and/or fats even more, depending on how your body responds.

Moderate Muscle-Building Range

(for anaerobic/aerobic activity of cross-training burning 500 calories or more for at least one hour)

> 30 percent protein
> 50 to 60 percent carbohydrate
> 10 to 15 percent fat

This is ideal for a high-performance program involving weight training combined with aerobic activity such as bicycling or running, where a combination of moderate muscular development, strength, and endurance is the goal. This range can also be used to maintain muscle mass with heavy anaerobic activity.

Minimum Muscle-Building Range

(for aerobic activity)

> 20 to 25 percent protein
> 60 to 70 percent carbohydrate
> 10 to 15 percent fat

This is ideal for all aerobic types of activity where improved performance, endurance, and body weight management is the goal.

LIGHT TO MODERATE

(aerobic activity for thirty minutes to one hour, burning 300 calories or less per hour)

> Stay at the low-end range of protein.
> Stay at the high-end range of carbohydrates.
> Stay in the middle range of fats to maintain body fat.
> Stay at the low-end range of fats and decrease total calories and/or increase energy expenditure to lose body fat.

MODERATE TO HEAVY

(aerobic activity for over one hour, burning 400 calories or more per hour)

> Stay at the high-end range of protein.
> Stay at the low-end range of carbohydrates.
> Stay at the high-end range of fats to maintain body fat.
> Stay in the middle range of fats and decrease total calories and/or increase energy expenditure to lose body fat.

This range can also be used to maintain muscle mass with moderate anaerobic activity.

These are general, not absolute, guidelines. It is suggested that you do several test runs using the formula that best suits your goal before settling into a pattern. Check how you look, feel, and perform, making adjustments when necessary. Then decide what works best for you, being ready to fine-tune as you improve.

How does this translate into calories and grams? Let's do some arithmetic. As an example, a 150-pound person is on a cross-training program burning 500 additional calories above a base light activity rate of 2500 calories. This person's total requirement is 3000 calories per day for moderate muscle building and high performance activity. The recommended dietary proportions selected from the cross-training Moderate Muscle-Building Range are:

30 percent protein
60 percent carbohydrate
10 percent fat

The person's actual portion of protein, carbohydrate, and fat calories from the total calories required is:

.30 x 3000 = 900 calories of protein
.60 x 3000 calories = 1800 calories of carbohydrate
.10 x 3000 calories = 300 calories of fat

Use this basic formula to convert calories into grams:

1 gram of protein = 4 calories
1 gram of carbohydrate = 4 calories
1 gram of fat = 9 calories

Therefore, the person's actual portion of protein, carbohydrate, and fat gram requirements is:

900 calories ÷ 4 grams = 225 grams protein
1800 calories ÷ 4 grams = 450 grams carbohydrate
300 calories ÷ 9 grams = 33.3 grams fat

To double-check the protein requirement/allotment per pound of body weight, use this formula:

225 grams protein ÷ 150 pounds = 1.5 grams protein (Ideal!)

LOSING FAT WITHOUT LOSING MUSCLE

Dieting for any person—a bodybuilder, an athlete, or just the average exerciser—is tough. It's more than a matter of losing fat, it's a matter of losing fat without losing muscle.

Extremely low-calorie diets never work for anybody for any length of time with the results they want. Besides burning up muscle, they deplete your body of nutrients, lower your metabolism, decrease your energy, promote binging, and leave your muscle tone flat and flaccid. The end result is a body that needs fewer calories to stay that way. Theoretically, you will have to stay on a diet for the rest of your life, which nobody can do, nor should do.

A diet consisting of a daily intake of less than 1000 calories for women and 1400 calories for men is considered starvation level by the body. When you sustain a low-calorie diet such as this, your body starts burning more muscle than fat for fuel. The body has an instinct all its own when it comes to survival. When faced with starvation, it will see to its energy needs first. Remember, muscle mass is a luxury, not a necessity. It requires more food and energy to obtain it, and it requires more food and energy to maintain it. So in starvation your body regards muscle as an enemy, something that needs to be gotten rid of for survival. Therefore it will use up muscle first, which needs more food and energy to maintain it, while it thinks food and energy are still available. It will save that slow-burning, protective layer of fat for last when it thinks food and energy will be scarce. Because of this, you also alter your metabolism and lower your setpoint, which is best described as the rate at which you burn calories, causing your body to need fewer calories to maintain more body fat. Then, when you begin eating normally again, your body will hoard the calories and store them as excess fat as if to prepare for the next starvation. It's looking out for your survival. And that is looking at it conservatively, because most people coming off of a starvation-level diet don't eat normally, they binge. Their body is depleted of energy and nutrients and they overeat all the things they shouldn't. The end result is less muscle fighting more fat with a slower metabolism than before. Your body doesn't stand a chance, and fat begins to take control. This is why the fat people who say they don't eat much are probably telling the truth. The real truth is that dieting like this offers only a temporary answer to a desperate situation, but eventually it becomes the problem instead of the solution.

By all practical methods you can lose only 2 to 3 pounds of fat per week safely without burning into muscle tissue. This is done most sensibly with a twofold method. First, you should drop your daily food intake by only 25 percent, or about 500 calories for women and 700 calories for men, below what is required for normal light activity. Depending on your muscle/fat body composition, this puts you at about the caloric intake required for your resting metabolic functions. Since it takes 3500 calories expended or reduced to burn off 1 pound of body fat, that will amount to a loss of 1 pound of fat per week for women and 1.4 pounds of fat per week for men. If calories are reduced any further below the resting metabolic rate without raising the metabolism above the light activity rate, the body will burn up muscle. Raising the metabolic rate will burn up fat, and this is where exercise comes in. Specifically, your caloric expenditure should equal your caloric reduction, leaving just the calories required for your basal metabolism to function, putting you in a neutral fat-burning, muscle-retaining zone. Therefore, by expending through exercise an additional 500 calories a day for women and 700 calories a day for men, the body will burn off another 1 pound of fat per week for women and 1.4 pounds of fat per week for men. That amounts to a solid fat loss of 2 pounds a week for women and 2.8 pounds a week for men. Any more than that and you risk burning into muscle. This is how weight loss works in numbers, but variables do come into play, especially if you have more muscle mass than the average person. And men, as a rule, have more muscle per pound of body weight than women. Therefore the resting metabolic rate will be higher in ratio. Experiment using this format and see what works best for you.

When starting a diet, the weight may come off quickly at first. Rest assured that this is not all fat. Some of it is water retained by the tissues. But as the diet progresses you may find that the weight comes off more slowly. If you are training, this could be due to an increase in muscle, which weighs more than fat. It could also be due to the fact that as you get closer to your goal and approach your essential weight, your body will automatically flip a metabolic switch to slow you down and keep you from going to a potentially dangerous low body weight, especially if you are training. In spite of the dangers, if you are training and dieting correctly, your body is in no way eager to lose hard-earned muscle (or necessary fat) and it's slowing you down from doing so. At this point, you should seek to maintain your present body weight until your system adjusts to the new level of fitness.

Muscle fights fat and it is the best safeguard you can have against being overweight. Muscle has fat-burning enzymes within its fibers and it also burns calories at a higher rate just resting than any other body tissues. It also has the capability of accumulating fat within its fibers intramuscularly when too much weight is gained. This kind of fat is the hardest to get rid of. The fatter you get, the more you lower muscle quality, thereby the ability to acquire it. Bodybuilders or athletes who ''bulk up'' (get fat) in their off-season between competitions and events are actually defeating their purpose. It hinders muscle growth. The body has to utilize the energy of body processes packing on fat when it's trying to build muscle, especially when compounded with the metabolic expending process of ultimately ''cutting up'' (losing fat). Since muscle mass and density play a big role in overall lean body composition, the more muscle there is in proportion to fat, the faster and more efficiently the body will burn it off and keep it off, leaving muscle tissue intact. To avoid a training burnout and muscle depletion, dieting should take place no more than four to six weeks before a competition. Therefore women should stay no more than 6 to 8 pounds, and men 8 to 10 pounds, away from their competitive body weight year-round.

THE TRAINING TABLE

When you are on a training program your diet becomes somewhat of a scientific effort. What you eat, how much you eat, and when you eat become important. And when your goal is to build muscle for peaks, power, performance, or the ultimate physique, protein and when you get it become even more important.

Your body can assimilate only 25 to 30 grams of protein at a meal. Anything over that will be converted to energy (or fat, if your total caloric intake is too high). For the 150-pound athlete who needs 225 grams of bodybuilding protein per day, this cannot be accomplished in a couple of meals. It requires seven or eight small meals throughout the day, each containing close to 30 grams of protein. Realistically that amounts to only a couple of ounces from a high-quality protein source. But there is not much margin for error here. Protein consumption must be based on maximum assimilation. This can be insured by several measures. Although you should eat protein with each meal to restore tissues, stabilize hunger, and keep the protein-digesting enzymes present, every meal should consist of not only protein, but also fats and carbohydrates in the balance that is recommended for your goals. Each meal should be complete. These macronutrients (proteins, fats, and carbohydrates), along with their micronutrients (vitamins and minerals), function best in synchronization with each other in providing energy and synthesizing protein. Eat a small amount of raw carbohydrate food first, such as a salad or a vegetable, to activate the digestive enzymes necessary to utilize the oncoming protein food with "raw" efficiency. Eat the majority of your protein foods next before getting to the majority of the carbohydrate foods. This allows your body to absorb as much protein as it can without confusion. It also eliminates the possibility of going overboard on carbohydrates, which can interfere with protein consumption and drive your blood sugar out of whack, or causing you to eat too many easy calories when you are hungry that can be stored as excess fat.

In your battle for the body, it is important to be aware of all the aspects that contribute to muscle growth. Muscles are generated by training and fueled by food, but they need rest for growth and repair. Training actually tears away at muscle fibers. To heal, they need cell-building protein along with complete recovery time to allow the nourishment to work. This is the period in which muscles grow and get stronger, able to conquer the next workout with more power and efficiency. In a sense, muscles need time in the trenches to build up in defense against unusual stress. Without it, your training and nutritional efforts will be squandered and you will not reach your maximum body-building potential.

Photo: Bob Gardner

—4—
COOKING GOOD

That simple little phrase "You are what you eat" sums up the principles in the chapters on Perfect Nutrition, Supernutrients, and the Dynamics of Diet. It's only logical that the physical nature and vitality of our bodies depend on the physical nature and vitality of the food we put into them. If we are going to preserve our health and build our bodies, we have to handle nourishment with the same careful regard. And cooking food the right way has everything to do with it.

Indisputably, it's not practical to eat all our foods in their raw basic state, and we don't. In fact, we eat most of our foods cooked, so it makes good sense to learn how to prepare foods with the least amount of destruction, retaining as much of their enzyme, nutrient, and fiber value as possible. The key is not to overkill food. Be aware and cook lightly. Keep in mind that you're going to get out of food what you put into it in terms of preparation. Long, lazy cooking treatments, repeated heat applications, and high-heat shortcuts are only going to shortchange you and your goals. So here is a rundown of the most healthful methods of cooking, along with helpful hints to keep you Cooking Good.

DRY COOKING

In a conventional oven, roasting and baking are the primary methods of cooking, but you should be careful with high and dry heats. Food is very exposed in the oven. Put the food as far away from the direction of the heat as possible. A cover or a piece of aluminum foil placed loosely over the top will help keep food from burning or drying out. Moist baking, a method of wrapping food "en papillote" (in parchment paper or foil), or by placing food in a Dutch oven or in ovenproof bags, is ideal for roasting or baking meats, fish, and vegetables without drying out their natural juices. When baking delicate foods such as breads or desserts, a pan of water placed on the bottom portion of the oven will deflect the intensity of the heat. It's always best to roast meats on a rack in a roasting pan to avoid contact with an overhot pan. This also keeps them out of their cooking fats and allows all-round cooking. A convection oven is an excellent alternative. It cooks foods, particularly meats, with circulating hot air and insures even doneness, brown all over on the outside, yet juicy and not overcooked on the inside. With a convection oven you have more control. It does about the same thing as a conventional oven, but in about two thirds of the time with a decrease of 25 to 50 degrees in oven temperature. That means less cooking to get the job done. It's also wonderful for warming and re-heating foods without overcooking them.

Broiling or indoor grilling are very good methods of cooking most meats and some vegetables. Done on a rack or grill placed either above or under the heating element, it allows food to cook on one side or both (depending on how well done you want it) and eliminates high heat coming from all directions. It also sears meat to help retain juices, yet allows outer fat to drip off. Meats or poultry with the fat or skin intact should be cooked no closer than 5 to 6 inches from the heat, otherwise the fat may catch fire and burn the meat. There's a method of "moist broiling" that calls for about ½ inch of water in the bottom of the broiler pan. This alleviates the high temperature of broiling and prevents burning. Fish (or vegetables) can be cooked a little closer to the heat, but for a much shorter period of time. One thing to watch out for is the word "grilled" when eating out. A grill is often just a griddle on which the food is fried in grease. You'll have to "grill" your food server to find out how a dish is prepared.

Probably the next best thing to owning a convection oven is an outdoor barbecue. Nothing makes plain food taste so good. Barbecuing meats causes the fast-melting fat to drip down onto the coals and explode with flavor, while it seals the outside of the meat, allowing it to retain its natural juices. You have wonderful juicy meat with the flavor of the fat—without the fat. If done correctly, barbecuing can be very safe and very healthy. It's always best to use ceramic or lava rock briquettes over a natural gas flame. Indoor portable barbecues that use an electric heating element under rock are also adequate, but they are not quite as versatile nor do they retain the flavor as much as outdoor barbecues. If you do use charcoal, make sure the coals are white-hot before cooking to burn off any dangerous chemicals. Should you have trouble lighting them, use starters made from bee's wax instead of lighter fluid. Leave the grill on the barbecue while the coals are getting hot. This will burn off any food or grease from previous cooking. You can also use a grill brush after the grill is hot to remove stuck-on food. Never use cleaning solvents. Cook food at least 6 inches from the coals. If food catches on fire while cooking, remove the grill with the food and splash a tiny bit of water on the flaming coals. For a really smoky outdoor flavor, use the addition of wood chips—mesquite, hickory, ash, alder, or oak. All of them are wonderful, but mesquite and oak are a bit more popular. Soak the chips in water for 30 minutes first, then spread them over ready-hot coals. Cook when they begin to smoke. Placing wet fresh herbs over coals will also add a savory flavor to barbecuing meats. To use dried herbs, soak them in water for 20 to 30 minutes before spreading them on the coals.

There are two ways to barbecue—directly and indirectly. The first method cooks food directly over the heat. This is best for searing chicken, hamburgers, fish and shellfish, and thinner cuts of meat such as steaks. The indirect method places food away from the hot coals, sometimes on the opposite side of the lit grill, and usually with the lid of the barbecue closed. This is considered best for slow-cooking whole fish, birds, roasts, and vegetables. You may also barbecue food wrapped in foil, placed directly over the heat. This is good for vegetables and foods that are too small for the grill or that may fall apart when cooking.

MOIST COOKING

Since most moist cooking is done on top of the stove, the best way to start off Cooking Good is to invest in a complete line of quality cookware with a non-stick surface. That includes all sizes of pots and pans and skillets (bakeware, too). This allows you the freedom to control your calories by cooking foods with very little fat or oil (or none at all). The nonstick surface also slows the evaporation of the low-calorie broths and liquids used in this book for stove-top cooking, enabling you to cook foods slowly and evenly, avoiding the use of fats. Then if you do choose to use any butter or oil, you can use just a small amount of it, and only for flavor. Low-calorie cooking sprays are a fair alternative, but are often made with inferior oils. You would do better to coat the pan with your own quality oil and wipe out the excess with a paper towel. The additional calories will amount to about the same.

Sautéing and stir-frying entail the same stove-top method of cooking, but differ somewhat in technique. Sautéing is usually done over medium heat. Cooking is brief and oil is optional, but some stock or liquid is necessary. Sometimes by covering a high-moisture food for a minute or two over low heat, it will develop its own liquid, just enough for sautéing. This method is good for browning small or ground pieces of meat and poultry, quick-cooking shellfish, and precooking cut vegetables. Stir-frying is generally done over medium to medium-high heat in a deep wok or skillet. A small amount of oil is used, but the addition of a small amount of liquid is helpful in cutting down on the need for oil. Food should be cut up fairly small for fast cooking, though cooking time will depend on size and variety. Vegetables should be cooked tender-crisp and meats, poultry, or fish should be ''just cooked'' and added last as they take less time to cook than vegetables. Liquid and/or a lid will speed up both the sautéing and stir-frying process, but lift the lid and allow time for the liquid to evaporate as the cooking finishes. You'll need to gauge your time accordingly.

Braising or stewing cooks food completely surrounded by liquid, which is meant to be consumed. The food is covered or partially covered and the heat ranges from low to medium, usually over a long period of time. This method is used for soups, stews, sauces, and grains, and for cooking tougher cuts of meat and poultry. Crock-Pot cooking also falls into this category and does the best job of slow controlled cooking without your having to stand over the pot.

Poaching is a method of cooking food completely covered with direct but gentle heat, with nothing added but a small amount of liquid (sometimes watery foods generate their own) that is meant to be consumed. Since a minimum of liquid is used, cooking is meant to be brief and is best suited for eggs, fish, and tender cuts of poultry.

Steaming is a method of cooking with indirect heat from steam, usually by placing the food in a steam tray above boiling water. It's ideal for vegetables, since the cooking water cannot touch them and leach out nutrients. Steaming is also satisfactory for seafood and some poultry, but it's best to wrap the food or line the steam tray with foil to avoid losing meat and fish juices in the water. Pressure cooking also falls into the category of steaming but with much more force and less time. It's best used for heartier vegetables and grains and must be closely monitored.

With a few exceptions, two methods of stove-top cooking to avoid are frying and boiling. Both denature foods in a different way. Frying or deep-frying requires fats and oils that when exposed to extreme heat convert to harmful "trans" fats and are very unhealthy. The combination of high heat along with damaged oil then becomes extremely dangerous and destructive to food. Boiling requires top heat. When food is placed for any length of time in boiling liquid (that is not meant to be consumed), not only does the food become overcooked very rapidly, but most of the vital juices and nutrients are leached out into the liquid. The only exceptions to boiling pertain to foods such as grains (the boiling liquid will be absorbed and eaten), eggs or shellfish (they have protective shells), whole unpeeled roots and tubers (potatoes, turnips, beets), and pastas, which of course can only be cooked by being boiled.

Microwave cooking, with or without liquid added, is considered a method of moist cooking in that foods are cooked by the agitation of water molecules within the food. But there are pros and cons concerning the properties of microwave cooking. This high heat caused by friction has the same effect on the healthfulness of food as conventional oven heat when its enzyme vitality is analyzed—the higher the heat, the more destruction. And due to the movement of molecules, the molecular structure of food is unusually altered, indicating that our own digestive enzymes may need further adaptation to microwave cooking to adequately utilize food cooked by this relatively modern method. Fat percentages in meat are decreased slightly more so it is better suited for fattier cuts, especially ground meats. And seafood, particularly shellfish, seems to fare well. But because molecular change inevitably alters the amino bond formations, it is advised that you keep the microwaving of protein foods down to a minimum. There is, however, evidence that more vitamins and minerals are retained when food is microwaved than cooked. Since fresh vegetables and grains have hardy fiber to protect their nutrients, they hold up better in microwave cooking than protein foods. Remember, though, that the cooking water leaches nutrients out of vegetables, so use as little as possible. And once again, even these foods should not be eaten cooked exclusively in the microwave. The microwave oven does have its place and it is indispensable for defrosting, reheating, and cooking some foods, especially when you are in a hurry. But don't overuse it. Be safe and moderate in its usage. There you have it—all you need to know to keep you Cooking Good and looking good! Make it part of your lifestyle plan of Bodybuilding Nutrition. And remember to cook lightly. Everything depends on it.

PART TWO

POWER FOODS

Photo: Bob Gardner

— 5 —
MEAT

POWERHOUSE ENTRÉES

Note:
Nutritional
calculations for
roasts and larger
pieces of meat are
based on
approximately 6
ounces of meat per
person.

Fast Tracks
For a savory flavor
when barbecuing,
use a sprig of
rosemary or other
hardy herb to baste
with instead of a
brush. Very
impressive.

Good red meat has been given a bad health rap in recent years—people say that it has too much saturated fat, that it is too high in cholesterol, that it has too many hormones—all of which are variable, relative, and based on a spectrum of controversy. If all the allegations made about meat in relationship to our health were proven to be fact, its advantages would still outweigh its disadvantages from a purely cell-building, life-giving standpoint. The truth is that animal meat, and that includes beef, veal, lamb, and pork, is the most totally nourishing form of protein on earth. If you ''never eat red meat,'' then you should start. Anyone who wants to build his body to its utmost potential cannot do so without some red meat in the diet. You might make some significant progress without it, but you'll never reach your peak.

Meat does the ultimate bodybuilding job in all ways. Fact: The protein in meat is the highest and most complete source of amino acids. Fact: The fat in meat, both saturated and unsaturated, is the most reliable food source of energy. Without either of these, there will be no intense training, no rapid recuperation, and no maximum gaining. Meat is also a superior source of the B-vitamins, particularly thiamin, riboflavin, niacin, and B–12. It is also high in the minerals phosphorus, sulfur, potassium, copper, and iron—both nonheme and heme. Heme iron is an element meat has that you cannot get anywhere else. It is the key to building red blood cells that unleash real strength and power when you train. Organ meats such as liver, heart, and kidneys all have even more concentrated doses of these nutrients (plus some more of their own), with generally more protein and less fat than muscle meats, so you can

Calorie Cuts
In place of oily marinades, try marinating meats, poultry, or fish in fruit juices, wines, or vinegars. Go with beef in raspberry vinegar, pork in pineapple juice, veal in lemon juice, lamb in sherry, chicken in orange juice, and fish in lime juice. If you like, add the seasonings of your choice to the marinade. Save some to baste with as you barbecue.

only go one better with these. The bottom line? Eat more first-quality red meat and get the steroid-free bodybuilding effect naturally.

The leaner the meat, the more nutritious it is in terms of vitamins, minerals, and protein. Some fat in meat is necessary in the diet and needed for energy, but if you get the leaner cuts of meats with all the visible fat removed, you will get as much fat as you need within the muscle fibers of the meat, without overdoing it.

To help you choose, here is a rundown of the "supercuts"—meats with less than 10 percent fat, starting with those that have the highest percentage of protein to the lowest percentage of total fat:

1. Kidney
2. Liver
3. London broil
4. Top round roast (lean)
5. Beef shank
6. Sirloin tip roast (lean)
7. Loin lamb chop
8. Round steak (lean)
9. Leg of lamb
10. Sirloin steak (lean)
11. Filet mignon
12. Veal cutlets
13. Porterhouse steak
14. T-bone steak
15. Veal chops
16. Rump roast (lean)
17. Rib-eye steak (lean)
18. Pork sirloin
19. Brisket (lean)
20. Pork steak (lean)
21. Rib roast (lean)
22. Cube steak (lean)
23. Ground beef (10 percent fat)
24. Flank steak (lean)

Next, take a look at the following Powerhouse Entrées, made exclusively with the supercuts of meat. They take protein to the max to help you build the body you want and make you a powerhouse in the gym. And you will enjoy the international herbs and seasonings and the trendy cooking methods that make them so wonderful. So get with it and put some muscle in your diet!

LONDON BROIL IN SHERRY-SOY MARINADE

Per serving:
314 calories
31 grams protein
20 grams fat
1 gram carbohydrate

⅓ cup low-sodium tamari
2 tablespoons sherry
1 tablespoon sesame oil
1 tablespoon rice vinegar
1 freshly pressed garlic clove
1 teaspoon raw honey
½ teaspoon ground ginger
¼ teaspoon ground red pepper
3-pound London broil

Mix all marinade ingredients together in a large baking dish or pan. Pierce the meat all over with a fork and place it in the marinade. Turn it several times to coat well, and marinate for at least 1 hour on each side. Prepare barbecue or broiler. Cook the meat 6 inches from the heat, 8 to 10 minutes on each side for medium-rare, basting several times with the marinade during cooking. Place the London broil on a large platter and slice it thinly on the bias. Serve in any meat juices and remaining marinade. *Serves 8.*

BUTTERFLIED LAMB IN MINT MARINADE

Per serving:
380 calories
26 grams protein
30 grams fat
0 grams
  carbohydrate

Grilling thought:
Spread a bunch of fresh wet mint leaves over the coals while cooking for added flavor.

⅓ cup rosé wine
¼ cup extra-virgin olive oil
2 freshly pressed garlic cloves
¼ cup minced fresh mint
1 tablespoon minced fresh oregano
Vegetable salt and freshly ground pepper to taste
5-pound leg of lamb, boned and butterflied
Cool Peach Yogurt Sauce (page 62)

Mix all marinade ingredients in a large baking dish or pan. Pierce the meat all over on both sides with a fork and place it in the marinade. Turn it several times to coat well and marinate for at least 2 hours on each side. Prepare coals on one side of the barbecue only. Cover and cook lamb on opposite side of coals until done as desired, depending on thickness. Turn once halfway through cooking to barbecue the lamb on both sides, basting with any remaining marinade. Serve with Cool Peach Yogurt Sauce. *Serves 8.*

STEAK STUFFED WITH HERBS AND ONIONS

Per serving:
444 calories
23 grams protein
37 grams fat
3 grams
  carbohydrate

1 tablespoon extra-virgin olive oil
2 large yellow onions, sliced
1 freshly pressed garlic clove
1 tablespoon each chopped fresh sage, parsley, and basil
2 tablespoons freshly grated Parmesan cheese
Vegetable salt and freshly ground pepper to taste
2½ pounds top sirloin steak, about 1 inch thick

Heat oil in a medium-size nonstick skillet. Sauté onions and garlic over medium heat for 3 to 4 minutes. Add herbs and continue to sauté several more minutes until onions begin to turn translucent. Remove skillet from heat and stir in Parmesan cheese and pepper to taste.

With a long, thin, sharp knife, cut an even pocket horizontally through the length and width of the steak, leaving a ½-inch edge around the rim, uncut. Stuff the pocket with the onion mixture and secure the opening shut with wooden toothpicks or small skewers. With your hand, gently flatten out the stuffed part of the steak so that the meat is somewhat uniform in thickness for cooking. Season with salt and pepper, if desired.

Place the steak on a broiler rack with the highest part about 6 inches from the heat. Broil 6 to 7 minutes on each side for medium-rare. Slice carefully crosswise into 1-inch-thick pieces. *Serves 8.*

BEEF FAJITAS

Per serving:
450 calories
32 grams protein
20 grams fat
38 grams
  carbohydrate

1½ pounds lean round steak, about ¾ inch thick
Juice of 1 lime
2 freshly pressed garlic cloves
¼ teaspoon cayenne
½ teaspoon ground cumin
8 corn tortillas, warmed
1 large red bell pepper, julienned
½ large ripe avocado
1 cup chopped ripe tomatoes
⅓ cup chopped scallions
½ cup plain nonfat yogurt
Cilantro sprigs
Tomato-Herb Salsa (page 123; optional)

Pound steak to a ¼-inch thickness. Mix together lime juice, garlic, cayenne, and ¼ teaspoon of the ground cumin in a large baking dish or pan. Marinate steak in the lime mixture for at least 6 hours. Turn several times to coat well.

Cook steak over hot coals or under a broiler 6 inches from the heat for about 2 minutes on each side. Slice it into thin strips.

Serve equal portions on four plates, each with 2 tortillas and an equal amount of red pepper, avocado, tomatoes, scallions, and a dollop of yogurt blended with the remaining cumin. Garnish with cilantro sprigs and serve with Tomato Herb Salsa, if desired. *Serves 4.*

THAI PORK IN SPINACH

Per serving:
413 calories
38 grams protein
24 grams fat
10 grams
  carbohydrate

2 teaspoons peanut oil
2 freshly pressed garlic cloves
1 white onion, diced
1¼ pounds boned lean pork steak, cut into 1½-inch strips
3 tablespoons tomato paste
2 tablespoons raw honey
2 tablespoons white wine vinegar
1 tablespoon chopped dried hot chilies (adjust to taste)
Vegetable salt to taste
1 bunch spinach leaves, about ½ pound

Heat oil in a large nonstick skillet and sauté garlic, onion, and meat over medium-high heat for about 5 minutes, until onion is translucent and meat is browned. Mix tomato paste, honey, and vinegar together and stir into pork mixture along with chilies. Season with salt if desired. Lower heat to medium and cook 10 to 12 minutes, stirring occasionally, until pork is done.

Place pork mixture in a serving bowl on a platter arranged with spinach leaves. To eat, spoon a small amount of Thai Pork onto a large spinach leaf, wrap it up, and eat it with your fingers. To eat the smaller leaves, wrap them along with the meat. *Serves 4.*

COOL PEACH YOGURT SAUCE

Per serving:
30 calories
3 grams protein
0 grams fat
5 grams
  carbohydrate

Here's a nice aside that makes a cool complement to barbecued lamb. Serve it over cucumbers, melons, or all by itself. It's also wonderful with any spicy meats.

> ⅔ cup plain nonfat yogurt
> 1 large ripe peach, pitted and peeled
> 2 tablespoons chopped fresh mint

Whir everything together in a blender until smooth and creamy. *Makes about 1¼ cups or 4 servings.*

SHISH KABOB

Per serving:
344 calories
37 grams protein
22 grams fat
4 grams
  carbohydrate

Interesting idea:
Try a real earthy delicacy and make kidney kabobs. Replace the lamb with lamb kidneys, skewering them lengthwise—they're just the right size.

> 1 pound lean boneless lamb chunks, cut from the leg or sirloin and about 1¼ inches thick
> 8 tiny white onions, peeled
> 8 fresh mushroom caps
> ½ cup dry red wine
> ¼ cup Chicken Stock (page 96)
> 1 tablespoon tomato paste
> 1 shallot, finely minced
> 1 teaspoon dried rosemary, finely crumbled
> 1 fresh parsley sprig, minced

Thread lamb, onions, and mushrooms alternately on 4 skewers. Mix remaining ingredients in a small bowl and brush all sides of the meat and vegetables generously with the sauce. Prepare barbecue coals. Place skewers on the grill 6 inches from the heat. Cook 4 to 5 minutes on each side for medium-rare, basting several times during cooking. *Serves 4.*

BEEF AND BROCCOLI IN
TOMATO-YOGURT SAUCE

Per serving:
316 calories
33 grams protein
12 grams fat
19 grams
  carbohydrate

8 ounces flank steak
1 tablespoon low-sodium tamari
1 freshly pressed garlic clove
1 teaspoon minced fresh ginger
2 tablespoons sake (or substitute white wine)
2 teaspoons sesame oil
½ pound broccoli florets
1 small white onion, sliced into strips
½ cup plain nonfat yogurt
1 ripe tomato, peeled, seeded, and finely chopped

Slice beef very thin. In a small bowl combine tamari, garlic, ginger, and 1 tablespoon of the sake. Add beef and let it stand coated in the marinade at room temperature for 1 to 2 hours.

In a large nonstick skillet or wok, heat 1 teaspoon of the oil over medium-low heat and stir-fry broccoli for several minutes until tender-crisp. Add the remaining 1 tablespoon of wine and braise broccoli another several minutes until semi-tender. Add water, if needed, for additional liquid during stir-frying. Arrange broccoli on a platter.

Heat remaining 1 teaspoon of oil over medium-low heat and sauté onion for about 1 minute. Drain beef, reserving the marinade. Add the beef to the onions and cook for another 1 to 2 minutes. Combine marinade, yogurt, and tomato and add to stir-fry. Cook 1 minute more until hot, stirring frequently. When done, pour mixture over the top of the broccoli. *Serves 2.*

SZECHUAN LAMB

Per serving:
347 calories
22 grams protein
22 grams fat
13 grams
  carbohydrate

2 lean loin lamb chops, about 4 ounces each
2 tablespoons chili sauce
2 tablespoons low-sodium tamari
1 tablespoon white wine vinegar
1 teaspoon peanut oil
2 freshly minced garlic cloves
1/4 pound fresh snow peas
1/4 pound fresh bean sprouts
1/4 pound sliced fresh mushrooms
1/4 cup Chicken Stock (page 96); more if needed
1/4 teaspoon red pepper flakes, crushed

Remove bone and any visible fat from the lamb chops and slice the meat very thin. In a small bowl combine 1 tablespoon of the chili sauce, tamari, and vinegar. Add lamb and let it stand coated in the marinade at room temperature for 30 minutes.

When done, heat oil over medium-low heat in a large nonstick skillet or wok. Add marinade and lamb and sauté with garlic for about 1 minute. Add vegetables and cook for several minutes more until tender-crisp. Use stock as needed for liquid. Combine the remaining 1 tablespoon chili sauce with red pepper flakes and blend into stir-fry. *Serves 2.*

MUSTARD-GRILLED FLANK STEAK

Per serving:
255 calories
38 grams protein
11 grams fat
2 grams
  carbohydrate

1/4 cup Dijon mustard
2 tablespoons freshly squeezed lemon juice
2 tablespoons low-sodium tamari
2 freshly pressed garlic cloves
Freshly ground pepper to taste
3-pound flank steak

Combine all marinade ingredients together in a large baking dish or pan. Add flank steak and turn on both sides to coat. Cover and marinate for at least 6 hours, or overnight. Prepare barbecue or grill. Cook meat 6 inches from the heat about 5 minutes on each side for medium-rare, basting occasionally with the marinade. Slice steak on the bias. Add more pepper to taste before serving. *Serves 8.*

GLAZED PORK TENDERLOIN WITH
PAPAYA-TOMATO RELISH

Per serving:
442 calories
46 grams protein
24 grams fat
8 grams
  carbohydrate

Tenderloin tip:
Pork tenderloin runs
thin and small, so be
sure not to overcook
it or it will be dry
and leathery.

Juice of 1 lime
2 tablespoons unsweetened pineapple juice concentrate
1 tablespoon raw honey
2 freshly pressed garlic cloves
½ teaspoon each ground sage and savory
Vegetable salt and freshly ground pepper to taste
1½ pounds pork tenderloin
Papaya-Tomato Relish (recipe follows)

Mix all ingredients together and baste pork tenderloin all over. Place it on a flat rack in a shallow roasting pan and tuck the tail under the meaty part of the roast to insure uniform thickness while cooking. Place a flat piece of foil loosely over the top of the meat and roast in a preheated 325-degree oven for 50 minutes to 1 hour, just until there is an absence of pink. (If you prefer to use a meat thermometer, insert it into the thickest part of the meat. When it registers 165 degrees, it is done.) Remove the foil and baste the pork with the glaze the last 10 minutes of cooking.

When done, place the tenderloin on a meat platter, top with any remaining glaze, and let it stand 5 minutes before cutting into ½-inch-thick slices. Serve with Papaya-Tomato Relish. *Serves 4.*

PAPAYA-TOMATO RELISH

Per serving:
62 calories
1 gram protein
0 grams fat
14 grams
  carbohydrate

1 large ripe papaya, seeded, peeled, and chunked
1 ripe tomato, seeded, peeled, and chunked
½ red bell pepper, seeded and chunked
1 tablespoon raw honey
1 small garlic clove
1 teaspoon grated lime peel
Juice of 1 lime

Put half the papaya chunks in a food processor or blender along with remaining ingredients and process to a coarse consistency. Add remaining papaya and process again briefly just until tiny chunks of papaya remain. Serve as a condiment with Glazed Pork Tenderloin. *Serves 4.*

VEAL SCALOPPINI IN
MUSHROOM-MADEIRA SAUCE

*Per serving (meat
and sauce):*
352 calories
38 grams protein
20 grams fat
3 grams
  carbohydrate

Re-veal-ing tips:
Because only gela-
tin is used as a
thickener, the longer
the sauce stands the
thicker it will
become; also, the
hotter the meat the
more liquid the
sauce will become.
Remember: The
best veal to use is
milk-fed veal less
than 3 months old.
If you can't obtain
it, soak the veal
scallops in nonfat
milk overnight.

Veal is often breaded and fried and served well done, but it shouldn't be, especially the lean and delicate scallops or cutlets. This recipe defies tradition and calls for lightly sautéed veal scallops in a lean sauce fragrant with Madeira.

The Sauce:

1 cup Chicken Stock (page 96)
½ cup Madeira wine
¼ cup thinly sliced fresh mushrooms
1 small freshly pressed garlic clove
2 teaspoons each minced fresh parsley and basil
1 packet unflavored gelatin

The Veal:

12 ounces veal scallops, about ¼ inch thick (or use veal cutlets pounded thin)
2 teaspoons butter

Put all the sauce ingredients, except for gelatin, in a medium-size saucepan. Boil uncovered over high heat for several minutes until mixture is reduced to a little more than half. Separately, dissolve gelatin in ¼ cup of the boiling liquid. Then pour the gelatin liquid back into the saucepan and stir for 1 minute more over high heat. Remove pan from heat and let sauce cool until it begins to thicken slightly.

Make several small cuts around the edge of each veal scallop to keep it from curling when cooking. Melt 1 teaspoon of the butter plus 1 tablespoon of the sauce over medium heat in a large cast-iron skillet. Make sure the bottom is well coated. Brown the veal scallops on one side, about 1½ minutes. Remove the veal from the skillet and melt the remaining 1 teaspoon of butter plus 1 tablespoon of sauce. Cook the scallops the same way on the other side for about 1 minute more, or until the inside is slightly pink. Do not overcook the veal until it is gray inside or it will toughen. Remove the veal scallops from the skillet and serve topped with sauce. *Serves 2.*

Healthful Hint
To peel and seed a tomato, stroke the skin with the dull edge of a paring knife until the skin is wrinkled. Cut in half crosswise to squeeze out the seeds, then peel it. This method of loosening the skin avoids the usual method of heating the tomato before peeling it.

Liquid assets:
Some liquid may form on the bottom of microwave dishes and casseroles, but don't pour it out. That is where a lot of the nutritious meat juices and valuable nutrients are.

FIT-AND-FAMOUS CASSEROLES

If you sometimes feel as if you are losing power in a hungry age of Spartan diets and strenuous workouts, you're right. When real hunger sets in you want real food, and lots of it. A big, beefy casserole would do just fine. But if you think you can't have it in your quest for perfection, you are wrong. These hardy but calorie-controlled casseroles were created to stick to your ribs, not to your abs. They're fit because they are made with only the essentials—fresh meats, vegetables, and whole grains—without the excess use of fats and starchy fillers. They're famous—well, just look at their world renowned origins. And they're fabulous. Every single one of them combines high-protein meat with complex carbohydrates, so you get more nutritional mileage for your calories in all ways. One is a power food, the other is a performance food. One does what the other doesn't. What one lacks in nutrients, the other makes up for. Both supply iron and protein—you know that, but bet you didn't know that when the heme iron and amino acids in meat accompany vegetables and grains in a meal, they boost the nonheme iron absorption of these carbohydrate foods by as much as ten times, and increase their protein value as well.

So don't set yourself up for a burnout, in the kitchen or the gym. These superfabulous main-dish meals have it all. And that includes three healthy methods of cooking to choose from: oven, stove-top, and one-step microwave. Take your pick, but don't take your time. Get with these no-nonsense casseroles and pump some iron into that body!

DENVER BEEF HASH

Per serving:
296 calories
27 grams protein
11 grams fat
22 grams
   carbohydrate

Done completely in one microwave process, this Wild West casserole uses no oil and does away with a lot of crazy frying.

2 russet potatoes, peeled and finely diced
1 red or green bell pepper, finely diced
1 yellow onion, finely diced
1 freshly pressed garlic clove
2 tablespoons "natural-style" catsup
1 tablespoon low-sodium tamari
1 pound lean beef, coarsely ground or chopped
Vegetable salt and freshly ground pepper to taste

Combine all ingredients well, except the beef and seasonings, in a 9 x 12-inch covered glass casserole dish. Crumble in beef and mix everything together once again. Cover and cook in a microwave oven on high for 14 to 16 minutes, stirring once halfway through cooking. Let stand, covered, for 5 minutes before serving. Season with salt and pepper, if desired. *Serves 4.*

BOEUF BOURGUIGNONNE

Per serving:
292 calories
37 grams protein
9 grams fat
7 grams
   carbohydrate

Braised note:
Add a little extra chicken stock if needed during braising.

1 cup burgundy wine
1 cup Chicken Stock (page 96)
1 teaspoon each dried marjoram and tarragon
1½ pounds lean boneless beef chunks
1 tablespoon extra-virgin olive oil
12 tiny white onions, peeled
1 bay leaf
3 whole peppercorns
1 carrot, chopped
1 cup fresh mushrooms, sliced
Vegetable salt
2 tablespoons snipped fresh parsley

Mix wine, stock, and herbs in a deep bowl. Add meat, toss to coat, and marinate overnight.

Heat oil in a large nonstick skillet. Add meat chunks, reserving leftover marinade. Toss them over medium heat until they are brown on the outside, about 5 minutes. Add onions and continue to toss just

until they are golden. Pour in reserved marinade and stir in seasoning and carrots. Simmer, covered, for 45 minutes. Add mushrooms and salt to taste. Simmer, covered, another 15 minutes. Top with snipped parsley. *Serves 6.*

DEADLIFT CHILI CON CARNE

Per serving:
245 calories
22 grams protein
9 grams fat
24 grams
 carbohydrate

Better than canned beans:
To prepare pinto beans, soak ½ cup dried beans overnight in enough water to cover. Drain and rinse. In a small saucepan, simmer beans in 1½ cups fresh water, covered, for 1½ hours (or pressure-cook them for 10 minutes). Drain again and add to chili.

This lighter version of chili con carne replaces half the amount of beans with corn, making it a complete protein combination.

2 pounds lean ground beef (10 percent fat)
2 freshly pressed garlic cloves
2 small yellow onions, chopped
2 cans (6 ounces each) tomato paste
2 cans (8 ounces each) tomato purée
4 cups Chicken Stock (page 96)
2 cups chopped and seeded tomatoes
2 jalapeño chilies, chopped and seeded
2 tablespoons chili powder
1 teaspoon ground cumin
½ teaspoon each dried oregano and cayenne
2 teaspoons raw honey
1 cup cooked pinto beans
1 package (10 ounces) frozen corn, rinsed and drained (or substitute 1½ cups
 fresh corn kernels)
2 cans (12 ounces each) "lite" beer (you may substitute chicken stock for any
 part of it)
Vegetable salt

In a large covered kettle or stockpot, crumble in beef and sauté over medium heat. Add garlic and onions and continue to sauté until meat is cooked and onions are translucent. Drain off any excess fat. Add remaining ingredients except beer and salt and simmer partially covered approximately 25 minutes. Add beer and salt to taste and simmer for another 5 minutes. *Serves 12.*

Chili max out: Serve with chopped fresh onions, avocados, and grated low-fat Cheddar cheese.

MOUSSAKA

Here's another internationally famous casserole made with ground lamb that is ideal for microwaving.

Per serving:
425 calories
27 grams protein
30 grams fat
14 grams
  carbohydrate

1 large eggplant, peeled and sliced ½ inch thick
1 freshly pressed garlic clove
1 teaspoon dried basil
½ teaspoon dried oregano
1 can (8 ounces) tomato sauce
2 large ripe tomatoes, sliced
2 ounces Parmesan cheese, freshly grated
1 pound lean ground lamb
Vegetable salt and freshly ground pepper to taste
2 ounces feta cheese

Arrange half the eggplant slices in a 10-inch round covered glass casserole dish. Stir garlic and herbs into the tomato sauce and spoon ½ can of the sauce evenly over the top of the eggplant. Arrange with 1 sliced tomato and sprinkle with half the Parmesan cheese. Crumble the ground lamb evenly over that. Then make another layer with the remaining eggplant, sauce, and tomato slices. Season with salt and pepper as you go, if desired. Crumble the feta cheese over the top of the casserole and sprinkle with remaining Parmesan cheese.

Cover and cook in the microwave on high for 18 to 20 minutes, rotating the casserole dish 180 degrees halfway through cooking. Let stand, covered, for 5 minutes before serving. *Serves 4.*

VEAL RAGOUT

Per serving:
376 calories
59 grams protein
11 grams fat
7 grams
  carbohydrate

4 veal shanks, about 1¼ pounds each
8 cups Chicken Stock (page 96), or substitute water for any part of it
2 thin slices of lemon
2 garlic cloves
1 teaspoon each dried marjoram and thyme
4 whole peppercorns
½ pound turnips, peeled and cut into small chunks
12 tiny white onions, peeled
2 ripe tomatoes, peeled, seeded, and chopped

12 fresh mushroom caps
¼ cup chopped fresh parsley
Vegetable salt to taste

Place veal shanks, stock, lemon, and herbs in a large covered kettle or stockpot. Bring to a boil, lower heat, and simmer uncovered for approximately 1 hour. When veal shanks are tender, remove them from the pot and strain the stock. Remove the meat from the bones in small chunks and put them back in the pot with the stock. Bring everything back to a boil and add vegetables. Lower heat and simmer, partially covered, for 15 to 20 minutes, or until vegetables are semitender. *Serves 6.*

MOROCCAN LAMB STEW

Per serving:
438 calories
45 grams protein
14 grams fat
34 grams
   carbohydrate

Chick-pea note:
To cook chick-peas (also known as garbanzo beans), soak ½ cup dried beans overnight in a small saucepan with enough water to cover. When done, add more water, just enough to cover if needed, and bring to a boil. Lower heat and simmer, covered, for about 2 hours, or until chick-peas are tender.

1 tablespoon extra-virgin olive oil
1½ pounds boneless lamb leg, cut into 1¼-inch chunks, all visible fat removed
2 small yellow onions, chopped
1 freshly pressed garlic clove
3 large ripe tomatoes, seeded and chopped
⅓ cup seedless golden raisins
½ teaspoon each paprika and dried savory
¼ teaspoon each ground cinnamon and coriander
1 cup Chicken Stock (page 96)
2 tablespoons chopped fresh parsley
Vegetable salt to taste
1½ cups cooked chick-peas

Heat oil in a large covered kettle or stockpot. Add lamb, onions, and garlic and sauté over medium heat for about 5 minutes. Add tomatoes, raisins, and seasonings and continue to sauté several more minutes. Stir in stock, parsley, and salt, if desired. Cover, lower heat, and simmer stew for about 30 minutes. Then add chick-peas and stir once more carefully, so as not to break the skins. Cover and simmer another 15 minutes, until done. *Serves 4.*

Stew in style: This makes a wonderfully exotic meal served over couscous, a Moroccan grain.

REUBEN CASSEROLE

Lean cuts of pork are the leanest of all the meats, with just 180 calories per 3 ounces. Pork is also the highest in niacin of all the meats. Have only the "supercuts" of pork ground for this layered high-protein casserole.

Per serving:
363 calories
41 grams protein
17 grams fat
9 grams
  carbohydrate

1½ pounds coarsely ground lean pork
3 cups finely shredded cabbage
1 freshly pressed garlic clove
1 teaspoon caraway seeds
Vegetable salt and freshly ground pepper to taste
3 large slices whole-grain rye bread, torn into small pieces
½ cup shredded low-fat Swiss cheese
6 egg whites, warmed to room temperature
2 egg yolks
1½ teaspoons dry mustard

Crumble pork and cabbage into a large nonstick skillet. Cover tightly and cook over low heat for about 5 minutes, until moisture begins to form. Using the pork's liquid for sautéing, raise heat to medium and add garlic and caraway seeds. Continue stirring over medium heat for about 5 more minutes, until pork is brown and cabbage is tender-crisp. Pour off any excess liquid and fat and sprinkle with salt and pepper to taste.

Place the pork and cabbage in a round 3-quart casserole dish. Arrange bread pieces over the top, covering it well. Sprinkle with Swiss cheese. With an electric mixer, beat egg whites in a medium-size bowl just until foamy. Stir in 2 egg yolks and dry mustard and season with more salt and pepper, if desired. Spread the egg-white mixture evenly over the top of the casserole. Bake uncovered in a preheated 350-degree oven for 30 to 35 minutes, until topping is golden brown. *Serves 6.*

STEAK AND KIDNEY PIE

Per serving:
336 calories
43 grams protein
12 grams fat
12 grams
  carbohydrate

1 pound beef kidney
1 pound boneless rib-eye steak
3 cups Chicken Stock (page 96)
2 teaspoons Worcestershire sauce
1 white onion, diced
1 celery rib, diced
1 carrot, diced
2 new white potatoes, peeled and quartered
⅓ cup chopped fresh parsley
1 cup coarse whole wheat bread crumbs
1 tablespoon butter, softened

Cut beef kidney in half crosswise. Remove outer membrane and cut out all visible gristle and fat. Cut any fat away from the steak. Chop the kidney and the steak into ¾-inch pieces. Add the pieces to a large nonstick skillet along with ¼ cup of the stock and 1 teaspoon of the Worcestershire sauce. Sauté them over medium heat for about 5 minutes, using more stock for liquid if necessary. When done, remove them from the skillet and place them in a 3-quart covered casserole dish.

In the same skillet, add onion, celery, and carrots along with an additional ¼ cup of the stock. Sauté over medium heat for another 5 minutes, using more stock if needed. When done, transfer vegetables to the casserole dish. Stir in remaining stock, Worcestershire sauce, potatoes, ¼ cup of the parsley, and pepper to taste. Cover and cook in a 350-degree oven.

After 1 hour, take the casserole out of the oven. Remove the potatoes and mash them with some of the cooking liquid until creamy. Stir back into the casserole. Mix the bread crumbs, butter, and remaining parsley together with fingers and crumble over the top. Put the pie back into the oven and bake another 10 minutes, uncovered, until topping is crispy. *Serves 6.*

THE MUSCULAR MEAT LOAF

Look out, here comes the new meat loaf, flexing its muscles all over the world! Say good-bye to the old meat loaf with its high fat content and starchy ingredients, and say hello to these seven lean and mean versions of that great American classic. And they're oh-so-healthy because no cheap hamburger meat, whole milk, or white bread crumbs are used. They have been replaced with extra-lean ground meats and fresh vegetable fillings, seasoned with savory herbs and spices. When you shop, be sure to get the leanest ground meat money can buy, with no more than 10 percent fat if possible. If it's not available, or you are not certain how much fat it contains, have a butcher grind cuts from the sirloin, round, or leg portions of the meat with all visible fat removed. If you are having poultry ground, have them remove the skin first. Choose a fine to medium grind. And have some fun with your meat loaf. Be willing to experiment with other fillings: chopped broccoli, cabbage, squash, and shredded potato or turnip. Add your favorite seasoning and you have a nutrition-packed, low-fat, high-protein meal. So rejoice, meat loaf lovers. The Muscular Meat Loaf has arrived!

For your good health: Have the butcher grind meat for you in a clean grinder that contains no previous scraps of pork or poultry. Better yet, grind it yourself. Always handle meat with clean hands. Store it in the coldest part of the refrigerator and plan on eating it within a day of buying it.

Note:
These meat loaves are best cooked in a 9 x 5-inch baking pan with a nonstick surface, but an alternate choice is an ovenproof glass pan. A loose foil cover over the meat loaf will keep it moist while it's cooking. It's hard to ruin a meat loaf, except if you overcook it and dry it out.

Power Booster
Talk about liquid protein! Warm up a jar of strained baby meat (any kind) liquefied with some stock or nonfat milk, season it your way, and eat it like soup. Or take it to work in a thermos.

SAVORY LAMB LOAF

Per serving:
222 calories
24 grams protein
9 grams fat
13 grams
   carbohydrate

1 pound lean ground lamb
1 cup grated carrots
1 small yellow onion, chopped
¼ cup seedless raisins
¼ cup chopped fresh parsley
1 teaspoon dried savory
½ teaspoon dried rosemary
Vegetable salt and freshly ground pepper to taste

In a medium-size bowl, combine all ingredients together well. Firmly pack lamb mixture into a 9 x 5-inch loaf pan. Loosely lay a piece of foil over the top and bake it in a 350-degree oven for 45 minutes. Remove the foil the last 5 minutes of baking to allow for browning. *Serves 4.*

MEAT LOAF PARMESAN

Per serving:
215 calories
26 grams protein
11 grams fat
4 grams
   carbohydrate

Positively eggplant Parmesan:
Replace the zucchini with an equal amount of peeled and chopped eggplant. You can also top the meat loaf with steamed eggplant slices instead of the tomato.

1 pound lean ground beef
1 cup grated zucchini
1 freshly pressed garlic clove
1 teaspoon dried basil
¼ teaspoon dried oregano
Vegetable salt and freshly ground pepper to taste
1 large ripe tomato, thinly sliced
2 tablespoons freshly grated Parmesan cheese

In a medium-size bowl, combine all ingredients together well, except the tomato and Parmesan cheese. Firmly pack beef mixture into a 9 x 5-inch loaf pan. Loosely lay a piece of foil over the top and bake in a 350-degree oven for 30 minutes. Remove foil, arrange the tomato slices across the top, and sprinkle with the Parmesan cheese. Continue to bake, uncovered, for 15 minutes more. *Serves 4.*

MEAT LOAF AND SALSA

Per serving:
202 calories
25 grams protein
10 grams fat
3 grams
   carbohydrate

1 pound lean ground beef
1 large bell pepper, diced
⅓ cup chopped yellow onion
1 freshly pressed garlic clove
2 teaspoons chili powder
Vegetable salt and freshly ground pepper to taste
½ cup Tomato Herb Salsa (page 123)

In a medium-size bowl, combine all ingredients, plus half the salsa, together well. Firmly pack beef mixture into a 9 x 5-inch loaf pan. Loosely lay a piece of foil over the top and bake in a 350-degree oven for 45 minutes. Remove the foil the last 5 minutes of baking to allow for browning. Top with remaining salsa and serve with additional salsa on the side, if desired. *Serves 4.*

LAYERED SPINACH AND VEAL LOAF

Per serving:
243 calories
39 grams protein
8 grams fat
3 grams
  carbohydrate

2 eggs, beaten
1 package (10 ounces) frozen defrosted chopped spinach (or substitute one large
    bunch freshly chopped spinach leaves, frozen, defrosted, and drained)
½ teaspoon freshly grated nutmeg
1 pound ground veal
2 scallions, finely chopped
½ teaspoon each dried marjoram and basil
Vegetable salt to taste

In a small bowl, combine eggs, spinach, and nutmeg and set aside. In a medium-size bowl, combine veal with remaining ingredients together well and divide the mixture in half. Firmly pack half the veal mixture into a 9 x 5-inch loaf pan. Add half the spinach mixture to the remaining veal mixture and blend them together well. Pack the combined mixture over the plain veal mixture. Spread the remaining spinach mixture over that. Loosely lay a piece of foil over the top and bake in a 350-degree oven for 45 minutes. Remove the foil the last 5 minutes of baking to allow for browning. *Serves 4.*

ORIENTAL MUSHROOM MEAT LOAF
(A little like Egg Foo Yung)

Per serving:
261 calories
31 grams protein
14 grams fat
3 grams
  carbohydrate

Optional topping:
Remove foil and
arrange sliced
pineapple (packed in
its own juice) over
the top of the meat
loaf halfway through
baking.

½ pound lean ground beef
½ pound lean ground pork
1 egg, beaten
1 cup chopped fresh mushrooms
⅔ cup fresh bean sprouts
2 scallions, chopped
1 freshly pressed garlic clove
2 tablespoons low-sodium tamari
1 teaspoon ground ginger
⅛ teaspoon red pepper flakes, finely crushed

In a medium-size bowl, combine all ingredients together well. Firmly pack meat mixture into a 9 x 5-inch loaf pan. Loosely lay a piece of foil over the top and bake in a 350-degree oven for 45 minutes. Remove foil the last 5 minutes of baking to allow for browning. *Serves 4.*

STEAK TARTARE WITH RED ONIONS

This is protein at its best.

Per serving:
251 calories
37 grams protein
4 grams fat
8 grams
  carbohydrate

Note:
Serve with thinly
sliced pumpernickel
bread, if desired.

1 large sweet red onion
1 egg yolk
1 tablespoon Dijon mustard
2 tablespoons finely minced parsley (reserve extra sprigs for garnish)
2 tablespoons capers
⅛ teaspoon freshly ground pepper
1 pound sirloin or round steak, ground medium

Peel and slice onion into ½-inch-thick rings. Finely mince 2 tablespoons of the onion (using smaller broken pieces) and mix lightly with remaining ingredients in a large bowl until just combined. Avoid packing the meat too tightly. Form a mound with the meat in the center of an iced platter. Surround it with the onion rings and garnish with sprigs of parsley. *Serves 4.*

LAMB TARTARE

Per serving:
248 calories
29 grams protein
22 grams fat
5 grams
  carbohydrate

½ cup finely ground bulgur wheat
⅓ cup cold water
1 pound lean lamb leg, finely ground
1 small white onion, finely minced or ground along with lamb
¼ cup finely chopped parsley (reserve extra sprigs for garnish)
⅛ teaspoon ground cumin
Pinch of cayenne
Vegetable salt to taste
2 large ripe tomatoes, cut into 6 wedges
Extra-virgin olive oil (optional)

Combine bulgur and water in a small bowl and let it stand 30 to 40 minutes to soften. Drain bulgur in a sieve, pressing it to squeeze out excess water.

In a large bowl, toss bulgur with remaining ingredients (except tomatoes and olive oil) until well combined. Heap the lamb mixture into six small mounds on a platter and chill for several hours. Garnish with sprigs of parsley and wedges of tomatoes brushed with a little olive oil, if desired. *Serves 6.*

Photo: Bob Gardner

— 6 —
POULTRY

COMPETITION CHICKEN

Calorie Cuts
Even if you don't eat cooked chicken skin, removing the skin before cooking will still save about 20 calories per piece.

The white meat of chicken is one of the best sources of low-fat protein. One half of a large chicken breast without the skin (6 ounces) has 284 calories, 54 grams of protein, and only 6 grams of fat, plus a heavy dose of essential amino acids. It is straight muscle-building food. But plain cooking methods without the fatty skin renders chicken dry and leathery, tasteless at best, and cooking it with the skin on leaves it with just a few too many calories. So now what? Get ready to perk up your taste buds and power up your diet. Here is just what you have been looking for—five new fast and flavorful ways to fire up a breast of chicken and help you make it to the finish line. Fabulously inventive, all are fast (the cooking time ranges from 3 to 25 minutes), all are skinless so they are good for you, and all are cooked with moist heat to keep them juicy and lock in the subtle flavors of herbs and seasonings. And, since no other ingredients are added, there are no added calories. So if you sometimes feel as if you are losing your footing on boring ground, let these fresh new ideas put some spring back into your step (and your chicken), and keep lean protein in your diet. Victory days are just ahead!

Cooking chicken: The recommended cooking times for chicken are fairly accurate, but since there are variations in the heating elements used and the size of the chicken breasts, cooking times may need to be adjusted. To be sure, when you are done cooking, check the center of a chicken breast to see that there is an absence of pink. If not, a minimum of additional cooking may be necessary. But be careful not to overcook it or the chicken will turn out tough and dry, even with moist heat. And don't forget, a couple of minutes of stove-top or oven cooking can translate into only a couple of seconds in the microwave.

MICROWAVE CHICKEN

Per serving:
284 calories
54 grams protein
6 grams fat
0 grams
   carbohydrate

2 skinless chicken breast halves (12 ounces)
½ teaspoon dried bouquet garni
2 twists of lemon peel
Vegetable salt and freshly ground pepper to taste

Place each breast half, meaty side up, in an individual microwave-safe plastic bag. Sprinkle each with ¼ teaspoon of the bouquet garni, add a twist of lemon, and seal each bag. Place one at a time in a microwave oven and cook on full power for 3 minutes. Remove each bag and let the chicken stand, sealed, for several more minutes before opening. Serve breasts in their own cooking juices and season with salt and pepper, if desired. *Serves 2.*

POACHED CHICKEN

Per serving:
284 calories
54 grams protein
6 grams fat
0 grams
   carbohydrate

Sober thought:
Liquor is added only for flavor, and since much of the alcohol evaporates during cooking, its calories won't count as long as you don't actually consume any excess poaching liquid.

2 skinless chicken breast halves (12 ounces)
½ cup sherry
2 garlic cloves, chopped
Vegetable salt and freshly ground pepper to taste

Place the breasts, meaty side down, in a large sauté pan with a cover. Add the sherry and garlic and cook, covered, over medium heat for 3 minutes. Turn the breasts over, spoon some of the poaching liquid over the top, and cover. Cook another 2 minutes over medium heat. Remove the pan from the heat and let it stand about 5 minutes more before uncovering. Serve the chicken topped with any of the remaining poaching liquid and season with salt and pepper, if desired. *Serves 2.*

STEAM-SMOKED CHICKEN

Per serving:
284 calories
54 grams protein
6 grams fat
0 grams
 carbohydrate

Subtle note:
The amount of liquid
smoke used in the
recipe produces a
subtle flavor. Use
more if a stronger
flavor is desired.

2 skinless chicken breast halves (12 ounces)
1 tablespoon liquid smoke
Vegetable salt to taste

Place the breasts, meaty side down, in a steam tray that will fit inside a medium-size saucepan. Fill the saucepan about ½-inch deep with water, along with the liquid smoke. Place the steam tray inside the saucepan (keeping the chicken about another ½ inch above the water line) and cover tightly. Bring water to a boil and let the chicken steam 8 to 10 minutes. Remove the saucepan from the heat and let it stand 5 minutes more before uncovering. Season with salt, if desired. *Serves 2.*

FLASH-BROILED CHICKEN

Per serving:
284 calories
54 grams protein
6 grams fat
0 grams
 carbohydrate

Broiling gauge:
Broiling differs
slightly with flame
and electric heat, so
let the orange slices
be your
thermometer. If they
become too charred
and start to burn,
lower the broiler
rack another notch
from the heating
element.

2 skinless chicken breast halves (12 ounces)
½ teaspoon dried fines herbes
1 large orange, cut into ¼-inch slices
Vegetable salt and freshly ground pepper to taste

Place the breasts, meaty side up, on a large piece of foil atop a broiler rack or tray. Sprinkle ¼ teaspoon of the fines herbes over each breast. Then arrange orange slices on top of each breast so that the meat is well covered. (Usually 3 slices will do it.)

Place the rack or tray about 6 inches below the heating element and broil chicken about 10 minutes. Remove the orange slices and turn the breasts meaty side down, to moisten them in their own juices. Continue to broil another 5 minutes. Remove from heat immediately and serve topped with cooking juices. Season with salt and pepper, if desired. *Serves 2.*

CHICKEN EN PAPILLOTE

Per serving:
284 calories
54 grams protein
0 grams fat
6 grams
   carbohydrate

*Low-cal serving
suggestion:*
Make a larger foil
packet and add
sliced fresh
mushrooms, celery,
or slivers of carrots
and zucchini,
cooking them along
with the chicken.

2 skinless chicken breast halves (12 ounces)
2 shallots, sliced
2 parsley sprigs, snipped
Vegetable salt and freshly ground pepper to taste

Place each breast half, meaty side up, in the center of a 12 x 12-inch piece of foil. Top with 1 sliced shallot and a sprig of snipped parsley. Bring opposite sides of the foil together and fold the edges just enough to seal tightly. Then roll the two ends just enough to seal tightly also. Each foil packet should be leak-free and slightly domed over the chicken. Pierce the foil to create one tiny air hole in the top of each packet.

Place the packets on a rack in the center of a preheated 450-degree oven and cook about 25 minutes. When done, remove packets from the oven and let stand several minutes before opening the foil. Serve breasts doused with their own cooking juices and season with salt and pepper, if desired. *Serves 2.*

Paper note: Cooking en papillote is traditionally done in parchment paper, but heavy-duty foil is less fussy, just as efficient, and produces quite a tasty result in its own right.

CHIC CUISINE

Nutritional note:
All chicken recipe
calculations are
based on 6 ounces of
chicken (or 1 large
breast half) per
person.

What can meet bodybuilding's lean high-protein requirements yet stand on its own two legs in the gourmet department? Chic Cuisine! Here are ten high-style recipes that take simple breast of chicken and turkey to new heights. You may recognize some of the old classics. They are true to tradition, but updated to satisfy today's trendy tastes in diet fare. And don't be afraid to try some of the newer creations, calorie-trimmed yet elegant. All require a minimum of cooking because the chicken is simply prepared. There is more emphasis on fresh herbs and vegetables and quick sauces rather than lengthy steps of breading, frying, and re-

Fast Tracks
The secret to a smooth sauce or gravy that becomes lumpy: whir it in the blender for a second or two. They'll never know!

Calorie Cuts
Draining cottage cheese of excess liquid removes the cream, which contains all the calories.

cooking that damage the health value of good food. Breast of chicken and turkey are one of the most digestible forms of meat you can eat, and for overall low-calorie protein, they can't be beat. Gram for gram they are fairly equal in protein and nutrients and are outstanding in the B-vitamins (especially niacin) and phosphorus. Also, for convenience they are virtually interchangeable in most of the recipes, as both are similar in flavor and texture.

Now you have the skinny on Chic Cuisine and you no longer have to be cooped up with the same old chicken thing to stay on a diet. With ten great gourmet recipes to explore, the world is your eggshell!

TURKEY KIEV

Per serving:
443 calories
64 grams protein
17 grams fat
6 grams carbohydrate

1 cup 1 percent low-fat cottage cheese
¼ cup chopped fresh parsley
1 large shallot
2 teaspoons freshly squeezed lemon juice
2 ounces blue cheese, crumbled
1½ pounds raw skinless turkey breast, sliced lengthwise in 4 pieces about ⅜ inch thick
½ cup buttermilk
⅓ cup chopped walnuts
2 tablespoons raw wheat germ

Using a large wire mesh strainer, drain any excess liquid from the cottage cheese so that it is less moist but not dry. Whir cottage cheese, parsley, shallot, and lemon juice in a blender until creamy. Stir in blue cheese.

Lay turkey slices out flat and spoon equal amounts of the blue cheese mixture lengthwise down the center. Roll each one up and secure with a toothpick. Brush rolls all around with buttermilk and place them on a baking rack and let them stand several minutes to dry. Finely grind walnuts and wheat germ together in a blender or food processor and place them in a shallow bowl. When turkey roll-ups are semidry, roll them all around in the walnut-wheat germ mixture until they are lightly coated.

Place rolls back on the baking rack, secured side down. Lay a piece of foil loosely over the top and bake them in a preheated 375-degree oven for 35 to 40 minutes until outsides are brown and crisp. *Serves 4.*

PEAR BLOSSOM CHICKEN

Per serving:
387 calories
56 grams protein
12 grams fat
14 grams
  carbohydrate

4 skinless, boneless chicken breast halves
½ teaspoon curry powder
¾ teaspoon ground ginger
2 large ripe pears, halved, cored, and peeled
½ cup plum wine (or substitute another fruity wine)
¼ cup chopped cashews

Arrange breasts close together in a 9 x 12-inch covered baking dish. Sprinkle each breast equally with the curry powder and ½ teaspoon of the ginger. Place a pear half, cut side down, on top of each breast. Pour plum wine over the chicken and pears, and sprinkle each pear with a pinch of the remaining ¼ teaspoon of ginger. Cover and poach in a preheated 350-degree oven for 30 minutes. Uncover, baste with the cooking liquid, and bake for another 5 minutes.

To serve, place each pear-topped breast on a plate. Spoon remaining liquid over tops equally and sprinkle with chopped cashews. *Serves 4.*

CHICKEN DIJON

Per serving:
332 calories
56 grams protein
9 grams fat
2 grams
  carbohydrate

4 skinless, boneless chicken breast halves
2 tablespoons Dijon mustard
½ cup evaporated nonfat milk
2 egg yolks
1 teaspoon balsamic vinegar
1 freshly pressed garlic clove
½ teaspoon dried tarragon
Freshly ground pepper to taste

Arrange chicken breasts spread slightly apart in a 9 x 12-inch baking pan. Spread ½ teaspoon of the Dijon mustard over the top of each breast. Loosely cover with a piece of foil and bake in a preheated 400-degree oven for 18 to 20 minutes.

Meanwhile, stir the remaining ingredients and the rest of the Dijon mustard together in the top of a double boiler with 2 inches of simmering, but not boiling, water. Cook the sauce for several minutes, stirring constantly. When it is hot and begins to thicken, remove it from the heat. When breasts are done, pour the sauce over each breast and serve. *Serves 4.*

TURKEY DIVAN

Per serving:
304 calories
49 grams protein
7 grams fat
9 grams
 carbohydrate

Asparagus tip:
If using frozen
asparagus, there is
no need to precook
them first.

Here's an elegant casserole made with precooked turkey and asparagus that is quickly finished off in the microwave oven.

1 cup reduced Chicken Stock (page 96)
1½ tablespoons arrowroot
½ cup 1 percent low-fat milk
¼ cup sherry
Vegetable salt and freshly ground white pepper to taste
1 pound asparagus, parcooked tender-crisp
4 tablespoons freshly grated Parmesan cheese
1¼ pounds precooked turkey breast, thinly sliced

Bring chicken stock to a boil in a small saucepan. Moisten arrowroot in milk and slowly stir it into the stock. Reduce heat to medium, add sherry, and continue stirring until mixture begins to thicken. Remove sauce from heat and season with salt and pepper, if desired.

Neatly arrange asparagus in a 9 or 10-inch covered microwave-safe dish. Pour half of the sauce over the top, covering the asparagus well, and sprinkle with half the Parmesan cheese. Lay the turkey slices evenly across the center of the asparagus and sauce, leaving the tips of the asparagus exposed. Cover the turkey well with remaining sauce and Parmesan cheese. Cook, covered, in the microwave on high for 5 to 6 minutes, just until hot. *Serves 4.*

CHICKEN ROUILLE

Per serving:
314 calories
54 grams protein
9 grams fat
2 grams
 carbohydrate

3 medium-size red bell peppers (or substitute one 7-ounce jar roasted peppers, rinsed and drained)
2 large garlic cloves
6 skinless, boneless chicken breast halves
½ cup Chicken Stock (page 96)
2 tablespoons Marsala wine
1 tablespoon extra-virgin olive oil
Vegetable salt and freshly ground pepper to taste

Place whole peppers and whole garlic cloves (with excess paper removed) on a piece of foil on a broiler rack 4 to 5 inches from the heat. Broil for about 20 minutes (or until they are semisoft and the skins are charred), turning them every 5 minutes or so. When done, enclose the

CHICKEN ROUILLE (*continued*)

peppers and garlic in a plastic bag and let them steam until they are cool enough to handle.

Next, place chicken breasts on a broiler rack about 6 inches from the heat and broil them 7 to 8 minutes on each side until done, lowering the rack if they start to char. (If you are using pre-roasted peppers, broil only the garlic along with the chicken.)

While the chicken is cooking, cut off the tops of the peppers to peel and seed them, and slip the skins off the garlic. Place both in a blender or food processor and purée along with the chicken stock. Pour purée into a medium-size saucepan and reheat just until hot. Stir in Marsala, olive oil, and salt and pepper to taste. Pour equal amounts of sauce over each chicken breast. *Serves 6.*

CHICKEN PAPRIKA

Per serving:
365 calories
59 grams protein
10 grams fat
8 grams
    carbohydrate

Thickening thought:
If you would like a thicker paprika sauce, moisten 1 tablespoon of whole wheat pastry flour in ¼ cup of the cooking liquid after the chicken is done. Add it to the skillet and stir until it begins to thicken. Add the yogurt last.

1 tablespoon butter
1 large yellow onion, chopped
2 tablespoons mild paprika
4 skinless, boneless chicken breast halves
2 cups Chicken Stock (page 96)
¼ cup chopped fresh parsley
Vegetable salt and freshly ground pepper to taste
1 cup plain nonfat yogurt

Melt butter in a large covered nonstick skillet. Add onion and sauté over medium heat for several minutes. Sprinkle in paprika and continue to sauté several minutes more, until onions are well coated.

Push the onions aside and in the same skillet add chicken breasts. Cook them about 1 minute on each side to quickly brown them in the paprika. Use a little of the stock as needed for liquid. Stir in the remaining stock, parsley, salt, and pepper. Bring stock to a boil and cover. Lower heat and braise for 25 to 30 minutes. Then add yogurt and stir until well blended and hot, but not boiling. Remove skillet from heat and serve. *Serves 4.*

CHICKEN MARENGO

Per serving:
384 calories
57 grams protein
13 grams fat
9 grams
  carbohydrate

1 tablespoon extra-virgin olive oil
2 freshly pressed garlic cloves
4 skinless, boneless chicken breast halves
12 tiny white onions, peeled
1 cup chopped and seeded Italian plum tomatoes
1 cup Chicken Stock (page 96)
½ cup dry white wine
¾ cup sliced fresh mushrooms
2 teaspoons chopped fresh basil
¼ cup sliced black olives
Vegetable salt and freshly ground pepper to taste
2 tablespoons chopped fresh parsley

Heat olive oil and garlic in a large covered nonstick skillet. Add chicken breasts, onions, and tomatoes and sauté briefly over medium heat. Add remaining ingredients, except parsley, and raise the heat to high until mixture begins to bubble. Cover, lower heat, and braise for about 20 minutes. Remove cover and simmer another 5 to 10 minutes to reduce stock slightly before serving. Sprinkle with parsley. *Serves 4.*

CHICKEN CACCIATORE

Per serving:
360 calories
57 grams protein
7 grams fat
15 grams
  carbohydrate

4 skinless, boneless chicken breast halves
1 yellow onion, quartered
1 green bell pepper, cut into strips
8 large fresh mushrooms, thickly sliced
3 cups Wine Marrow Sauce (page 156)
¼ cup chopped fresh parsley

Arrange chicken and vegetables in a large covered baking dish. Pour sauce over the top to cover everything well. Cover and bake in a 375-degree oven for 1 hour. Uncover and bake for another 15 minutes. Garnish the top with parsley. *Serves 4.*

TURKEY PICCATA

This herb-fresh version of a piccata requires no breading or frying in a lot of oil.

Per serving:
330 calories
52 grams protein
11 grams fat
5 grams
 carbohydrate

Fast Tracks
We all know that turkey meat is high in protein. But bet you were wondering what to do with those big old boring turkey legs or breasts. Insert slivers of garlic into the deepest part of the uncooked meat and throw them on the barbecue. Or roast them in the oven surrounded by sprigs of fresh herbs and a splash of wine. Simple.

⅓ cup freshly squeezed lemon juice
⅓ cup dry white wine
1 freshly pressed garlic clove
12 ounces raw skinless turkey breasts, sliced on the bias to ¼-inch thickness
2 teaspoons extra-virgin olive oil
Vegetable salt and freshly ground pepper to taste
1 teaspoon chopped fresh thyme
2 tablespoons chopped fresh parsley
1 teaspoon arrowroot

Mix together 2 tablespoons each of the lemon juice and wine along with the garlic in a shallow bowl. Add turkey slices and turn to coat well in the mixture. Let them stand about 30 minutes.

Heat 1 teaspoon of the olive oil in a medium-size covered nonstick skillet. Add turkey slices, cover partially, and cook on one side over medium heat for 2 to 3 minutes. Repeat cooking process on the other side with the remaining teaspoon of olive oil. Transfer turkey slices to a serving platter. Season them with salt and pepper to taste.

In the same skillet over medium heat, stir in remaining lemon juice along with thyme and 1 tablespoon of the parsley. Moisten arrowroot in remaining wine and add it to the skillet. Stir for about 1 minute, until sauce begins to thicken. Immediately pour it over the turkey slices and garnish with remaining parsley. *Serves 2.*

COQ AU VIN

Per serving:
354 calories
55 grams protein
12 grams fat
4 grams
 carbohydrate

1 tablespoon butter
1 freshly pressed garlic clove
8 whole shallots
4 skinless, boneless chicken breast halves
½ cup Chicken Stock (page 96)
1 small bay leaf
1 tablespoon each chopped fresh chervil and parsley
1 teaspoon chopped fresh thyme
½ cup red Bordeaux wine

French suggestion:
Serve with tender
cooked *petit pois*
(baby peas).

1 cup thickly sliced fresh mushrooms
⅛ teaspoon freshly ground pepper
Vegetable salt to taste

Melt butter in a large covered nonstick skillet. Over medium-low heat, sauté garlic briefly. Add shallots and toss to lightly brown them. Remove ingredients from skillet and set aside.

Add chicken breasts, along with stock and herbs, and sauté over medium heat until liquid evaporates and chicken has browned on the outside. Pour in wine, cover, and lower heat. Braise over medium-low heat for about 15 minutes. Then stir in mushrooms, pepper, and salt, if desired. Simmer, partially covered, for another 10 to 15 minutes, stirring in shallots the last 5 minutes. Remove the bay leaf before serving. *Serves 4.*

CHEEP CONCOCTIONS

Fast Tracks
To congeal fat faster
when chicken stock
is warm or at room
temperature, drop a
few ice cubes into
the pot until fat
forms around them.
Then simply lift the
ice cubes out along
with the fat.

What is economical in terms of cost, time, and calories, and cheaper by the dozen? Cheep Concoctions. And boy are they cheap! The following twelve clucking-good recipes are made with whole birds and less expensive cuts of poultry to keep you on your budget. You'll also find plenty of clever calorie-saving measures to keep you on your diet, plus some nifty time-saving dishes to keep you from running around the kitchen like a chicken without a head.

Yes, Cheep Concoctions are a bargain, but nutrition is the real deal. The dark meat of poultry is packed solid with protein, iron, and B-vitamins, particularly thiamin and riboflavin. Dark meat is good for you, but the combination of light and dark meat is even better. Together they make the vitamin-B complex and amino acid network complete, and are a superior form of protein.

And no, we didn't forget about taste. In this collection of body-building recipes you'll find succulent Cornish hens roasted with a Cognac-based vegetable stuffing and chicken baked in the "world's best barbecue sauce," along with some calorie-trimmed ethnic favorites. Wait until you try them and you'll have to agree that Cheep Concoctions were made to keep you on target and flying high.

APPLE-STUFFED TURKEY LOAF

Per serving:
250 calories
36 grams protein
8 grams fat
9 grams
   carbohydrate

1 pound ground raw turkey
1 egg, beaten
2 tablespoons nonfat milk
⅔ cup finely chopped celery with leaves
1 small white onion, finely chopped
1½ tablespoons poultry seasoning
Vegetable salt and freshly ground pepper to taste
1 large apple, cored, peeled, and sliced

In a medium-size bowl, combine all ingredients except the apple. Firmly pack half the turkey mixture into a 9 x 5-inch loaf pan. Arrange the apple slices across the top. Then pack the remaining turkey mixture carefully over the apples so they are completely covered. Loosely lay a piece of foil over the top of the loaf and bake in a 350-degree oven for 45 minutes. Remove foil the last 5 minutes of baking to allow for browning. *Serves 4.*

SWEET-AND-SOUR TURKEY STIR-FRY

Per serving:
393 calories
54 grams protein
8 grams fat
24 grams
   carbohydrate

1 teaspoon peanut oil
1 freshly pressed garlic clove
1 red onion, sliced into strips
1 green bell pepper, cut into bite-size chunks
½ teaspoon minced fresh ginger
½ cup unsweetened pineapple juice
12 ounces raw turkey breast, skinned and sliced into thin strips
1 tablespoon raw honey
1 tablespoon red wine vinegar
1 tablespoon tomato sauce
1 tablespoon low-sodium tamari (optional)

Heat oil over medium-low heat in a large nonstick skillet or wok. Add garlic, onion, green pepper, and ginger. Cook until vegetables are heated through but crunchy. Stir frequently, adding some of the pineapple juice for liquid if necessary. Add turkey and continue stir-frying for several minutes more. When turkey turns white, combine remaining pineapple juice, honey, vinegar, and tomato sauce and stir into the skillet. Add tamari, if desired. *Serves 2.*

TURKEY AND FRUIT BROCHETTE

Per serving:
301 calories
44 grams protein
5 grams fat
19 grams
  carbohydrate

Fast Tracks
Brush the "world's best barbecue sauce" on cut fruits or vegetables and barbecue them for several minutes on each side along with turkey, chicken meat, or fish.

¼ *cup freshly squeezed grapefruit juice*
¼ *cup unsweetened apple juice concentrate*
2 *tablespoons low-sodium tamari*
1¼ *pounds raw turkey breast, skinned and cut into 1-inch chunks*
1 *cup fresh pineapple chunks*
4 *fresh apricots, halved*

Prepare barbecue coals. Mix grapefruit juice, apple juice concentrate, and tamari together. Thread turkey and fruit chunks alternately on 4 skewers. Brush them all over with the juice blend. Barbecue 6 inches from the heat over medium-hot coals, about 6 minutes on each side. Baste well with the juice blend several times during cooking and once when done. *Serves 4.*

SAVORY CHICKEN AND RICE

(Another microwave favorite!)

Per serving:
384 calories
45 grams protein
7 grams fat
38 grams
  carbohydrate

Leg extensions:
Nutritional calculations are based on a 6-ounce portion of leg meat per person.

1 *large celery rib with leaves, finely chopped*
1 *large carrot, finely sliced*
1 *yellow onion, finely diced*
8 *chicken drumsticks, skinned*
½ *teaspoon each dried sage and thyme*
1 *snipped fresh parsley sprig*
1 *cup Chicken Stock (page 96)*
1 *cup uncooked quick-cooking brown rice*
Vegetable salt and freshly ground pepper to taste

Arrange all ingredients except rice and seasonings in a 3-quart covered microwave-safe dish. Cover and cook on high for 15 minutes. Add rice, making sure the grains are well covered with liquid. Cover again, rotate dish 180 degrees, and continue cooking on high for 7 to 8 minutes more. Let stand, covered, for 5 minutes or until rice has absorbed cooking liquid before serving. Season with salt and pepper, if desired. *Serves 4.*

TERIYAKI TURKEY STICKS

Per serving:
283 calories
51 grams protein
6 grams fat
5 grams
  carbohydrate

⅓ cup low-sodium tamari
2 tablespoons rice vinegar
1 tablespoon raw honey
2 freshly pressed garlic cloves
1 teaspoon ground ginger
2 pounds raw turkey breast, skinned and cut into 1-inch chunks

Fast Tracks
When baking or grilling indoors, liquid smoke added to the basting or barbecuing sauce for flavor is an excellent alternative to outdoor barbecuing.

Combine marinade ingredients in a large shallow bowl. Add turkey chunks and mix until they are well coated with the marinade. Let stand refrigerated 2 to 4 hours, tossing several times to marinate turkey evenly.

Prepare barbecue coals. Thread equal amounts of turkey chunks on 6 skewers and place on the grill about 6 inches over medium-hot coals. Barbecue 5 to 6 minutes on each side, basting with any remaining marinade. *Serves 6.*

BARBECUE-BAKED CHICKEN

Baked in the "world's best barbecue sauce," this chicken tastes just as if it's been cooked outdoors.

Per serving:
270 calories
42 grams protein
7 grams fat
9 grams
  carbohydrate

1 can (8 ounces) tomato puree (or substitute "natural-style" catsup)
2 tablespoons low-sodium tamari (or substitute 1 tablespoon Worcestershire
    sauce)
1½ tablespoons raw honey
1 tablespoon red wine vinegar
1 tablespoon finely grated onion
2 freshly pressed garlic cloves
1 tablespoon chili powder
1½ teaspoons dried mustard
1 teaspoon ground cumin
½ teaspoon liquid smoke
Dash of Tabasco sauce (adjust to taste)
6 whole chicken legs, skinned

Thigh note:
Nutritional calculations are based on a 6-ounce portion of leg and thigh meat per person.

Thoroughly blend all ingredients except chicken. Arrange chicken legs, meaty side up, fairly close together in a medium-size baking dish or pan. Pour a portion of the barbecue sauce over the chicken so that it is well coated. Loosely cover pan with foil and bake in a preheated 350-degree oven for 45 minutes. Remove foil the last 10 minutes of baking and baste the chicken with the remaining sauce. Continue baking, uncovered, for another 10 minutes, or until done. *Serves 6.*

CHICKEN LIVER STEW

Per serving:
287 calories
34 grams protein
5 grams fat
25 grams
  carbohydrate

2 new red potatoes, peeled and chunked
1 carrot, sliced
1 small white onion, sliced
1 green bell pepper, sliced
1 pound chicken livers, cut up
2 tablespoons chopped fresh parsley
2 freshly pressed garlic cloves
1 teaspoon dried tarragon
1 teaspoon Worcestershire sauce
1 can (8 ounces) tomato puree
1 cup Chicken Stock (page 96), or substitute water
½ cup dry red wine
Vegetable salt and freshly ground pepper to taste

Place all ingredients in order listed above in a large Crock-Pot. Stir gently, cover, and cook on low for 8 to 12 hours or on high for 4 to 6 hours. *Serves 4.*

FITNESS FRIED CHICKEN

It's fit to be fried, but it's not! Fatty chicken skin is replaced with an oat bran crumb coating and baked crisp in the oven.

Per serving:
299 calories
45 grams protein
7 grams fat
12 grams
  carbohydrate

Six-piece ensemble:
Nutritional
calculations are
based on a 6-ounce
portion of light and
dark meat per
person.

1 frying chicken, about 3½ pounds, cut up and skinned (legs and breast only)
2 egg whites
½ cup uncooked rolled oats
½ cup oat bran flakes
¼ teaspoon each ground nutmeg and turmeric
Vegetable salt and paprika to taste

Dip chicken pieces in egg whites to coat them well and place on a baking rack for several minutes to dry a little. Grind rolled oats into a coarse flour in a blender or food processor. Add oat bran flakes and seasoning and grind once more to a semifine consistency. Place oat crumbs in a large shallow bowl. When chicken pieces feel sticky, roll each one in the oat crumbs until lightly coated. Arrange the pieces, meaty side up and spread slightly apart, on the baking rack and bake in a preheated 375-degree oven for 35 minutes, until brown and crisp. *Serves 4.*

CHICKEN ENCHILADA CASSEROLE

Per serving:
354 calories
38 grams protein
7 grams fat
34 grams
  carbohydrate

1 can (19 ounces) enchilada sauce
12 corn tortillas
1½ pounds ground raw chicken
4 ounces grated low-fat Monterey Jack cheese
½ cup chopped scallions
1 jar (2 ounces) chopped pimientos (or substitute mild chopped green chilies)

Pour enchilada sauce into a large shallow bowl. Dip tortillas in the sauce to coat them well; drain off the excess. Arrange 6 of the dipped tortillas in the bottom of a large round covered casserole dish. Spoon one quarter of the enchilada sauce over the tortillas and evenly crumble in the ground chicken. Sprinkle with half the cheese then with half the scallions. Spread with a layer of pimientos, leaving a few for garnish. Spoon another quarter of the sauce over that. Arrange remaining 6 dipped tortillas over the top of the casserole and spoon another quarter of the sauce over the top. Sprinkle evenly with remaining cheese.

Cover and bake in a 350-degree oven for 45 minutes. To serve, spoon the last amount of the sauce over the top and sprinkle with remaining scallions. Dot with pimiento garnish. *Serves 6.*

Casserole olé: Serve topped with a dollop of plain nonfat yogurt, chopped olives, ripe avocado slices, or Chunky Guacamole (page 189). For an all-in-one-meal, add a layer of thinly sliced raw zucchini between the tortillas and the chicken before cooking. For a real taste treat, replace all or part of the chicken with tiny fresh or frozen defrosted shrimp. You can also use precooked shrimp, chicken, or turkey in this recipe and cut the cooking time by 10 to 15 minutes. And this casserole is ideal for the microwave oven. Microwave it, covered, on high for 22 to 24 minutes instead of baking it in the oven.

CORNISH HENS WITH SUMMER SQUASH STUFFING

Per serving:
442 calories
59 grams protein
9 grams fat
31 grams
   carbohydrate

Squab note:
Nutritional
calculations are
based on an 8-ounce
portion of light and
dark meat per
person.

½ cup reduced Chicken Stock (page 96)
2 cups chopped yellow or green summer squash
⅔ cup peeled and chopped green apples
¼ cup chopped yellow onion
2 tablespoons seedless golden raisins
½ teaspoon each dried marjoram, thyme, and ground sage
⅛ teaspoon ground allspice
Vegetable salt and freshly ground pepper to taste
3 tablespoons Cognac
2 Cornish hens, 1 pound each
¼ cup apple cider

Heat chicken stock in a medium-size covered nonstick skillet. Add remaining ingredients, except the cognac, hens, and cider and stir well. Cover and cook over medium-low heat for 3 to 4 minutes, until squash is tender-crisp. Uncover, raise heat to medium, and cook several minutes more until liquid has evaporated. When done, stir in 1½ tablespoons Cognac and remove skillet from heat.

Spoon half the mixture into the cavity of each squab and seal it off with string or skewers. Space the hens apart on a rack in a shallow roasting pan and roast in a 325-degree oven for 50 minutes to 1 hour. Mix remaining Cognac and apple cider together and baste hens with the mixture several times during the last 15 minutes of roasting, using any pan drippings, if desired. *Serves 2.*

CHICKEN STOCK

There's a lot to be said for the chicken soup theory, or any poultry soup for that matter. The healing properties are in the stock, and are the result of a very high ratio of protein to calories, approximately 4 grams of protein per 22 calories—about the same as chicken meat itself. The concentration of amino acids in the protein restores the living cells that are essential for tissue growth and repair when you are ill or injured.

Make a pot of stock and freeze it in 1-cup containers. When ready to use, thaw it and you have an instant base to make any kind of soup or stew. Keep it on hand and use it as a flavorful cooking liquid instead of water for rice, vegetables, or potatoes. Cut calories by substituting it for oil in sautéing and stir-frying. Or put some in a thermos and take it to work or the gym for a healthful, low-cal perk-me-up. And bet you didn't know that warm protein stock or broth is a natural appetite depressant. Its versatility is endless.

For a more concentrated, tastier stock, boil it uncovered longer than the recommended time until its amount is reduced to about two thirds. (When a recipe calls for reduced chicken stock, the amount given refers to the quantity remaining after it has been reduced.)

Per cup:
22 calories
4 grams protein
1 gram fat
2 grams
   carbohydrate

Stock exchange:
This chicken stock is used as an ingredient for many recipes in this book, but you can substitute commercial low-sodium chicken broth or bouillon.

One more tip:
Precooked chicken (or even turkey) can be used in this recipe, but starting with fresh uncooked meat and bones will give you a nutritional edge—and a more flavorful stock.

3 pounds chicken backs, necks, or wings
3 quarts water
1 yellow or white onion, chopped
3 celery ribs with leaves, chopped
1 carrot, chopped
2 fresh parsley sprigs
1 bay leaf
½ teaspoon dried thyme
4 cloves
6 white peppercorns

Place all ingredients in a large covered kettle or stockpot. Bring to a boil, reduce heat, and simmer partially covered for approximately 2 hours, or until liquid is reduced by half. Strain stock through a fine sieve or colander lined with a wet paper towel. (Bone the chicken and reserve the meat for other uses, if desired.) Chill to remove any fat that solidifies at the top. *Makes about 6 cups.*

POWER-BASE CHICKEN SOUP

Using only stock, nonfat milk, and egg as your power base, "get rich quick" with this delicious low-cal cream of chicken soup.

Per serving:
181 calories
24 grams protein
5 grams fat
10 grams
  carbohydrate

1 cup reduced Chicken Stock (page 96)
2 teaspoons arrowroot
1 cup nonfat milk
1 egg, beaten
4 ounces chopped cooked chicken (reserved from stock)
Vegetable salt and freshly ground pepper to taste
1 tablespoon minced fresh parsley

Bring chicken stock to a boil in a medium-size saucepan. Dissolve arrowroot in nonfat milk. Add egg to milk and arrowroot and whisk until well blended. Slowly pour mixture into boiling stock, whisking constantly 1 to 2 minutes until soup thickens. Add chicken. Remove saucepan from heat and season with salt and pepper, if desired. Serve sprinkled with parsley. *Serves 2.*

Photo: Matti Klatt

— 7 —
SEAFOOD

FLAMBUOYANT FISH

Fish is one of the bodybuilder's greatest natural resources. Freshly caught, it is flavorful in its own right, never really needing more than a squeeze of lemon. But that's just a bonus: Nutrition is what fish is all about. Since only a small percentage of its calories are comprised of fats and carbohydrates, the remainder is pure protein, high in the essential amino acids. It is rich in vitamin A, the B-vitamins (especially B–12, folic acid, and niacin), and the minerals phosphorus and zinc. And everything you have heard about fish preventing heart disease is true. All fish contains saturated fats, but cold-water fish (some of which are characteristically oily, containing over 5 percent fat) is extremely high in the Omega-3 fatty acids, an unsaturated fat that significantly lowers blood cholesterol and inhibits the clotting that can lead to heart attacks.

But some people still think that fish is just another word for "blah," and don't eat it as often as they should, which is at least twice a week. Although fish will always be one of the healthiest and most complete sources of protein, it doesn't have to be the dullest, especially when we add a few of our own resources—an herb here, a spice there, a little bit of sherry, or some sun-dried tomatoes. Suddenly we have Flambuoyant Fish! If you notice, each and every recipe here was created with a different method of dry or moist cooking. And better yet, they were designed to add no more than 10 to 100 additional calories to each 6-ounce serving of fish. Imagine, all this and nutrition too. Very "ef-fish-ent."

BAKED COD ALASKA

Per serving:
240 calories
40 grams protein
7 grams fat
5 grams
  carbohydrate

4 cod fillets, 6 ounces each
2 tablespoons freshly squeezed lemon juice
2 egg whites, warmed to room temperature
½ cup plain nonfat yogurt
1 tablespoon finely minced onion
½ cup nonfat milk
1 tablespoon Dijon mustard
1 freshly pressed garlic clove
1 teaspoon dried dill weed
Vegetable salt and freshly ground pepper to taste

Arrange fillets on a nonstick baking sheet. Sprinkle the top with lemon juice. In a small bowl, beat egg whites with an electric mixer until soft peaks form. Fold in 2 tablespoons of yogurt, along with the minced onion and salt to taste, if desired. Spoon equal portions of the egg white topping over each fillet. Bake in a preheated 375-degree oven for about 20 minutes.

Meanwhile, blend the rest of the yogurt along with the remaining ingredients in a small double boiler. Cook over a full boil until mustard mixture is hot, 10 to 15 minutes.

When fish is done, remove each fillet with a spatula and place on individual serving plates. Pour equal amounts of the mustard sauce over each one. *Serves 4.*

ORIENTAL STIR-FRIED TUNA

Per serving:
375 calories
51 grams protein
16 grams fat
7 grams
  carbohydrate

2 teaspoons sesame oil
2 freshly minced garlic cloves
12 ounces fresh tuna steaks, cut into 1-inch cubes
2 scallions, chopped
2 teaspoons grated fresh ginger
3 tablespoons low-sodium tamari
1 tablespoon rice vinegar
½ teaspoon raw honey

Heat oil in a large nonstick skillet or wok. Add garlic and sauté for about 30 seconds over medium heat. Add tuna chunks, scallions, and ginger. Raise heat to medium-high and toss fish to lightly brown it. Mix tamari and vinegar together and add as needed for liquid during cooking. Sauté 5 to 6 minutes, until liquid has evaporated and fish flakes easily with a fork. *Serves 2.*

Stir-frying thought: To cut down on calories, a tiny bit of sesame oil is used—only for flavor. The darker the sesame oil, the stronger it is and the less you will need. It is also less refined and better for you.

PORT-STEAMED HALIBUT WRAPPED WITH VEGETABLES

Per serving:
306 calories
44 grams protein
12 grams fat
6 grams
   carbohydrate

Healthful Hint
When steaming ordinary fish, line the steam tray with lettuce leaves to catch valuable fish juices that seep out during cooking.

1 cup port wine
2 cups water
4 bay leaves
4 large romaine lettuce leaves
4 halibut steaks, 6 ounces each
1 small leek bulb, thinly sliced
4 ounces roasted red peppers, cut into strips (see Chicken Rouille, page 85,
   for roasting directions; or substitute prepacked roasted red peppers,
   rinsed and drained)
4 thin orange slices

Bring port, water, and bay leaves to a boil in a covered saucepan large enough to accommodate a steam tray. Using tongs, immerse each lettuce leaf, one at a time, in the boiling liquid for 25 to 30 seconds. When it is limp and bright green, drain it and lay it out flat, ridge side down, on a paper towel. After all 4 leaves are done, remove the saucepan from the heat and scoop out the bay leaves.

Place each halibut steak in the center of a lettuce leaf. Top each one with a bay leaf, leek slices, and roasted red pepper strips. Finish off with a splash of the port liquid and an orange slice. Carefully package-wrap a lettuce leaf around each fish bundle and secure with toothpicks.

Arrange the wrapped fish in a steam tray and place it in the saucepan of port liquid. Cover tightly, bring the liquid back to a boil, and steam the fish for 8 to 10 minutes. Before serving, douse the fish bundles with a little more of the port liquid, if desired. *Serves 4.*

SWORDFISH BAKED IN FOIL WITH
SUN-DRIED TOMATOES

Per serving:
307 calories
50 grams protein
11 grams fat
4 grams
  carbohydrate

Flambuoyant idea:
Drizzle a few drops
of extra-virgin olive
oil over each fish
steak before serving.

4 swordfish steaks, 6 ounces each
⅓ cup dry-packed sun-dried tomatoes, chopped
4 freshly chopped garlic cloves
1 teaspoon each dried thyme and basil
Juice of 1 lemon
Freshly ground pepper to taste

Place each swordfish steak in the center of a 12-inch square piece of foil. Top each one with equal portions of the sun-dried tomatoes, garlic, basil, thyme, and lemon juice. Season with pepper to taste. Bring two parallel sides of the foil together above the fish; fold the ends over several times and crimp them, leaving a slight domed space between the fish and the foil. Make the packet airtight by sealing the two side ends using the same crimping method.

Bake in a preheated 400-degree oven for 15 minutes. Remove the fish from the oven and let it stand several minutes before carefully opening the foil packets. Remove foil before serving. *Serves 4.*

CARIBBEAN POACHED SEA BASS

*Per serving (including
coconut milk):*
258 calories
40 grams protein
9 grams fat
4 grams
  carbohydrate

4 sea bass fillets, 6 ounces each
⅔ cup Coconut Milk (recipe follows)
3 tablespoons light rum
⅔ cup chopped fresh pineapple (or substitute an 8-ounce can crushed
  unsweetened pineapple)

Arrange fish fillets in a 10- or 12-inch covered nonstick skillet. Pour coconut milk and rum over the top. Then spread equal portions of pineapple across the top of each fillet. Cover tightly and poach over medium heat for about 8 minutes, or until fish is flaky. Remove fillets with a spatula and pour poaching liquid over them. *Serves 4.*

COCONUT MILK

Per cup:
86 calories
1 gram protein
8 grams fat
3 grams
  carbohydrate

1 cup boiling water
1 cup freshly grated coconut

Pour boiling water over grated coconut. Let it stand for 10 minutes. Then press the liquid through a cheesecloth-lined or very fine sieve. (You may substitute finely shredded dried unsweetened coconut for the fresh coconut, but let it stand about 30 minutes before pressing.) *Makes about 1 cup.*

MICROWAVED SCROD WITH MUSHROOMS, SHALLOTS, AND SHERRY

Per serving:
215 calories
37 grams protein
6 grams fat
3 grams
  carbohydrate

2 scrod fillets, 6 ounces each
½ cup thinly sliced fresh mushrooms
2 shallots, thinly sliced
2 tablespoons snipped fresh parsley
⅓ cup sherry
¼ cup Chicken Stock (page 96), or substitute water
Freshly ground pepper to taste

Place the fish fillets in a microwave-safe dish. Arrange the mushrooms, shallots, and parsley on the bottom around the fish. Pour the sherry and stock over the fish, cover tightly, and microwave on high for 2 to 3 minutes. Uncover, stir the mushrooms and shallots, and baste the fish with the liquid, rotating the dish 180 degrees. Cover and continue cooking for 2 to 3 minutes more, or until the fish is flaky. Serve the fish topped with the mushrooms and sherry liquid. Season with pepper, if desired. *Serves 2.*

SUNNY BROILED SOLE WITH
LITE TARTAR SAUCE

Per serving (not
including sauce):
260 calories
37 grams protein
10 grams fat
4 grams
  carbohydrate

4 sole fillets, 6 ounces each
1 egg white, lightly beaten
1/4 cup raw sunflower seeds, coarsely ground
2 tablespoons raw wheat germ
1 tablespoon dried parsley
Vegetable salt and freshly ground pepper to taste
Lite Tartar Sauce (recipe follows)

Arrange fillets on a nonstick baking sheet and brush the tops with egg white. Mix remaining ingredients together and sprinkle over the fillets. Place the baking sheet under a broiler, about 8 inches from the heat. Broil for 7 to 8 minutes, until fish is flaky and topping is browned. Serve fillets with Lite Tartar Sauce.

LITE TARTAR SAUCE

Here's a low-fat, low-calorie tartar sauce that is great with any kind of fish, plain or fancy.

Per serving:
97 calories
1 gram protein
7 grams fat
8 grams
  carbohydrate

1/3 cup reduced-calorie safflower oil mayonnaise
1/4 cup plain nonfat yogurt
1/3 cup peeled, seeded, and finely chopped cucumber
1 tablespoon finely minced shallots
1 tablespoon raw honey
1 tablespoon cider vinegar
2 teaspoons chopped capers
1/2 teaspoon grated lemon peel
1/8 teaspoon each dry mustard and celery seed

Thoroughly mix all ingredients and let stand in refrigerator several hours before serving. *Makes about 1 cup, enough for 4 servings.*

BARBECUED SALMON WITH ORANGE-CHILI BASTE

Per serving:
279 calories
41 grams protein
11 grams fat
2 grams
   carbohydrate

⅓ *cup freshly squeezed orange juice*
1 tablespoon freshly squeezed lime juice
1 teaspoon chili powder
½ *teaspoon each ground cumin and red pepper flakes*
4 salmon steaks, 6 ounces each

Prepare barbecue coals. Combine basting ingredients in a small bowl; baste both sides of salmon steaks with orange-chili mixture. Place the fish on the grill approximately 6 inches above medium-hot coals. Barbecue 4 to 5 minutes on each side, basting once during barbecuing and again just before serving. *Serves 4.*

CATFISH WITH CAJUN SPICES

Per serving:
350 calories
38 grams protein
21 grams fat
1 gram carbohydrate

4 catfish fillets, 6 ounces each
2 freshly pressed garlic cloves
1½ *tablespoons peanut oil*
2 teaspoons dried parsley, finely crumbled
½ *teaspoon freshly ground pepper*
½ *teaspoon each dried marjoram and thyme*
¼ *teaspoon each dried oregano and paprika*
Vegetable salt to taste
4 lemon wedges

Place catfish fillets on a flat rack in a baking pan. Pat them dry with a paper towel to make sure they are free of moisture. Mix garlic and peanut oil together. Lightly brush both sides of the fillets with the garlic oil. Mix remaining ingredients together except the lemon. Sprinkle both sides of the fillets with all the seasoning. Bake uncovered in a preheated 375-degree oven for 10 to 12 minutes. Garnish with lemon wedges. *Serves 4.*

TURBOT IN RED ROQUEFORT SAUCE

Per serving:
357 calories
41 grams protein
15 grams fat
16 grams
  carbohydrate

1 tablespoon olive oil
2 freshly pressed garlic cloves
1 small white onion, finely chopped
1 cup Chicken Stock (page 96), or substitute water
1 can (8 ounces) tomato puree
2 tablespoons tomato paste
1 pound Italian plum tomatoes, seeded and finely chopped
1 teaspoon each minced fresh thyme and basil
2 tablespoons minced fresh parsley
Freshly ground pepper to taste
2 ounces Roquefort cheese
4 turbot fillets, 6 ounces each

Heat oil in a large nonstick skillet. Add garlic and onion and sauté for several minutes over medium heat until onion is translucent. Use a little of the chicken stock for liquid if needed during sautéing. When done, stir in remaining ingredients except for cheese and fish. Cover and simmer sauce for 20 to 25 minutes. Add cheese and stir for about 5 minutes until it has melted into the sauce.

Remove the sauce and arrange the fillets on the bottom of the skillet. Pour the sauce back into the skillet over the fish. Cover and simmer the fish in the sauce over medium heat for 10 to 12 minutes, or until the fish is flaky. Serve each fillet in equal portions of red sauce. *Serves 4.*

INDIVIDUAL CRAB PUFF CASSEROLES

Per serving:
188 calories
29 grams protein
5 grams fat
9 grams
  carbohydrate

½ cup Chicken Stock (page 96)
1 freshly pressed garlic clove
⅓ cup finely chopped white onion
⅓ cup finely chopped celery
⅓ cup shredded carrots
⅓ cup chopped fresh mushrooms
1 tablespoon each minced fresh dill and parsley
2 teaspoons Dijon mustard
12 ounces shredded fresh or frozen defrosted crabmeat
4 egg whites, warmed to room temperature
¾ cup shredded low-fat Swiss cheese
Vegetable salt and freshly ground pepper to taste

Heat stock in a large nonstick skillet. Add garlic, onion, celery, carrot, mushrooms, dill, and parsley. Cook them over medium heat for about 5 minutes, until they are tender-crisp. Stir in crabmeat and remove skillet from heat.

In a large bowl, beat egg whites with an electric mixer until stiff but not dry. Fold egg whites into crab mixture along with shredded cheese. Season with salt and pepper, if desired. Turn into four individual casserole dishes. Bake in a preheated 350-degree oven for 30 to 35 minutes, until tops are golden brown. *Serves 4.*

Tasty treat:
Substitute your favorite variety of smoked cheese for the low-fat Swiss cheese.

Power Boosters
Place whole live oysters on a hot grill. Make sure the shells are closed. When cooked, they will open up and be ready to eat right out of the shell. Serve with Tomato Herb Salsa (page 123) or a simple wedge of lemon or lime.

Want to try something a little more civilized? Place freshly shucked whole oysters (cooked or raw) inside mushroom caps and serve with a seafood sauce or Lite Tartar Sauce (page 104).

SHELLFISH DELITES

Shellfish are the ocean's greatest treasure of high-protein and low-fat seafood. These delectable delicacies have fewer calories overall than fish for their protein value, and they are rich in important nutrients: vitamin A, the B-vitamin complex, as well as impressive minerals like copper, iodine, zinc, and iron. The whole-bodied bivalves—mussels, clams, and oysters—are particularly concentrated in these nutrients, and calorie for calorie they get a rating as nature's top power food. Pop a couple of oysters—you won't need any supplements, but you will train like an animal! And what you've heard about avoiding shellfish because of its high cholesterol content is ungrounded. Natural dietary cholesterol does not necessarily cause harmful blood cholesterol. Nature has provided shellfish with the correct ratio of beneficial fatty acids that act as a built-in neutralizer to cholesterol. So without further guilt, go ahead and indulge in these Shellfish Delites and really feel the power of the sea!

NONFAT NEW ENGLAND CLAM CHOWDER

Wonderfully aromatic, this chowder contains no butter, cream, whole milk, or flour and is thickened only with potatoes.

Per serving:
125 calories
10 grams protein
1 gram fat
18 grams
  carbohydrate

Sea note:
If you want a thicker chowder, omit some of the stock and mash more of the potatoes.

1 bottle (16 ounces) clam juice
2 cups Chicken Stock (page 96) or substitute water
4 new red potatoes, peeled and diced
1 small white onion, diced
1 celery rib with leaves, diced
1 bay leaf
½ teaspoon dried marjoram
1 cup evaporated nonfat milk (or substitute 1 percent low-fat milk)
10 ounces fresh or frozen defrosted clams, chopped
Vegetable salt and freshly ground pepper to taste
¼ cup minced fresh parsley

In a large nonstick saucepan, bring clam juice, chicken stock, potatoes, celery, bay leaf, and marjoram to a boil over high heat. Cook 7 to 8 minutes until potatoes are fork-tender. With a slotted spoon, take out about one half of the cooked potatoes and mash them fine with a fork. Remove the bay leaf and discard. Stir the mashed potatoes back into the chowder and add milk, clams, and salt and pepper, if desired. Lower heat to medium and simmer, but do not boil, the chowder for about 5 minutes more. Serve sprinkled with parsley. *Serves 6.*

LOBSTER TAILS WITH ANCHOVY BUTTER

This lobster bake is short on calories and long on flavor because the dipping butter is cut with lemon juice and spiked with anchovies.

Per serving:
349 calories
38 grams protein
20 grams fat
3 grams
  carbohydrate

3 tablespoons sweet butter
⅛ teaspoon anchovy paste
2 lobster tails (about 1¼ pounds), split
2 tablespoons freshly squeezed lemon juice, strained

Melt butter in a small saucepan or in a microwave oven. Add anchovy paste and stir until well blended. Keep anchovy butter warm without letting it bubble. Place lobster tails, meat side up, on a baking sheet in a preheated 375-degree oven. Bake 12 to 15 minutes, basting several times with the anchovy butter.

When done, remove lobster meat from the shells. Combine remaining anchovy butter with lemon juice and serve on the side as a dipping sauce or drizzle it over the lobster meat. *Serves 2.*

Lobster broil: You can also broil the lobster tails by placing them, shell side down, on a broiler rack. Broil them 8 inches from the heat for 7 to 8 minutes. Try substituting extra-virgin olive oil for the butter. (Use it as a dipping sauce for other shellfish as well, or drizzle it over salads or vegetables.)

STUFFED SHRIMP ROMANO

Per serving:
237 calories
25 grams protein
11 grams fat
9 grams
  carbohydrate

1 tablespoon extra-virgin olive oil
1 freshly pressed garlic clove
¾ cup finely chopped mushrooms
½ teaspoon dried basil
¼ teaspoon dried oregano
2 tablespoons finely chopped black olives
2 tablespoons freshly grated Romano cheese
Freshly ground pepper to taste
8 large shrimp, shelled and deveined, with tails left on
2 brown rice cakes, finely crushed

Heat olive oil in a small nonstick skillet. Sauté garlic briefly over medium heat. Add mushrooms, sweet basil, and oregano and continue to sauté about 5 minutes, until mushrooms are cooked and free of moisture. Stir in the black olives, 1 tablespoon of the Romano cheese, and pepper to taste. Set stuffing aside.

To butterfly the shrimp, cut a slit lengthwise along the outer side with the tip of a small sharp knife. Be sure not to make the cut all the way through the body of the shrimp, and leave the tails on.

Lay the shrimp out, cut side up, on the rack of a broiler pan lined with foil. Spoon equal portions of the stuffing across the top of the shrimp. Sprinkle the tops with equal portions of crushed rice cakes and the remaining Romano cheese. Place the rack of shrimp under the broiler 6 to 8 inches from the heat and broil 5 to 6 minutes, until shrimp begin to turn pink. *Serves 2.*

POACHED OYSTERS IN
COCONUT-CREAMED SPINACH

Per serving:
200 calories
15 grams protein
10 grams fat
15 grams
    carbohydrate

Thicker oyster liquor:
Add 1 to 2
teaspoons arrowroot
moistened in the
oyster liquor and
wine to the boiling
coconut milk. Stir
until it begins to
thicken before
adding the spinach.

Delicate in taste but iron-strong, one serving of this savory dish will provide 9 mg. of iron, nearly the recommended daily amount for men and half for women.

> 2 teaspoons butter
> 1 freshly pressed garlic clove
> ½ teaspoon each dried marjoram and savory
> 1 small white onion, diced
> 1 cup Coconut Milk (page 103), or substitute 1 percent low-fat milk
> ½ pint freshly shucked oysters with liquor (about 6)
> ¼ cup semidry white wine
> 1 large bunch chopped spinach leaves, about ½ pound (or substitute one
>   10-ounce package frozen spinach, defrosted and drained)
> Freshly ground pepper to taste

Melt butter over medium heat in a covered 8- or 9-inch nonstick skillet. Briefly sauté garlic, marjoram, and savory. Stir in onion and sauté about 2 minutes. Add coconut milk, raise heat to medium-high, and bring it to a slow boil.

Drain the liquor from the oysters and set the oysters aside. Stir oyster liquor, white wine, spinach, and pepper into the hot coconut milk. Let it cook for about 2 minutes, stirring occasionally.

Place oysters, several inches apart, on top of the bed of creamed spinach, cover tightly, and poach for 4 to 5 minutes, until oysters are firm. Serve oysters on top of spinach. *Serves 2.*

BEER-STEAMED SHRIMP WITH BAYOU HOT SAUCE

The Sauce:

Per serving:
175 calories
34 grams protein
2 grams fat
6 grams
    carbohydrate

> ½ cup tomato sauce
> 4 ounces roasted red peppers (see Chicken Rouille, page 85, for roasting
>   directions; or substitute prepacked roasted red peppers, rinsed and drained)
> 2 tablespoons hot pepper sauce (adjust amount to taste)
> 1 tablespoon Worcestershire sauce
> 2 garlic cloves

Optional brew:
Add beer to the final sauce if a thinner consistency is desired.

1 teaspoon dried basil
½ teaspoon each dried oregano and thyme
Pinch of allspice

The Shrimp:

1 bottle (12 ounces) strongly brewed beer
2 freshly chopped garlic cloves
½ teaspoon red pepper flakes
¼ teaspoon allspice
24 large shrimp, peeled and deveined with tails left on

Puree all the sauce ingredients in a blender and pour into a small saucepan. Simmer, uncovered, over medium heat for about 15 minutes, until sauce is slightly reduced.

While the sauce is simmering, pour beer and spices into a covered saucepan large enough to accommodate a steam tray. Place the tray in the saucepan and add shrimp. Cover tightly, and bring beer to a boil. Steam 3 to 4 minutes, just until shrimp turn pink. Serve with hot sauce for dipping. *Serves 4.*

SPICY BOMBAY SHRIMP

Per serving:
157 calories
22 grams protein
6 grams fat
3 grams carbohydrate

1 tablespoon butter
1 freshly pressed garlic clove
1 teaspoon curry powder
½ teaspoon dry mustard
¼ teaspoon red pepper flakes, crushed
1 tablespoon minced fresh chives
2 teaspoons freshly squeezed lime juice
½ pound medium-size shrimp, peeled and deveined

Place butter in a medium-size microwave-safe dish. Cook on high for about 1 minute, until butter has melted. Stir in remaining ingredients, except shrimp, and cook about 30 seconds more. Add shrimp and toss them well to coat in the seasoning sauce. Cook them on high for 2 to 3 minutes, stirring once during cooking, until they just turn pink. *Serves 2.*

STIR-FRIED PRAWNS WITH PAPAYA

Per serving:
277 calories
21 grams protein
9 grams fat
29 grams
    carbohydrate

1 teaspoon peanut oil
1 freshly pressed garlic clove
2 scallions, chopped
8 large prawns, peeled and deveined
1 ripe tomato, peeled, seeded, and chopped
1 small ripe papaya, peeled, seeded, and sliced into 1-inch-thick strips
¼ cup Chicken Stock (page 96), or more if needed
1 tablespoon low-sodium tamari
1 teaspoon raw honey
1 teaspoon freshly squeezed lemon juice
¼ cup shredded unsweetened dried coconut

Heat oil over medium-low heat in a large nonstick skillet or wok. Add garlic and scallions and sauté for about 1 minute. Add prawns and tomato and cook for another minute, until prawns are slightly opaque. Stir frequently. Toss papaya into stir-fry and continue to cook until papaya is just heated through. Stir gently so that the papaya does not break apart, using stock if more liquid is needed.

Blend tamari, honey, and lemon juice together with a little of the stock and stir into the skillet. Toss in coconut, reserving a little to sprinkle over the top. *Serves 2.*

QUICK-MARINATED SCALLOP BROCHETTE

Per serving:
120 calories
20 grams protein
0 grams fat
9 grams
    carbohydrate

1 pound large scallops
¼ cup low-sodium tamari
¼ cup mirin
¼ cup sake
2 freshly pressed garlic cloves
1 large zucchini, sliced ¾ inch thick
1 red bell pepper, cut into eighths
1 small white onion, quartered

Place scallops in a large shallow dish. Bring tamari, mirin, sake, and garlic to a boil in a small saucepan. Remove marinade from heat and pour over scallops. Turn several times to coat well. Let stand 15 minutes and prepare barbecue coals.

When done, thread equal portions of scallops, zucchini, peppers, and onion on each of 4 skewers, alternating the seafood and vegetables.

Brush brochette all around with remaining marinade. Cook 6 to 8 inches from the coals for 4 to 5 minutes on each side. Baste several times during cooking and serve in any leftover marinade. *Serves 4.*

SEAWORTHY SPECIALTIES

Get your "net worth" from these power-packed seafood deals. Except for the sashimi, which is raw and more than worthy all by itself, these nutritious recipes all get their protein from more than one source. Whether it be milk, cheese, eggs, tofu, or fish, it all adds up to more protein value and nutrients for your calories. Some of these delicious dishes are highly concentrated in the hard-to-get nutrients, such as calcium and phosphorus. For example, canned fish with bones (salmon, sardines, and mackerel) is one of the most potent sources of assimilable calcium you can get. Vitamins A and D are another precious nutrient combination found in the edible bones and oils of whole canned fish. And every single one of these recipes contains some complex carbohydrate, so they are great training foods as well. Any way you cut it, you can't go off course with these Seaworthy Specialties.

Per serving:
182 calories
19 grams protein
8 grams fat
8 grams
 carbohydrate

*Good salmon
suggestion:*
Serve with Lite
Tartar Sauce (page
104) or the mustard
sauce from Baked
Cod Alaska (page
100), or one of the
cheese sauces from
the section on Slim
Pastabilities (pages
152 and 154).

GOOD SALMON BURGERS

Do your heart good with oat bran, calcium, and the Omega-3s, all rolled into one little burger. Or substitute whole mackerel or sardines for the salmon; just be sure to rinse and drain them of their packing oils.

1 can (15½ ounces) pink or red salmon, including fine edible bones
½ cup oat bran flakes, crushed
¼ cup uncooked quick-cooking oats
2 egg whites
⅓ cup finely chopped white onion
2 tablespoons reduced-calorie safflower oil mayonnaise
2 tablespoons freshly squeezed lemon juice
2 teaspoons prepared horseradish
Freshly ground pepper to taste

Mix everything together well in a medium-size bowl. Make 6 well-formed patties and place them on a baking rack. Bake in a 350-degree oven for 12 to 15 minutes, until tops are browned. *Serves 6.*

LEFT-HOOK FISH CAKE

Need more steam in the gym and less in the kitchen? Get a power punch from this mild and tasty fish dish. One batch is worth at least a couple of rounds, so you'll have energy to spar!

Per serving:
254 calories
35 grams protein
6 grams fat
15 grams
   carbohydrate

Look out! Here are some power-packed pointers:
- Mix 4 ounces of soft tofu into fish mixture before cooking.
- Replace ¼ cup of the bread crumbs with wheat germ.
- Add some noninstant nonfat dry milk.
- Or how about a couple of scoops of unflavored protein powder?

2 cups grated raw red snapper (or substitute any other mild-tasting firm-flesh fish)
1 cup whole wheat bread crumbs
3 egg yolks, beaten
¾ cup evaporated nonfat milk
½ teaspoon paprika
Vegetable salt to taste
6 egg whites, warmed to room temperature

In a large soufflé dish, combine fish, bread crumbs, egg yolks, evaporated milk, and paprika. Season with salt, if desired. In a large bowl, beat egg whites with an electric mixer until soft peaks form. Fold egg whites into fish mixture. Place soufflé dish in a deep large pan with water halfway up the sides of the dish. Bake, uncovered, in a preheated 350-degree oven for 1 to 1¼ hours, or until a knife inserted into the center comes out clean.

You can also opt for more steam in the kitchen by placing the soufflé dish in a large pot of simmering water. Cover the pot and steam the fish cake for about 1 hour. Eat it as you would a custard, hot or cold. *Serves 4.*

TUNA-TOFU CASSEROLE

Here's a "new-tritional" twist on an old favorite. Tofu replaces the standard cream of mushroom soup used as a thickener, boosting the casserole with additional protein and calcium.

Per serving:
214 calories
17 grams protein
8 grams fat
18 grams
   carbohydrate

2 cans (6½ ounces each) water-packed tuna, rinsed and drained
1 cup sliced fresh mushrooms
1 small yellow onion, finely chopped
⅔ cup grated low-fat Cheddar cheese
1 cup snipped fresh parsley
4 ounces soft tofu

½ cup evaporated nonfat milk
1 garlic clove
½ teaspoon ground turmeric
½ recipe cooked Whole Wheat Fettuccine (page 151)
Vegetable salt and freshly ground pepper to taste

In a 2-quart casserole dish, toss tuna, mushrooms, onion, cheese, and parsley together. Whir tofu, milk, garlic, and turmeric in a blender until creamy, and pour over tossed tuna. Mix everything together, then combine with fettuccine. Season with salt and pepper, if desired. Bake in a preheated 350-degree oven for 30 to 35 minutes, until top is brown and crusty. *Serves 6.*

SOFT TUNA TACOS

This recipe does away with greasy deep-fried tortillas, and the unpalatably dry tuna is made moist and tasty mixed with a taco sauce and yogurt.

Per serving:
353 calories
25 grams protein
12 grams fat
35 grams
    carbohydrate

Taco tip:
You may also make soft chicken or turkey tacos by substituting 2 cups of cooked shredded chicken or turkey breast for the tuna.

½ cup taco sauce
½ cup plain nonfat yogurt
2 cans (6½ ounces each) water-packed albacore, rinsed and drained
2 cups shredded lettuce
1½ cups chopped ripe tomatoes
1 cup shredded low-fat Cheddar cheese
½ cup diced yellow onion
1 ripe avocado, diced
12 corn tortillas

Mix taco sauce and yogurt together in a small serving bowl. Crumble tuna into a medium-size serving bowl. Add half the taco-yogurt sauce and toss well with the tuna. Arrange remaining sauce, tossed tuna, lettuce, tomatoes, cheese, onion, and avocado in separate small serving bowls. Lay serving implements next to each bowl.

To prepare tortillas, heat 4 at a time in a microwave oven for 30 seconds, or wrap them all in a small towel and place them in a steam tray, away from the water. Steam them for 5 minutes. Being careful not to break them, fold them in half and serve immediately with accompaniments, including additional plain taco sauce if desired. *Serves 6, with two tacos per person.*

SEAFOOD EN PIPERADE

1 tablespoon extra-virgin olive oil
3 freshly pressed garlic cloves
1 large red onion, thinly sliced
1 red bell pepper, seeded and sliced
1 green bell pepper, seeded and sliced
4 tablespoons tomato paste
3 cups Chicken Stock (page 96)
1 cup clam juice
2 fresh jalapeño or chili peppers, seeded and chopped
½ teaspoon each dried oregano, basil, and cayenne
2 ripe tomatoes, seeded and chopped
1 bay leaf
1½ pounds white fish, cut into 1-inch chunks
½ pound large scallops
½ pound large shrimp, shelled and deveined
½ pound crab meat chunks
Grated rind of 1 lime
¼ cup chopped fresh cilantro

Heat oil in a large covered kettle or stockpot. Sauté garlic and onion over medium heat for about 1 minute. Add bell peppers and continue to sauté 4 to 5 minutes, using a little stock as needed for liquid. When peppers are tender-crisp, add remaining stock and clam juice and stir in tomato paste, chili peppers, herbs, and tomatoes. Cover and simmer for 25 to 30 minutes.

When done, raise heat to medium-high and stir in white fish and scallops and cook, uncovered, for 2 minutes. Stir in shrimp and cook another 3 minutes. Stir in crab meat and cook 1 minute more. Remove stockpot from heat and stir in grated lime rind. Remove bay leaf and serve sprinkled with cilantro. *Serves 6.*

SASHIMI LOVER'S SPECIAL

Per serving (including sauce):
216 calories
28 grams protein
6 grams fat
12 grams
   carbohydrate

Sashimi serving suggestion:
Try serving the fish on a bed of *wakame* (Japanese sea vegetable) instead of lettuce and offer brown rice as an accompaniment (more sauce may be needed).

Safety catch:
If kept in the coldest part of the refrigerator, raw fish will be good for several days. If all the alarming reports you've heard about raw fish concern you, however, freezing it at 10 degrees below zero for 7 days before preparing it will kill any possible parasites.

This raw fish duo is definitely not for sashimi lovers only. In fact, fish only tastes "fishy" when it is cooked. Here are two of the best-tasting fish choices for sashimi. Dine on them in the raw and glow in good health!

The Sashimi:

½ pound raw salmon
½ pound raw yellowtail
1 cucumber, peeled, seeded, and slivered
½ carrot, pared and slivered
¼ small turnip, peeled and slivered
1 bunch scallion tops (5 to 6 inches long)
6 to 8 large leaves of butter lettuce
1 ripe nectarine, pitted, peeled, and cut into thin slices
1 ounce gingerroot, peeled and thinly sliced

The Dipping Sauce:

⅓ cup low-sodium tamari
1 tablespoon rice vinegar
1 teaspoon prepared hot Chinese mustard (adjust to taste)
1 teaspoon raw honey

Go to a market where you can get fish that has been caught within the last 24 hours. Tell the butcher you are buying it for sashimi, so he will give you only the freshest steaks. Ask him to skin and bone both fish. If he is willing to accommodate you further, have him cut the fish crosswise into slices ⅜ to ¼ inch thick, 2 inches long. If not, freeze fish about 30 minutes, until semisolid. Then, with a thin sharp knife, slice the fish accordingly. Roll salmon and yellowtail slices around equal slivers of cucumber, carrot, and turnip. Tie each one in a bundle with a scallion top. Arrange sashimi on a serving platter lined with lettuce leaves. Garnish with nectarine and ginger slices.

Mix all the dipping sauce ingredients together in a small serving bowl. Place alongside the platter of sashimi. *Serves 6.*

Photo: Kevin Carasco

— 8 —
EGGS

THE OMELET CLUB

Calorie Cuts
Tofu is similar to the taste and texture of cooked eggs. It just about equals eggs in protein but has only one-third the calories and fat. You can cut the calories of egg dishes by substituting 2 ounces of soft tofu (plus 1 tablespoon water) for each whole egg you plan to use in a quiche, frittata, or scrambled egg dish. Mash the tofu into the egg mixture, replacing no more than one third of the eggs called for.

Eggs are one of nature's most exceptional diet foods. One egg contains about 80 fast-burning calories, 7 grams of protein, and only 6 grams of fat. The egg provides all the essential amino acids plus vitamins A, B–2, D, E, niacin, biotin, and the minerals iron, copper, and phosphorus. One thing the egg doesn't contain is harmful cholesterol. Although the egg does contain dietary cholesterol, it does not cause or promote harmful effects in the body if your diet is otherwise good. As we have established, the actual cause of harmful blood cholesterol is consuming a diet too high in processed, saturated fats (such as ice cream and fried foods) and leading a sedentary lifestyle. This causes a raised level of circulating triglycerides in the blood, which in turn causes a buildup of the kind of cholesterol that clogs the arteries. Aside from all that, the egg is the richest known source of choline, which is found in lecithin, and is a neutralizing property that keeps the natural cholesterol in the egg emulsified.

If you are concerned about cholesterol, before you go about eliminating natural foods such as eggs from your diet, start by cutting out the junk foods and adding plenty of fresh fruits, vegetables, and whole grains, and you'll never have to worry about things like eggs again. So go from agony to "egg-stasy" and join the Omelet Club today. Treat yourself to these healthy high-protein culinary creations and rediscover perfection in a pan.

Great white note: You may substitute egg whites for yolks in any of these recipes. For a satisfactory egg dish, though, use at least one egg yolk per three whites, and make sure the volume of the yolks and whites combined equals the volume of the whole eggs called for.

EGGPLANT STRATA

Per serving:
267 calories
20 grams protein
9 grams fat
29 grams
    carbohydrate

1 eggplant, peeled and sliced ½ inch thick
4 eggs
1½ cups nonfat milk
2 freshly pressed garlic cloves
¾ teaspoon oregano, finely crumbled
Vegetable salt and freshly ground pepper to taste
4 thick slices whole wheat bread
1 pound ripe tomatoes, sliced ¼ inch thick
1 small white onion, thinly sliced and separated into rings
½ cup shredded part-skim mozzarella cheese

Arrange eggplant slices evenly over the entire bottom of an 8- or 9-inch-square baking pan. In a shallow bowl, beat together eggs, milk, garlic, ½ teaspoon oregano, and salt and pepper to taste. Soak each bread slice in the egg mixture on both sides until fully saturated. Lay the bread slices in a layer over all the eggplant slices. Pour any remaining egg mixture over the bread.

Arrange tomato slices and onion rings evenly over the top. Sprinkle with remaining oregano then with mozzarella cheese. Cover and let stand, refrigerated, several hours.

Bake, uncovered, in a preheated 350-degree oven for 40 minutes. *Serves 4.*

TUNA TIMBALES

Here's a neat high-protein idea—zesty egg and tuna muffins to go. Take a bunch for lunch or a power snack. Store them in a cool place and have them nuked, or as they are.

Per serving:
53 calories
7 grams protein
2 grams fat
2 grams
    carbohydrate

4 eggs
1 cup nonfat milk
½ teaspoon Worcestershire sauce
½ teaspoon dry mustard
⅓ cup chopped fresh chives
1 tablespoon chopped fresh parsley
2 teaspoons minced fresh dill
1 can (6½ ounces) water-packed albacore, rinsed and drained
Freshly ground pepper to taste

In a large bowl, beat eggs, milk, Worcestershire sauce, and mustard together well. Stir in remaining ingredients until well combined. Line a 12-cup muffin tin with cupcake liners. Spoon equal amounts of the mixture into each liner until about three-quarters full.

Set the muffin tin into a larger pan with water just under the rim of the tin. Place in a preheated 350-degree oven and bake for 20 to 25 minutes, until egg is firm and golden. Remove muffin tin from the oven to cool. *Makes 12 timbales or servings.*

SHRIMP AND VEGETABLE QUICHE
WITH BROWN RICE CRUST

Per serving (including crust):
308 calories
23 grams protein
11 grams fat
34 grams carbohydrate

6 eggs
1½ cups nonfat milk
2 tablespoons freshly grated Parmesan cheese
6 ounces fresh or frozen defrosted tiny shrimp
½ cup each chopped carrots and cauliflower florets
¼ cup chopped celery with leaves
1 teaspoon each minced fresh tarragon and thyme
Vegetable salt and freshly ground pepper to taste
1 Brown Rice Crust (page 146)

In a large bowl, beat eggs and milk together well. Stir in remaining ingredients until well combined and pour into prepared brown rice crust. Bake in preheated 350-degree oven for 35 to 40 minutes, until egg is firm and golden. Top with additional Parmesan cheese, if desired. *Serves 6.*

HERBED CHEESE AND ARTICHOKE FRITTATA

Per serving:
199 calories
18 grams protein
11 grams fat
7 grams
  carbohydrate

1 cup 1 percent low-fat cottage cheese
1½ tablespoons extra-virgin olive oil
2 tablespoons chopped fresh basil
1 tablespoon chopped fresh sage
2 freshly pressed garlic cloves
1 cup shredded part-skim Gruyère cheese
6 eggs
1½ cups nonfat milk
8 ounces steamed or frosted defrosted artichoke hearts, quartered
Vegetable salt and freshly ground pepper to taste
Tomato-Herb Salsa (page 123), optional

Using a large sieve, drain cottage cheese of excess creamy liquid. In a blender or food processor, blend cottage cheese, 1 tablespoon of the olive oil, herbs, and garlic just until green flecks remain. Combine with shredded Gruyère cheese. In a large bowl, beat eggs and milk together well. Using a spatula, fold one half the herbed cheese mixture into the egg mixture. Mash and stir until blended. Add half the artichokes and salt and pepper to taste, and stir again to mix.

Place the remaining ½ tablespoon of olive oil in a large flame-proof or cast-iron skillet. Using a paper towel, rub the olive oil all around to coat, then wipe out the excess. Pour the frittata mixture into the skillet and place it on the stove over medium-low heat. Cook, uncovered, for 3 to 4 minutes, until frittata is partly set, but still wet on top. Scatter in remaining artichokes and herbed cheese.

Place the frittata under the broiler 4 to 5 inches from the heat and cook for 2 to 3 minutes more, until eggs are set and golden. Serve with Tomato-Herb Salsa, if desired. *Serves 6.*

HARD WOK OMELET

Per serving:
361 calories
28 grams protein
25 grams fat
9 grams
  carbohydrate

1 teaspoon sesame oil
1 freshly minced garlic clove
1 large scallion, chopped (reserve green top)
⅓ cup sliced fresh mushrooms
¼ cup coarsely chopped fresh bamboo shoots
1 tablespoon low-sodium tamari (more is optional)
2 ounces firm tofu, cut into small cubes
3 large eggs (plus 1 tablespoon water)

Heat oil in a nonstick omelet pan. Sauté garlic and scallion briefly over medium heat. Add mushrooms, bamboo shoots, and tamari and continue to sauté several minutes more, just until mushrooms are soft and bamboo shoots are tender-crisp. Add tofu and toss lightly for about 1 minute more, until hot. If desired, add more tamari as needed for liquid or flavor. Remove filling from pan and keep it warm.

In a small bowl, whisk eggs and water together until well blended and light yellow. Wipe the omelet pan clean with a paper towel dabbed in sesame oil. Pour the egg mixture into the pan and cook over medium heat (medium-low if you are using an electric stove). As the eggs begin to set, run a spatula around the sides of the omelet, lifting it enough to allow the uncooked portion to flow underneath. Then let it cook a few moments undisturbed. When eggs are shiny but set, spoon the filling in a row across the center. Using the spatula, carefully lift one side of the omelet over the filling and then the other side, forming an overlapping closure. Remove the pan from the heat. Lift the pan at an angle and gently slide the omelet, with the help of the spatula, to an inverted position on a warm serving plate. Sprinkle with reserved chopped scallion top. *Serves 1.*

TOMATO-HERB SALSA

Per cup:
68 calories
3 grams protein
1 gram fat
12 grams
 carbohydrate

Salsa note:
If you like a thinner salsa, add a little chicken stock while blending to the consistency desired.

This is a fresh, zesty, versatile salsa that can be used with meats, fish, vegetables, or egg dishes. It's also wonderful as a dip for chips and vegetable appetizers.

1 pound ripe tomatoes
1 celery rib, chopped
½ green bell pepper, seeded and quartered
2 tablespoons chopped fresh basil
1 tablespoon chopped fresh thyme
1 shallot
Vegetable salt and freshly ground pepper to taste
Dash of Tabasco sauce (adjust to taste)

Cut tomatoes in half crosswise and gently squeeze out the seeds. Place half the tomatoes along with the remaining ingredients in a food processor or blender and process until coarsely chopped. Add the remaining tomatoes and continue to process to a chunky-smooth consistency. *Makes about 2 cups.*

EGGS DINARDO

Here's a healthier version of eggs Benedict, using prosciutto instead of ham. Good prosciutto (Italian ham) is naturally cured but raw, and a superior source of protein. The dish is then topped with a delicate butter-free hollandaise sauce.

The Sauce:

Per serving:
300 calories
21 grams protein
17 grams fat
16 grams
  carbohydrate

⅓ cup nonfat milk (or substitute reduced Chicken Stock, page 96)
4 large egg yolks
2 tablespoons freshly squeezed orange juice
⅛ teaspoon cayenne
Sea salt to taste

The Eggs:

2 whole wheat English muffins, halved and toasted
6 ounces thinly sliced prosciutto
4 eggs, lightly poached
1 sprig Italian parsley, snipped

Heat milk in the top of a small double boiler over simmering water. Whisk egg yolks together with orange juice. Slowly pour mixture into the hot milk in a thin stream, whisking constantly for 1 to 2 minutes, until sauce becomes hot and thick. Do not boil. When done, remove sauce from the heat and stir in cayenne and salt. Cover to keep warm.

Place each muffin half on a plate and layer with one quarter of the prosciutto slices; top with a poached egg. Spoon equal amounts of the sauce over each egg and top with snipped parsley. Serve immediately. *Serves 4.*

APPLE PAN CAKE

Per serving:
284 calories
11 grams protein
7 grams fat
46 grams
  carbohydrate

½ cup apple cider
2 cups peeled and sliced apples
½ teaspoon cinnamon
4 eggs
½ cup nonfat milk
½ cup whole wheat pastry flour
½ cup buttermilk
2 tablespoons raw honey
2 teaspoons freshly squeezed lemon juice
Pinch of sea salt (optional)

Heat apple cider in a large covered nonstick ovenproof skillet. Add apple slices, cover, and simmer over medium heat for 5 to 10 minutes, until apples are tender-crisp. Stir once halfway through cooking, adding the cinnamon. Cook, uncovered, for several minutes if necessary, to evaporate excess liquid.

In a large bowl, beat eggs with an electric mixer until foamy and light yellow. Blend milk and flour together and gradually fold into the eggs. Blend buttermilk, honey, lemon juice, and sea salt together and stir into the egg-and-milk combination just enough to mix.

Pour entire mixture into the skillet with apples and stir briefly. Place the skillet in a preheated 375-degree oven and bake uncovered for 20 to 25 minutes, until cake is light brown and fluffy. Serve topped with some reserved apples, more raw honey, or even unsweetened apple-sauce if desired. *Serves 4.*

HUEVOS RANCHEROS

Per serving:
344 calories
28 grams protein
25 grams fat
9 grams
   carbohydrate

1 tablespoon corn oil
1 freshly pressed garlic clove
1 yellow onion, diced
1 celery rib with leaves, diced
1 cup low-sodium tomato juice
½ pound Italian plum tomatoes, chopped
1 teaspoon each chopped fresh oregano and basil
1 sprig each chopped fresh mint and cilantro
Vegetable salt and freshly ground pepper to taste
4 corn tortillas
8 eggs, beaten
½ large ripe avocado, thinly sliced
¼ cup plain nonfat yogurt

Heat 1 teaspoon of the oil in a medium-size nonstick saucepan and add garlic, onion, celery, tomato juice, tomatoes, herbs, and salt and pepper. Simmer over medium heat for 15 minutes.

Meanwhile, brush both sides of the tortillas with the remaining oil. Place them on a baking sheet and bake in a preheated 375-degree oven for 6 to 7 minutes, until they are crisp and slightly golden.

Wipe a medium-size nonstick skillet with a paper towel dabbed in corn oil. Pour in eggs and scramble them over medium heat until just set. Place 1 tortilla on each of four plates. Spoon an equal portion of eggs onto each tortilla and top with simmering ranchero sauce. Garnish with avocado slices in a pinwheel pattern and top each with 1 table-spoon yogurt. *Serves 4.*

THE CLUB OMELET

Here's the ultimate omelet, consisting of four tiers of egg with a filling of smoked turkey, onions and olives, and zucchini and mushrooms, each between a layer of egg omelet, and topped with a fresh tomato-herb salsa. If you're creative, you can substitute your own fillings of cheeses, avocado, tuna, or different kinds of precooked meat and vegetables. This tiered egg creation is high in protein, low in fats and calories, and makes a spectacular showing for a breakfast, brunch, or lunch.

The Turkey Filling:

Per serving (including salsa):
337 calories
31 grams protein
18 grams fat
13 grams carbohydrate

Brunch accompaniments: Cantaloupe halves filled with fresh strawberries, warm whole wheat tortillas or bagels, and freshly squeezed orange juice.

⅓ cup Chicken Stock (page 96)
⅛ teaspoon liquid smoke
1½ cups diced cooked turkey breast

The Onion-Olive Filling:

1 teaspoon extra-virgin olive oil
1 white onion, thinly sliced
1 can (2¼ ounces) sliced black olives, rinsed and drained
1 tablespoon minced fresh parsley
Vegetable salt and freshly ground pepper to taste

The Zucchini-Mushroom Filling:

1 teaspoon extra-virgin olive oil
1 small freshly minced garlic clove
2 zucchini, thinly sliced
½ cup sliced fresh mushrooms
1 teaspoon chopped fresh oregano
Vegetable salt and freshly ground pepper to taste

The Omelet:

8 large eggs
3 tablespoons water
Extra-virgin olive oil
Tomato-Herb Salsa (page 123)

For the turkey filling, mix stock and liquid smoke together and drizzle it over diced turkey breast while tossing it to moisten it well. Set aside until ready to use.

For the onion-olive filling, heat oil in an 8-inch nonstick omelet pan. Add onion and toss over medium-high heat for 2 to 3 minutes, until it is almost tender, adding a little water if needed during cooking. Remove the pan from the heat and stir in olives, parsley, and seasoning. Transfer the filling to an ovenproof dish and keep it warm until ready to use.

For the zucchini-mushroom filling, heat oil in an 8-inch nonstick omelet pan. Brown garlic quickly over medium heat. Add zucchini, mushrooms, and seasonings and sauté for 3 to 4 minutes, stirring occasionally, until vegetables are tender-crisp. Add a little water if needed during cooking. Place the filling in an ovenproof dish and keep warm until ready to use.

Whir eggs and water together in a blender for a few seconds until light yellow but not foamy. Rub an 8-inch nonstick omelet pan well with a paper towel dabbed in olive oil. Heat pan over medium-high heat. Pour one quarter of the mixture in the pan. As egg mixture begins to get firm around the sides, lift edges with a rubber spatula to allow uncooked portion of the omelet to flow underneath. Continue to cook until the top of the eggs are just set. Using the spatula, slide the omelet flat into the center of a large serving plate. Spread a few tablespoons of the salsa over the egg, then the reserved turkey over the top. Keep it warm.

Repeat the omelet-making procedure with an equal amount of the egg mixture and place the second omelet flat on top of the turkey filling. Spread the top of the egg with the onion-olive filling. Keep it warm while making the third omelet with equal mixture. Place it on top of the onion-olive filling and arrange the zucchini-mushroom filling over the top of the egg. Keep it warm once more while making the last omelet. Place it over the zucchini-mushroom filling and top generously with Tomato-Herb Salsa. Carefully cut pie-shaped wedges to serve. *Serves 4.*

SKILLET EGGS LYONNAISE

This is a fabulous French-style onion and potato frittata made without any oil or butter.

Per serving:
240 calories
17 grams protein
11 grams fat
20 grams
  carbohydrate

6 eggs
2 tablespoons water
1 teaspoon dried marjoram
½ cup reduced Chicken Stock (page 96)
1 freshly pressed garlic clove
1 white onion, thinly sliced into 1-inch strips
2 russet potatoes, peeled and finely diced
Vegetable salt and freshly ground pepper to taste
½ cup shredded low-fat Swiss cheese
1 parsley sprig, snipped

In a medium-size bowl, whisk eggs and water along with marjoram and set aside. In an 8- or 9-inch nonstick covered skillet, heat 2 tablespoons of the stock over medium heat and add garlic and onion. Cook for 3 to 4 minutes, tossing occasionally until onions are tender-crisp. Add potatoes and continue to cook another 8 to 10 minutes, until potatoes are almost tender. Add stock anytime during the cooking process, 1 tablespoon at a time, if needed for liquid. Season with salt and pepper if desired.

When done, the onion-potato mixture should be free of liquid but moist. Flatten it lightly and evenly on the bottom of the skillet. Sprinkle the cheese over the top. Then pour in the egg mixture, cover, and continue to cook over medium heat (medium-low if you are using an electric stove) for about 5 minutes, until eggs are shiny but set. Sprinkle with snipped parsley and cut into wedges to serve. *Serves 4.*

THE 17-CALORIE EGG
(And that's no yolk!)

If you love those whole egg recipes but avoid them because of their fat and calorie content, don't worry, everything is "all white!" Luscious things like quiches and soufflés are all right here—they're made entirely with egg whites. Make no mistake: The whole egg is a complete food. The nutrients in the yolk and the white interact to provide total nourishment. However, eating just the whites is an excellent way to cut back on fats and calories as a temporary or occasional diet measure. The big bodybuilding bonus: The white of the egg contains almost twice the amount of amino acids (including the eight essential amino acids) as the yolk, and only about 25 percent of its calories. Furthermore, one egg white supplies nearly 20 percent of the daily limiting amino acid requirement (methionine) for the average man and 25 percent for the average woman. Although bodybuilders require up to three times more protein than the average person, when the daily limiting amino acid requirement has been met, the protein needs have been met. All that for only 17 fat-free calories per egg white!

These updated and upgraded recipe renditions of old favorites are not only high in protein and low in calories, but also pennywise and simple to prepare. Most are even shorter on cooking time, too. Now I ask you: Can you think of a better way to get enough protein, get all your amino acids, get ripped, and have fun at the same time? I didn't think so.

Cheese Cuts
Cheese is very high in protein but also high in fat. For your reference, here is a list of the top 30 cheeses starting with those that have the highest amount of protein to the lowest amount of fat. Cottage cheese is number 1 at 48% protein, 1% fat. The list ends with Roquefort at 17% protein and 22% fat.

Cottage cheese, dry
Cottage cheese, 1% low-fat
Cottage cheese, 2% low-fat
Cottage cheese, creamed
Monterey Jack, low-fat
Cheddar, low-fat
Swiss, low-fat
American, low-fat
Parmesan
Mozzarella, part-skim
Romano
Gruyère, low-fat
Swiss, full-fat
Provolone

Gruyère, full-fat
Gouda
Mozzarella, full-fat
Ricotta, part-skim
Camembert
Monterey Jack, full-fat
Muenster
Brick
Brie
Cheshire
Limburger
Blue cheese
Cheddar, full-fat
Colby
Feta
Roquefort

NO-BAKE SALMON SOUFFLÉ

Here is a deliciously simple and versatile soufflé that contains only five ingredients and takes five minutes to cook, yet satisfies high nutritional requirements—including 50 percent of the minimum daily requirement of calcium.

Per serving:
312 calories
47 grams protein
12 grams fat
5 grams
   carbohydrate

3 egg whites, warmed to room temperature
½ teaspoon ground cumin
1 can (6½ ounces) salmon, rinsed and drained
1 scallion, chopped
1 jar (2 ounces) chopped pimientoes, rinsed and drained

In a medium-size bowl, beat egg whites with an electric mixer. When peaks begin to form, add cumin and finish beating until whites are stiff but not dry. Set aside.

Crumble salmon, along with the fine edible bones, into an 8- or 9-inch nonstick omelet pan with a high cover. Add scallions and sauté lightly over medium heat until just softened. Stir in pimientoes. Add several tablespoons of the beaten egg whites to the salmon mixture and blend well, spreading it evenly across the bottom of the pan. Pour in remaining egg white topping, and, with a rubber spatula, neatly arrange it to form a dome. Cover, lower heat, and cook 2 to 3 minutes.

To remove the soufflé, run the spatula around and under the sides, tilt the pan, and slide it onto a serving plate. *Serves 1.*

STOVE-TOP CHICKEN AND BROCCOLI QUICHE

This quick quiche has a potato crust, a great natural source of complex carbohydrates.

Per serving:
154 calories
16 grams protein
4 grams fat
14 grams
   carbohydrate

1 tablespoon extra-virgin olive oil
1 freshly pressed garlic clove
3 new white potatoes, peeled and thinly sliced crosswise
6 egg whites, lightly beaten
½ cup evaporated nonfat milk
⅔ cup steamed or frozen defrosted broccoli florets
1 cup diced cooked chicken breast
½ cup shredded part-skim mozzarella cheese
½ teaspoon each dried marjoram and basil
Vegetable salt and freshly ground pepper to taste

Heat oil in a 10-inch nonstick covered skillet. Cook potatoes with garlic uncovered over medium heat for 10 to 15 minutes, until potatoes are fork-tender and lightly browned on both sides. Remove skillet from heat and arrange potato slices evenly on the bottom and around the sides of the skillet.

In a large bowl, thoroughly mix remaining ingredients and pour into the potato-lined skillet. Cover and cook over medium heat for 5 to 6 minutes, or until egg mixture is set. Cut into wedges to serve. *Serves 6.*

SLIM STUFFED PEPPERS

An all-time favorite made even more nutritious with egg whites replacing extra ground beef.

Per serving:
182 calories
15 grams protein
8 grams fat
13 grams
  carbohydrate

Nifty note:
You may substitute
any other ground
meat for the beef.
Just be sure it's
extra lean.

4 green bell peppers
¾ pound lean ground beef
4 egg whites, lightly beaten
2 tablespoons tomato paste
1 freshly pressed garlic clove
2 tablespoons minced fresh parsley
½ teaspoon dried oregano
Vegetable salt and freshly ground pepper to taste
1 cup dried whole wheat bread crumbs
⅓ cup freshly grated Parmesan cheese
¼ cup raw wheat germ
1 tablespoon extra-virgin olive oil

Cut peppers in half lengthwise. Remove stems and membranes and set the peppers aside. In a medium-size bowl, mix beef, egg whites, tomato paste, garlic, and herbs together, along with salt and pepper, if desired. Add ¾ cup of the bread crumbs along with half the Parmesan cheese to the beef mixture and blend well. Stuff each pepper half with the beef mixture and arrange them, stuffed side up, in a large covered baking dish. Add water so that it is about ¼ inch deep in the bottom of the dish. Cover tightly and cook in a 350-degree oven for 45 minutes.

Meanwhile, toss the remaining ¼ cup of bread crumbs along with the wheat germ, olive oil, and remaining Parmesan cheese to make a crumbly topping.

After 45 minutes of cooking, uncover the stuffed peppers and sprinkle the tops equally with the topping. Continue to bake the peppers, uncovered, about 10 minutes more until the topping is crispy. *Serves 8.*

CURRIED CARROT
AND CAULIFLOWER CASSEROLE

Per serving:
67 calories
9 grams protein
1 gram fat
5 grams
  carbohydrate

2 carrots, peeled and sliced
2 cups cauliflower florets
1/3 cup finely minced white onion
1 teaspoon curry powder
4 egg whites, warmed to room temperature
1/2 cup nonfat milk
2/3 cup grated low-fat Cheddar cheese

Steam carrots and cauliflower for 7 to 8 minutes, until they are par-cooked to tender crunchy. Arrange them in an 8-inch round nonstick baking pan or dish. Sprinkle the tops with the minced onion and half the curry powder.

In a large bowl, beat egg whites with an electric mixer just until they are foamy. Mix milk, grated cheese, and remaining curry powder together and fold it into the egg whites. Pour the mixture over the top of the vegetables and spread it around evenly. Bake, uncovered, in a preheated 350-degree oven for about 15 minutes, until top is golden brown. *Serves 6.*

CHILE RELLEÑO LITE

It's baked, not deep-fried, so no oil is used. Part-skim ricotta replaces hard cheese and cuts calories to a third. And extra egg whites replace whole eggs, giving you more for less. Totally lite!

Per serving:
103 calories
9 grams protein
4 grams fat
7 grams
  carbohydrate

1½ cups part-skim ricotta cheese
2 scallions, finely minced
1 tablespoon minced fresh sage
8 mild green chili peppers, whole (fresh-roasted or canned, rinsed
      and drained)
6 egg whites, warmed to room temperature
1 teaspoon chili powder
Pinch of vegetable salt
1 can (10 ounces) enchilada sauce

In a small bowl, combine ricotta, scallions, and sage together and set aside. Slit one side of each chili and remove seeds. Arrange them flat in a circular fashion in a 9- or 10-inch nonstick pie tin. Spoon equal amounts of the ricotta filling across the top of each chili.

In a large bowl, beat egg whites with an electric mixer until stiff, moist peaks form, sprinkling in chili powder and salt while beating. Spread meringue in a dome shape evenly over chilies and bake in a 350-degree oven for 20 to 25 minutes, until top is golden. Warm the enchilada sauce and pour equal amounts into shallow serving dishes. Cut chile relleño into 8 wedges and serve it over the sauce. *Serves 8.*

MICROWAVE FRENCH TOAST
WITH ORANGE-YOGURT TOPPING

Per serving:
140 calories
7 grams protein
1 gram fat
26 grams
    carbohydrate

Sticky note:
Instead of the topping, just drizzle a mixture of warm honey and orange juice over the French toast. It's delicious. But be careful not to overcook the French toast. Bread tends to toughen when microwaved. Check about halfway through cooking just to see if the egg is already set.

Nuked, not fried, and made with egg whites only, this version of French toast is healthy, low-calorie, and quick.

4 egg whites
⅓ cup nonfat milk
2 tablespoons raw honey (or substitute NutraSweet to taste)
4 slices whole wheat bread
½ cup plain nonfat yogurt
¼ cup freshly squeezed orange juice
¼ teaspoon pure vanilla extract

In a medium-size shallow bowl, lightly whisk egg whites, milk, and 1 tablespoon of the honey together. Soak both sides of each bread slice in the egg white mixture. Place the four slices of bread on a flat microwave ovenproof dish and microwave them on medium-high for 1 to 1½ minutes. Turn the slices over and microwave them another 1 to 1½ minutes, or until the egg-soaked bread is moist but firm. (If you are cooking one slice at a time, microwave for 30 seconds on each side.)

In a small bowl, blend together yogurt, orange juice, vanilla, and remaining honey (or NutraSweet). Spoon equal amounts of the topping over each piece of French toast and serve. *Serves 4.*

MUSCLE-BUILDING BREAKFAST DRINKS

If you are training regularly, you know you need extra protein to build muscle. If you are watching your diet too (as in cutting back on calories), you also need extra protein to keep from losing muscle. The kind of protein you need is lean, high-quality protein containing all eight of the essential amino acids in the right proportions. Remember, if one of these eight essential amino acids is out of balance or missing in dietary protein, protein synthesis in the body will drop or stop completely, limiting muscular growth and repair.

This essential amino acid requirement is best met with meat, fish, poultry, and dairy products—a safe spectrum that seems simple enough to cover. But there's a catch. If you have been following the Perfect Nutrition program, you know that the protein in foods is up to 80 percent more utilizable when foods are eaten raw, which means you would need as little as 20 percent of your normal amount to meet your protein requirement. A great calorie saver. But unless you are a modern caveman, that can be a problem when it comes to meat, fish, and poultry.

One way to beat the meat dilemma is with eggs. Eggs have the highest protein-efficiency ratio of all the protein foods, and are a healthy, low-calorie food, high in vitamins, minerals, and essential fatty acids, and protein-rich in all the essential amino acids. You can throw a couple of raw eggs into the blender with fresh fruit or juices and have a high-quality, 100 percent protein-efficient meal.

The white and the yolk each play a role in making an egg the nutritionally perfect food. The white is where most of the protein and amino acids are, and the yolk is where most of the vitamins and minerals are. But the yolk is also where most of the fat and calories are, a snag to bodybuilders (and dieters) looking for some fast cuts. So consuming just the whites is a great temporary solution to get the results you want, as long as you are taking vitamin and mineral supplements. Throw a couple of whites in that blender, and now you have it all—a high-quality, 100 percent protein-efficient meal that is low-calorie too.

These Muscle-Building Breakfast Drinks call for three egg whites plus fresh fruits to make them even more nutritious. For a super boost, you can beef up your drink with your favorite protein powder. A good protein powder just about equals the egg white in its perfect 4:1 ratio of calories to protein. Just be sure it's free of sugar and fillers, and made with a minimum of heat processing. Or make the drink really complete by adding a tablespoon each of raw wheat germ and bran to the blender.

If the fruits aren't naturally sweet enough, add a little raw honey or NutraSweet to taste while the drinks are blending. Simply toss all the ingredients in a blender and whir, and you'll get one big frosty drink.

Have one of these deliciously satisfying drinks to start your day off with a real energy high, or have one at the end of the day when your muscles are at rest and repair and can use the extra protein. Or you can even have one to replace a meal. This will knock off a few calories and help you lose weight without losing muscle. (You can do this indefinitely if you use the whole egg.) So let these Muscle-Building Breakfast Drinks go to work for you while you get on with the job of bodybuilding.

But first, here are some important notes about the egg: An enzyme called avidin in the raw egg white can interfere with the absorption of the B-vitamin biotin over a long period of time. However, since most of the biotin is in the yolk, you are not getting enough biotin from the egg source to worry about it anyway. But if you plan to use whole eggs—or you just want to take a precautionary measure—simply place the uncracked eggs under very hot tap water for one minute and the avidin will be inactivated.

In view of the recent health warnings about eggs, always be sure to buy the freshest eggs available (check the date on the carton). Don't use raw eggs that are over one month old. Make sure they have been stored in a cool (40 degrees or below), dry place. Never rinse or wash the eggshells before you use them and never use cracked eggs. If you can obtain fertile eggs, by all means do so. They are usually found farm-fresh or in health food stores, are generally produced with greater care, and are more nutritious.

SPICED PEAR ENERGIZER

Per serving:
331 calories
13 grams protein
1 gram fat
73 grams carbohydrate

3 egg whites
1 ripe juicy pear, cored
¼ cup seedless golden raisins
½ cup unfiltered apple juice
⅛ teaspoon cinnamon
2 cloves, crushed
3 to 4 ice cubes

Whir all ingredients in a blender until thick and frosty. *Makes 1 large drink serving.*

BLUE MOON FROSTY

Per serving:
181 calories
13 grams protein
1 gram fat
33 grams
  carbohydrate

3 egg whites
⅔ cup fresh or frozen unsweetened blueberries
⅔ cup freshly squeezed orange juice
¼ teaspoon pure vanilla extract
3 to 4 ice cubes

Whir all ingredients in a blender until thick and frosty. *Makes 1 large drink serving.*

CHERRY CHEESECAKE SHAKE
(Tastes a little like cheesecake)

Per serving:
246 calories
17 grams protein
2 grams fat
40 grams
  carbohydrate

3 egg whites
⅔ cup fresh sweet or frozen unsweetened pitted cherries
½ cup plain piima or kefir milk
⅓ cup unfiltered apple juice
¼ teaspoon each pure vanilla and almond extract
3 to 4 ice cubes

Whir all ingredients in a blender until thick and frosty. *Makes 1 large drink serving.*

Per serving:
229 calories
14 grams protein
1 gram fat
45 grams
  carbohydrate

BANANA BERRY SMOOTHIE

3 egg whites
1 ripe banana
½ cup fresh or frozen unsweetened strawberries
½ cup freshly squeezed orange juice
3 to 4 ice cubes

Whir all ingredients in a blender until thick and frosty. *Makes 1 large drink serving.*

Berry good idea: Instead of strawberries, you may also use any of your favorite seasonal berries. If you use frozen ones, make sure they are unsweetened.

PIÑA COLADA CRUSH

Per serving:
261 calories
18 grams protein
8 grams fat
30 grams
  carbohydrate

3 egg whites
²⁄₃ cup fresh pineapple chunks
¹⁄₃ cup shredded fresh or unsweetened dried coconut
¹⁄₂ cup nonfat milk
¹⁄₂ teaspoon pure vanilla extract
3 to 4 ice cubes

Whir all ingredients in a blender until thick and frosty. *Makes 1 large drink serving.*

PEACH FIZZ

Per serving:
144 calories
13 grams protein
1 gram fat
24 grams
  carbohydrate

3 egg whites
1 large ripe peach, pitted
¹⁄₂ cup freshly squeezed orange juice
¹⁄₄ teaspoon pure vanilla extract
1 to 2 ice cubes
¹⁄₂ cup sparkling mineral water

Whir all ingredients, except mineral water, in a blender until thick and frosty. Briefly stir in mineral water and serve. *Makes 1 large drink serving.*

Fizzy solution: You may substitute your favorite diet soda sweetened with NutraSweet or fructose for the sparkling mineral water.

— PART THREE —
PERFORMANCE FOODS

Photo: Chris Lund

— 9 —
GRAINS

GOING WITH THE WHOLE GRAIN

Power Booster
Make healthy,
energy-bursting
peanut butter 'n
honey wheat snacks
with a mix of raw
peanut butter, wheat
sprouts, raw honey,
and pitted chopped
dates. Make them
into gooey balls and
roll them in a
coating of raw wheat
germ. Wow!

In our modern culture, grains are regarded as an ingredient rather than a staple, and are generally synonymous with breads and cereals. Unfortunately, most all breads and cereals are milled and processed to some degree. Milling makes whole grains into flour by grinding the grain and sifting out the bran and germ, where most of the nutrients are. The flour is then used exclusively for cooking and baking, a process that further eliminates most nutrients.

Bread, as we know it, is a fairly recent food. Centuries ago, when people didn't have fuel or oven facilities, or when wood wasn't always available for burning in the crude ovens used for baking bread, they ate their bread raw. Grains or seeds were ground and soaked until they softened, then were formed into glutinous masses or loaves, and stored to be eaten as "bread." Breadwise, the people then were probably better off. Eating this way often kept them going in hard times when other foods, such as fresh meats, fruits, and vegetables weren't around. Sad, but this little tidbit of anthropology gives us a strong insight into the importance of eating natural earth foods.

Uncooked whole grains, including rice, supply generous amounts of the B-vitamins and vitamin E. They also supply numerous minerals, especially calcium, phosphorus, and iron. They contain a substantial amount of protein and are a wonderful source of complex carbohydrate and cellulose fiber—the type of fiber that hastens food through the digestive system, fighting fat, various digestive problems, and colon cancer.

Cooking and processing, especially with commercial products, greatly alters these beneficial properties. Since nearly all grain products

Fast Tracks
The secret to fluffy rice: Soak the grains in enough cold water to cover for 6 to 8 hours (overnight for wild rice), then drain and cook them according to directions in a large (not cramped) saucepan so that the grains have room to expand. Do not lift the lid or stir until cooking time is up.

are cooked, what can we do about it? How do we choose the best grains? First of all, when buying commercial breads, cereals, or grain products (such as pasta), it's not a matter of choosing the best, because there is no "best" once they are processed and devitalized. It becomes a matter of choosing your grain foods with the least amount of initial destruction. Go for grains that have been regularly cooked over instant; unbleached flour over white flour; sprouted grain over whole grain, etc. Look for fewer ingredients on package labels; these products are usually purer and less processed because fewer damaged ingredients have been added. Next, don't think "flour" when buying grain products for baking. Instead, think "whole grain" and grind your own flours if you have to. Last but not least, sprout your own grains (or beans) once in a while, or buy them already sprouted and eat them fresh (see Sprouted Wheat Salad; page 146). This is how you really preserve and culture the life force of a grain seed, thereby enjoying its complete nutritional benefits.

Using chicken stock instead of water makes rice more flavorful. For a shortcut, omit stock and add low-sodium tamari or a dash of Worcestershire sauce to the cooking water along with a sprinkle of garlic or onion powder. A bit of oil in the cooking water keeps the grains from sticking together.

There are thousands of grain products on the market to choose from, and many of them are inferior. But your careful knowledge and freedom of selection is all you really have to rely on, so let this bit of advice lead you to a healthier way of life. Check out these delicious, nutritious recipes—all made with whole grains, of course. You'll find in this section, too, helpful hints on boosting the nutritional value of these grain dishes, as well as steps for sprouting grains. Nowadays, you can't ask for more than that.

SUPER-START QUINOA CEREAL

Per serving:
285 calories
8 grams protein
2 grams fat
59 grams carbohydrate

This super grain of South American origin is 16 percent protein (wheat is next highest, with 14 percent). Two ounces of uncooked quinoa supplies 9 grams of protein and all 8 essential amino acids in balanced proportions. It is also higher in calcium, phosphorus, and iron than wheat, rice, or corn. It's easy to cook and has a sweet, nutty taste. To boost protein value, substitute it for a portion of other cooked whole grains. Quinoa is readily available in health food stores.

2 cups water
1 cup uncooked quinoa grains
½ cup seedless raisins
1½ teaspoons ground cinnamon
Pinch of freshly grated nutmeg
½ teaspoon pure vanilla extract
¼ cup pure maple syrup

Rinse and drain quinoa first. Bring water and quinoa to a boil in a medium-size covered saucepan. Reduce heat, cover, and simmer for about 10 minutes. Stir in remaining ingredients, cover again, and continue cooking over a low heat for another 5 minutes, until cereal becomes a thick (but not dry) mush. Serve as is or with any of the breakfast boost topping suggestions (see left). *Serves 4.*

ZUCCHINI BRAN MUFFINS
(Fruit juice sweetened!)

Per muffin:
134 calories
3 grams protein
5 grams fat
20 grams
  carbohydrate

1¼ cups whole wheat flour
¾ cup raw bran
2 teaspoons baking powder
½ teaspoon each ground cinnamon and ginger
1 egg, beaten
⅔ cup unsweetened apple juice concentrate
2 tablespoons safflower oil
½ teaspoon pure vanilla extract
¾ cup shredded zucchini
¼ cup finely chopped dried pineapple
⅓ cup finely chopped walnuts

Mix flour, bran, baking powder, cinnamon, and ginger together in a medium-size bowl. In a large bowl blend together egg, apple juice concentrate, oil, and vanilla. Then stir in zucchini, pineapple, and walnuts. Add dry mixture to liquid mixture and stir until just combined. Drop equal tablespoonfuls of the batter into a nonstick 12-cup muffin pan. Bake in a preheated 375-degree oven for about 30 minutes, or until tops are brown and firm to the touch. *Makes 12 muffins.*

ROSEMARY POLENTA

Per serving:
135 calories
5 grams protein
3 grams fat
23 grams
    carbohydrate

Appetizing idea:
Make prosciutto
polenta. Lay slices
of prosciutto over
polenta before
topping with sauce.
Or wrap thin slices
of prosciutto around
small chunks of
polenta. Secure with
toothpicks and serve
as an appetizer with
a marinara dipping
sauce.

4 cups water
1 teaspoon dried rosemary, finely crumbled
1 tablespoon extra-virgin olive oil
Sea salt to taste
1 cup stone-ground yellow cornmeal
3 cups Wine Marrow Sauce (page 156), warmed (or substitute "natural-style"
    marinara sauce)
Freshly grated Parmesan cheese (optional)

In a large saucepan or stockpot, bring 3 cups of water along with rose-mary, olive oil, and sea salt to a rolling boil. Thoroughly moisten corn-meal in the remaining cup of water and stir it into the boiling water. When it just begins to thicken, lower heat to medium, and stir con-stantly for about 5 minutes, until the polenta is the consistency of thick (but not dry) mush. Serve topped with equal portions of Wine Marrow Sauce and Parmesan cheese, if desired. *Serves 6.*

HARVEST RICE

Wild rice is an extremely nutritious grass seed that contains twice as much protein as brown rice. The woody flavor of wild rice is enhanced when mixed with sweet, nutty brown rice in this autumn-inspired dish. This rice blend will cook up best when soaked overnight in water.

Per serving:
179 calories
6 grams protein
4 grams fat
3 grams
    carbohydrate

½ cup uncooked wild rice
½ cup uncooked brown rice
2½ cups Chicken Stock (page 96)
1 freshly pressed garlic clove
⅓ cup finely chopped yellow onion
1 celery rib with leaves, finely chopped
1 large apple, peeled, cored, and thinly sliced
1 teaspoon ground sage
Pinch of allspice
¼ cup finely chopped pecans
Vegetable salt and freshly ground pepper to taste

After soaking overnight, drain combined rices. In a large covered saucepan, bring rice to a boil in 2 cups of the stock. Cover tightly, lower heat, and simmer for about 50 minutes.

Meanwhile, heat ¼ cup of the remaining stock in a medium-size covered nonstick sauté pan. Add garlic, onion, and celery. Cover and simmer over medium-low heat for 3 to 4 minutes, until onion and celery are tender-crisp. Stir in apples, sage, and allspice. Add remaining stock as needed for liquid. Cover and continue simmering for another 3 to 4 minutes, until apples are semisoft. Add pecans and continue sautéing uncovered, stirring occasionally, for several more minutes, or until all liquid has evaporated.

Remove sauté pan from the heat. When rice is cooked, stir in sautéed apple mixture and season with salt and pepper, if desired. *Serves 6.*

CALIFORNIA RICE

Sweet Wehani is called for here, but you can use any of the aromatic and hybrid rices or rice blends to make this simple, healthy dish. They lend a more exciting flavor and appearance than the standby brown rice and are available in health food and specialty food stores.

Per serving:
212 calories
6 grams protein
2 grams fat
43 grams
  carbohydrate

Nutty note:
Top with or add in
finely chopped
unsalted green
pistachio nuts.

1½ cups Chicken Stock (page 96), or substitute water
1 cup uncooked Wehani rice
1 teaspoon butter
1 large shallot, finely chopped
½ teaspoon each dried marjoram and savory
1 small bunch spinach leaves (about ½ pound), chopped
Vegetable salt and freshly ground pepper to taste

In a large covered saucepan, bring all ingredients to a boil except spinach and seasoning. Lower heat, cover tightly, and simmer for about 20 minutes. Remove the cover, pack in chopped spinach leaves and cover again. Turn off the heat and let the rice and spinach stand for several minutes until the leaves are just wilted. Stir to mix in the spinach and season with salt and pepper, if desired. *Serves 4.*

BROWN RICE CRUST

Here's a versatile rice crust for just about anything. Pour in an egg mixture and bake a quiche; add a fish, poultry, or meat entrée in a sauce and make a casserole; or spread with cooked vegetables and top with cheese to make a handy vegetable, grain, and dairy combo.

Per serving:
175 calories
7 grams protein
4 grams fat
29 grams
   carbohydrate

1 cup uncooked brown rice
2 cups water, or substitute Chicken Stock (page 96)
1 cup nonfat milk
2 eggs, beaten
¼ cup freshly grated Parmesan cheese
2 tablespoons chopped fresh chives or parsley
Vegetable salt and freshly ground pepper to taste

In a medium-size covered saucepan, bring rice and water to a boil for 5 minutes. Lower heat, cover tightly, and simmer for 35 to 40 minutes, until rice is tender and fluffy. Combine remaining ingredients with cooked rice and turn into a 9- or 10-inch nonstick (or lightly oiled) pie tin. Press sides and center down with a large wet spoon to form a crust. Cover loosely with foil and bake in a preheated 350-degree oven for 30 to 35 minutes. Remove foil the last 5 minutes of baking to allow crust to brown. *Makes a crust for 6 servings.*

SPROUTED WHEAT SALAD

Sprouted whole grains and beans are the most practical way to eat these foods uncooked in order to obtain their full nutrients. Sprouting greatly increases their amino acid value and generates higher amounts of vitamins A, B, C, and E.

The Salad:

Per serving:
364 calories
6 grams protein
20 grams fat
42 grams
   carbohydrate

4 cups fresh whole wheat sprouts
1 green bell pepper, diced
1 small carrot, grated
2 small celery ribs, diced
1 scallion, minced
2 ripe tomatoes, cut into eighths

The Dressing:

⅓ cup safflower oil
3 tablespoons cider vinegar
1 tablespoon freshly squeezed lemon juice
1 freshly pressed garlic clove
1 teaspoon Dijon mustard
1 teaspoon minced fresh dill
½ teaspoon raw honey
Vegetable salt and freshly ground pepper to taste

Good egg idea:
Sprinkle the salad tops with grated hard-boiled eggs, or just the whites.

To make sprouts, soak 1 cup of whole wheat seeds in a ½-gallon glass or plastic container filled with 1 quart warm water. Cover the container with cheesecloth and secure it with a tight rubber band or string. Place the container in a warm dark place for about 10 hours; drain the seeds through the cheesecloth. Rinse and drain them once more, through the cheesecloth, leaving no water in the jar. Lay the container back into its resting place, on its side so that the seeds are evenly spread out. Repeat this rinsing procedure at least twice a day until seeds begin to sprout, 2 to 4 days. Use them as soon as the sprouts are as long as the seed. Although the sprouting time and sprout length will vary, you can use these directions to sprout most whole seeds and beans.

For the salad, arrange a bed of whole wheat sprouts on four salad plates. Mix remaining vegetables and place four equal amounts of the mixture in the center of the sprouts. Garnish each with four tomato wedges. Whisk dressing ingredients together and drizzle equal amounts over each salad. *Serves 4.*

SLIM PASTABILITIES

Healthful Hint
It's a mineral madness! When boiling pasta (or soups and even cereals), drop a mineral supplement tablet into the boiling water and the pasta will soak up the minerals.

Presenting pasta—the hottest star on the American cuisine scene! Basic pasta contains only flour and eggs, so it's a relatively high-protein, low-calorie food that provides necessary bulk. It is also an excellent source of complex carbohydrate, so essential for supplying energy during hard endurance training. But as our passion for pasta grows, so does our fear of those menacingly rich sauces that make it taste so good. Careless amounts of oil, butter, cheese, heavy cream, and nuts are the culprits. And of course white-flour pastas are a no-no. The following whole grain pasta and sauce recipes offer lighter versions with less amounts of these ingredients, or none at all. Without sacrificing flavor, you can go with

Noodle note:
These pasta recipes call for whole eggs. You may substitute 2 egg whites for each whole egg, and 1 egg white for each yolk called for with satisfactory results.

Calorie Cuts
To make the lightest of cream sauces, simply toss a dollop of plain nonfat yogurt in with plain hot pasta. Add none, one, or any of the following ingredients: freshly pressed garlic, extra-virgin olive oil, freshly grated Parmesan or Romano cheese, prepared mustard, dried herbs such as parsley, oregano, or basil, and vegetable salt and freshly ground pepper to taste.

the combination of ingredients that suits your diet. Or eat your pasta mixed with only steamed vegetables, meat, or fish. You'll find these recipes so delightfully delicious that you may even be satisfied with just plain pasta, especially when it's homemade.

Homemade pasta is a real treat and relatively easy to make. If you are using pureed vegetables in your dough, you'll probably want to use a food processor. If you are making it by hand, all you need is a rolling pin, a large sharp knife, and a pasta crimper if you want. Should you have the time and the wizardry, you can invest in a pasta machine and open up a whole new area of experimentation and fun. Or you can also buy these fresh and fancy pastas at delis, Italian markets, and specialty food stores. And most markets, as well as health food stores, now carry the superior whole grain pastas. For the record, the "semolina" grain popularly used in commercial pastas is a high-grade but refined flour that unfortunately has been nutritionally depleted in the milling process.

Here is the basic procedure for making pasta dough by hand. Pile the flour onto a large flat surface and make a well in the center. Drop in the moist or liquid ingredients and blend them together, using your fingers or a fork. Recommended flour amounts are given in the recipes, but use as much or as little as you need to form a firm but cohesive ball of dough. Knead the dough for 5 to 10 minutes with the heel of your hand, folding and turning as you go, until it does not stick to your hands or the work surface. Cut the dough into four sections and form each one into a ball. If you're using a pasta machine, follow the manufacturer's instructions at this point. If you proceed by hand, flatten each piece of dough with a rolling pin, stretching it outward in all directions until it is a very thin sheet. Let the sheets of dough rest at room temperature for 40 minutes to 1 hour. Just before they become brittle, cut the pasta.

For noodles, loosely roll each sheet in jelly-roll fashion and cut it crosswise to the desired width. Then unroll and cut to the desire length.

For ravioli, spoon the filling onto one sheet of dough, about 1 inch apart. Cover with a second sheet of dough. Press dough down between the filling with your fingers to seal ravioli off. Then cut out squares with a knife or pasta crimper.

Let the pasta dry out for about 1 hour before cooking by separating the pieces or squares and laying them out flat on paper towels or wax paper. If you wish to save some pasta after it has dried, store it in a tightly sealed plastic bag or airtight container in the refrigerator or freezer (ravioli should be frozen), but do not defrost it before cooking, or it will become mushy.

Boil each pound of pasta in approximately 6 quarts of water. Add a tiny bit of oil to keep the strands from sticking together. Putting the pasta in already boiling water will also keep this from happening. A little salt added to the water will make it taste better, and boiling it in a mixture of water and stock will give it even more flavor. Homemade pasta cooks faster than store-bought pasta, so you don't want to over-cook it. "Al dente," or slightly chewy, is the traditional way to eat it. Drain the pasta in a colander and keep warm by placing it in a covered casserole dish in a very low oven.

To reheat pasta with sauces or in casseroles, place it in a covered oven-proof casserole dish in a 275 to 300-degree oven until palatably hot. For plain pasta, drop it in a pot of very hot or boiling water for 1 to 2 minutes, then drain.

Yes, pasta has hit the big time, but not the big calories. Add these gourmet diet recipes to your menu, and meet the star that has captured America's heart—and stomach!

CONFETTI PASTA

The Pasta Verde:

⅓ cup steamed and pureed beet, collard, kale, or turnip greens, pressed free of
    liquid
1 egg
1¼ cups whole wheat pastry flour

The Carrot Pasta:

⅓ cup steamed and pureed carrots, pressed free of liquid
1 egg
1¼ cups whole wheat pastry flour

The Tomato Pasta:

3 tablespoons tomato paste
1 egg
1 cup whole wheat pastry flour

To make these vegetable pastas, it is more efficient to use a food processor to puree the vegetables first, so proceed with making the dough in the processor also. For individual recipes, puree the vegetables by

CONFETTI PASTA (*continued*)

processing several times with 1-second pulses using a metal blade. Add the egg, process again, then add the flour. Continue processing with 1-second pulses until dough forms small beads. Roll each piece of dough into a ball, wrap in plastic, and set aside for 20 to 30 minutes before rolling out to make noodles.

Follow the directions in the introduction for completing the pasta-making process. Each recipe makes about ½ pound of dough. Serve all three colored pastas in one dish. Top with one of the two following variations of pesto sauce. *Serves 6 as a side dish.*

TOMATO-POTATO PESTO
(*Contains no cheese or nuts*)

Per serving:
61 calories
1 gram protein
5 grams fat
4 grams
   carbohydrate

2 tablespoons extra-virgin olive oil
½ cup torn fresh basil leaves
¼ cup chopped fresh parsley
4 garlic cloves
1 large ripe tomato, seeded, peeled, and chopped
1 new red potato, cooked, peeled, and mashed
Vegetable salt and freshly ground pepper to taste

Blend all ingredients in a blender or food processor until smooth and tiny green flecks remain. Warm pesto, if desired, and serve tossed with hot pasta. *Makes 6 servings, or enough for 1½ pounds of pasta.*

LITE PESTO
(*Contains no oil or nuts*)

Per serving:
21 calories
2 grams protein
1 gram fat
1 gram carbohydrate

Pesto pizzazz:
Try adding a little crumbled anchovy or anchovy paste to this recipe. Mamma mia!

1 cup reduced Chicken Stock (page 96)
½ cup torn fresh basil leaves
3 garlic cloves
4 tablespoons freshly grated Parmesan cheese
Freshly ground pepper to taste

Blend all ingredients in a blender or food processor just until tiny green flecks remain. Warm pesto, if desired, and toss with hot pasta. *Makes 6 servings, or enough for 1½ pounds of pasta.*

WHOLE WHEAT FETTUCCINE

Per serving:
277 calories
11 grams protein
8 grams fat
41 grams
   carbohydrate

2 cups whole wheat flour
2 eggs
1 tablespoon extra-virgin olive oil
Chicken and Zucchini Béarnaise (recipe follows)

Make pasta according to directions on page 148. Top with Chicken and Zucchini Béarnaise. *Makes about 1 pound, enough for 4 servings.*

CHICKEN AND ZUCCHINI BÉARNAISE
(Contains no butter, cheese, cream, or oil)

Per serving:
206 calories
32 grams protein
8 grams fat
2 grams
   carbohydrate

1½ cups reduced Chicken Stock (page 96)
¾ cup 1 percent low-fat milk
2 shallots, finely minced
1 tablespoon chopped fresh parsley
1 teaspoon chopped fresh tarragon
1 tablespoon freshly squeezed lemon juice
2 egg yolks
1 pound chicken breasts, skinned, cooked, and diced
2 zucchini, steamed and sliced
¼ teaspoon cayenne
Vegetable salt to taste

Bring stock and milk to a slow boil in a double boiler. Add shallots, parsley, and tarragon and continue cooking for several minutes. Lower heat to a simmer. Blend lemon juice and egg yolks and slowly stir into stock mixture until heated through. Do not boil. Toss in chicken, zucchini, cayenne, and salt, if desired, and stir until just hot. Remove from heat and spoon sauce over hot Whole Wheat Fettuccine. *Serves 4.*

BAKED EGG NOODLES
AND CHEESE WITH TOMATOES

This is a takeoff on the all-time favorite macaroni and cheese, but with fresh tomatoes added.

The Noodles:

Per serving:
140 calories
7 grams protein
4 grams fat
21 grams
  carbohydrate

1½ cups whole wheat pastry flour
2 eggs
1 egg yolk

Make pasta according to directions on page 148. *Makes about 1 pound, enough for 6 side-dish servings.*

The Cheese Sauce: *(contains no butter, cream, or oil)*

Per serving:
79 calories
9 grams protein
4 grams fat
2 grams
  carbohydrate

⅔ cup nonfat milk
3 ounces Neufchâtel cheese
1 cup shredded low-fat Cheddar cheese
2 tablespoons finely minced white onion
½ teaspoon dry mustard
Vegetable salt and freshly ground pepper to taste

Topping option:
If you like a cheesy crust that has crunch, sprinkle wheat germ over the top of the cheese before baking.

Bring milk and Neufchâtel to a simmer in a double boiler. Add Cheddar cheese, onion, mustard, and salt and pepper to taste and continue to stir over a slow boil until cheese has melted. Toss cheese sauce with noodles (save a little to pour over the top), turn into a 3-quart casserole dish, and mix in 2 large, ripe tomatoes (chopped, seeded, and drained). Top with remaining sauce and bake, uncovered, in a 350-degree oven for 10 to 12 minutes, until top is golden. *Serves 6.*

ORIENTAL NOODLE SALAD

The Noodles:

Per serving:
127 calories
6 grams protein
2 grams fat
21 grams
    carbohydrate

1 cup whole wheat pastry flour
½ cup brown rice flour
2 eggs

Make pasta according to directions on page 148. *Makes about ¾ pound, enough for 6 side-dish servings.*

The Salad:

Per serving:
87 calories
4 grams protein
6 grams fat
7 grams
    carbohydrate

1 cup small broccoli florets
1 cup mung bean sprouts
½ cup sliced fresh mushrooms
2 scallions, chopped
4 ounces firm tofu, cubed

The Dressing: *(contains no oil, cheese, or cream)*

½ cup plain nonfat yogurt
¼ cup rice vinegar
2 tablespoons sesame oil
2 tablespoons low-sodium tamari
1 tablespoon raw honey
1 teaspoon minced fresh ginger

Combine salad ingredients with noodles in a large serving bowl. Blend dressing ingredients together and toss well with noodle salad. *Serves 6.*

SPINACH AND CLAM QUENELLES
(French dumplings)

Per serving:
213 calories
14 grams protein
7 grams fat
24 grams
  carbohydrate

1 cup whole wheat pastry flour
2 teaspoons baking powder
1 tablespoon butter
4 ounces chopped fresh or frozen clams, drained
½ cup chopped fresh or frozen spinach, drained
¼ cup nonfat milk
2 egg whites
2 eggs
Yogurt Mornay Sauce (recipe follows)

Mix flour and baking powder together in a medium-size bowl. Using your fingers or a pastry blender, cut in butter until mixture forms coarse crumbs. In a food processor, puree clams and spinach with milk. Add egg whites and process until mixture is foamy. Blend in flour mixture a little at a time, processing after each addition. Add whole eggs and blend well. Chill mixture to firm it.

Flour hands and form 8 oval-shaped dumplings. Drop them into a large kettle of simmering water (do not overcrowd them) and poach 10 to 12 minutes. Remove quenelles with a slotted spoon and drain. Top them with Yogurt Mornay Sauce. *Serves 4.*

YOGURT MORNAY SAUCE
(Contains no butter, cream, or oil)

Per serving:
65 calories
7 grams protein
2 grams fat
4 grams
  carbohydrate

⅔ cup plain nonfat yogurt
½ cup reduced Chicken Stock (page 96)
¼ cup shredded low-fat Swiss cheese
¼ cup freshly grated Romano cheese
⅛ teaspoon paprika

Blend all ingredients in a double boiler over simmering water. Stir until cheese melts, but do not boil. Serve over spinach and clam quenelles. *Serves 4.*

HERB RAVIOLI WITH VEAL

The Pasta:

Per serving:
196 calories
9 grams protein
4 grams fat
36 grams
  carbohydrate

2 scallions, chopped
¼ cup packed fresh basil leaves
2 eggs
1½ cups whole wheat pastry flour

Finely chop scallions and basil in a food processor with 1-second pulses. Add eggs and process until mixture is pureed. Add flour and continue to process until small beads form. Wrap dough in plastic and set it aside for 20 to 30 minutes. Then follow the directions on page 148 for making ravioli. *Makes between ¾ to 1 pound, enough for 4 servings.*

The Veal Filling: (contains no butter, cheese, cream, or oil)

Per serving:
238 calories
29 grams protein
13 grams fat
2 grams
  carbohydrate

1¼ pounds ground veal
2 freshly pressed garlic cloves
½ cup chopped fresh chives
½ cup finely chopped fresh mushrooms
1 teaspoon each minced fresh basil and thyme
½ teaspoon minced fresh oregano
Vegetable salt and freshly ground pepper to taste
Wine Marrow Sauce (page 156), optional
Freshly grated Parmesan or Romano cheese (optional)

Crumble veal into a large nonstick skillet. Brown it over medium-low heat along with garlic. When done, add chopped chives, mushrooms, herbs, and salt and pepper to taste. Continue to sauté several more minutes. Proceed as instructed in the introduction for making ravioli. If desired, top with Wine Marrow Sauce and grated cheese. *Serves 4.*

GNOCCHI
(Potato dumplings)

Here is my grandmother's authentic recipe for gnocchi (or *cavatil*). It is an Old World legacy, very basic, and easy to make.

Per serving (not including sauce):
272 calories
8 grams protein
4 grams fat
53 grams
  carbohydrate

1 pound russet potatoes, whole
1 egg yolk
1 cup whole wheat flour
2 teaspoons butter, melted
Wine Marrow Sauce (recipe follows)
Freshly grated Parmesan cheese (optional)

Steam or boil potatoes until tender. Drain and peel. Mash them fine and let them sit at room temperature for 1 hour to dry out excess moisture. Blend in egg yolk, add flour, and combine, using your fingers or a fork. Add butter and work mixture into a ball of dough. Form into 4 smaller balls. With the palms of your hands roll each ball into long, skinny, finger-thick rolls. Cut each roll into 1-inch lengths. Form a ''shell'' by making a depression with a rolling motion in the center of each piece with your thumb or middle finger.

Boil gnocchi in a large kettle or stockpot of simmering water for 10 minutes, or until they rise to the top. Scoop them out with a slotted spoon and drain. Serve topped with Wine Marrow Sauce and Parmesan cheese, if desired. *Makes about 2 pounds, enough for 6 servings.*

WINE MARROW SAUCE
(Contains no oil or cheese)

Per serving:
113 calories
4 grams protein
1 gram fat
21 grams
  carbohydrate

3 cans (8 ounces each) tomato sauce
1 can (8 ounces) tomato puree
1 pound beef or veal marrow bones
2 freshly pressed garlic cloves
1 teaspoon dried basil
½ teaspoon dried oregano
1 bay leaf
2 parsley sprigs, chopped
1 cup dry red wine
Vegetable salt and freshly ground pepper to taste

Put all ingredients, except wine and seasonings, in a large covered saucepan. Simmer slowly for 45 to 50 minutes, stirring occasionally. Add wine and simmer, partially covered, another 10 to 15 minutes. Remove bay leaf and marrow bones and season with salt and pepper, if desired. Serve over Gnocchi. *Serves 4.*

PIZZA PLUS

There's no excuse for pizza except that this pizza is a great excuse for getting your complex carbohydrates and protein in one fun and fabulous dish. You've got your complex carbohydrates in fresh vegetable toppings and a whole grain pizza crust. And you've got your protein in high-quality meat, shellfish, and cheese toppings. Even the crust is high in protein.

Included in this stylishly healthy collection of pizza recipes are all the nutritional tips you'll need to know to rise above the pitfalls of traditional pizza. These wonderful toppings and seasonings are full of pizzazz, but they're just a start really. Personalize your pizza; there are hundreds of combinations to choose from, depending on what you like. You'll even find a shortcut suggestion with each recipe, calling for a ready-made minicrust instead of the baked Protein-Plus Pizza crust. What's even better is that these pizzas are best done in the microwave oven. Cook them on high, starting with 30 seconds. Work your way up, depending on the number and size of your crusts. So if you're looking for a good excuse to have pizza, look no further. Get away from the unnatural and get into the supernatural ingredients. Try one of these new Pizza Plus creations and take a big, wholesome step beyond pizza!

Here's a helpful hint for healthful pizza making: Cut down a little on your pizza sauce and add freshly chopped tomatoes. If you don't want a tomato-based pizza sauce, make a garden sauce. Stew until soft: chopped eggplant (peeled), zucchini, scallop squash or yellow crookneck squash, along with chopped leek or shallots in just enough Chicken Stock (page 96) to cover. Then puree them in a blender, using the cooking stock to achieve the consistency you desire. Add a dash of sherry for something unique. Substitute this for simple pizza sauce. It's also excellent over pasta instead of the usual marinara sauce.

A minimum of the lowest-fat cheeses are used in these recipes, but if you don't want to use cheese at all, pizza can be marvelous without. The real flavor is in the olive oil and seasonings anyway. Or you can sprinkle on a tiny bit of freshly grated Parmesan or Romano cheese (Romano is stronger) for a cheesy zip. Or make a skinny-cheese topping with a mix of 1 percent low-fat cottage cheese (drained) and Romano cheese creamed together. You may also spread on Neufchâtel, a low-fat type of cream cheese. However, these cheeses don't do well exposed to high and dry temperatures for any length of time, so you should add them, along with the topping, to a prebaked crust and bake them for only a few minutes as suggested in the directions for Protein-Plus Pizza Crust.

Most pizza recipes call for parcooked vegetables to make them more palatable. The vegetables are then cooked again at high heat on top of the pizza. You don't need to do that. To preserve their nutritional goodness as much as possible so that parcooking isn't necessary, you can finely chop or grate raw, chunkier vegetables to make them cook faster on top of the pizza. If you use frozen vegetables, defrost them, then rinse and drain them. Just a few minutes of oven time on top of the pizza will be enough. The same goes for canned vegetables. For larger pieces of fresh vegetables, cut them to size and freeze them. Then defrost them on paper towels to absorb the moisture that drains out of them. Defrost watery vegetables such as eggplant, zucchini, and other summer squash between several layers of paper towels. When they are soft and fully defrosted, press down gently on the paper towel to squeeze out the excess moisture. (Salting the vegetables before cooking helps dry them out too.) This method of freezing and defrosting raw vegetables partly softens them, just as if they were parcooked, yet leaves most of the enzymes, nutrients, and fiber intact. They are then ready for the pizza topping. All you need to do is cook them 5 or 10 minutes at most, on a prebaked pizza crust. Use this freezing procedure for most of the heartier vegetables in the recipes that follow.

Marinate bland meats, previously frozen fish or shellfish, frozen or canned vegetables—condiment-type vegetables are the only thing you should buy in a can or a jar—or even cubes of tofu in a blend of vinegar and wine (or sherry), along with garlic or herbs, before cooking them on top of the pizza. This makes a low-calorie alternative to the usually spicy, fatty meats used in commercial pizzas.

PROTEIN-PLUS PIZZA CRUST

Wheat gluten is substituted for half the normal amount of wheat flour. This nearly triples the protein value of the crust. Gluten makes a lighter, crispier, and more delicate tasting crust, and is readily available in health food stores.

Per slice:
126 calories
9 grams protein
2 grams fat
17 grams
   carbohydrate

1 packet active dry yeast
1 teaspoon raw honey
1½ cups warm water
2 tablespoons extra-virgin olive oil
1½ cups whole wheat flour
1½ cups wheat gluten
½ teaspoon sea salt (optional)

Hot tomato idea:
Bake tomato right into the dough. Substitute tomato juice for water in the crust-making procedure. You can even sprinkle herbs into the dough that complement the topping you are going to use.

In a small bowl, dissolve yeast and honey in water and stir in olive oil. In a large bowl, sift together flour, gluten, and salt, if desired. Then add the liquid mixture to the dry mixture and combine to make a soft dough. Turn it out onto a lightly floured surface and knead for about 5 minutes, until smooth and elastic. Cover the dough and let it rise for about 30 minutes.

Divide the dough into two balls. With a rolling pin, roll each one into a 12-inch circle, making it as thin as possible. Transfer the dough onto two pizza pans rubbed with a paper towel dabbed in olive oil. Press the dough up the sides of the pan to form a slight raised edge. Brush the tops with a little extra olive oil before adding the sauce or topping, if desired. You may also prebake these crusts to avoid over-cooking fresh toppings. Pierce the dough with the tines of a fork and bake them for 12 to 15 minutes in a preheated 425-degree oven. All they need then are a few additional minutes in the oven to melt the cheese and warm the toppings. *Makes two pizza crusts, or 12 slices total; wrap and freeze one crust if you like.*

SIMPLE PIZZA SAUCE

Per cup:
104 calories
4 grams protein
0 grams fat
23 grams
    carbohydrate

You don't want your pizza sauce to overwhelm the flavor of other ingredients and herbs. So, use 1 cup of tomato puree or crushed tomatoes and stir in 2 tablespoons of minced fresh Italian parsley. In addition, you may also add another herb or tablespoon of extra-virgin olive oil if it complements your topping, but that is optional. Spread a cup of this sauce over one pizza crust as a basic undercoating. *Makes 1 cup.*

ARTICHOKE, TOMATO, AND CHEESE PIZZA

Per slice (including crust and sauce):
232 calories
16 grams protein
7 grams fat
26 grams
    carbohydrate

1 freshly pressed garlic clove
1 cup Simple Pizza Sauce (recipe above)
1 Protein-Plus Pizza Crust (page 159)
¼ cup chopped fresh basil (save a few leaves for garnish)
1 cup shredded part-skim mozzarella cheese
2 ripe tomatoes, thinly sliced
4 steamed or frozen defrosted artichoke hearts, quartered
1 tablespoon extra-virgin olive oil
Freshly ground pepper to taste

Complementary toppings:
Freshly grated Parmesan cheese, fresh tuna, anchovies, fresh mushrooms, chives, marjoram, tarragon, parsley.

Stir garlic into sauce. Spread sauce over dough, leaving a ½-inch rim around the edges. Sprinkle with half the chopped basil. Scatter with cheese and bake in a preheated 450-degree oven for 15 minutes. Remove the pizza from the oven and top with tomatoes and artichokes. Sprinkle with remaining chopped basil and bake another 3 minutes. Drizzle with olive oil and season with pepper to taste. Garnish with reserved basil leaves. *Makes 6 slices.*

Shortcut crust:
Whole wheat sourdough English muffins.

MEXICAN PIZZA

Per slice (including crust and sauce):
222 calories
16 grams protein
6 grams fat
26 grams
  carbohydrate

Complementary toppings:
Low-fat Monterey Jack cheese, pinto beans, fresh jalapeño peppers, red onions, fresh salsa, cilantro, chili powder (mild), red pepper flakes (hot).

Shortcut crust:
Corn tortillas.

1 can (10 ounces) enchilada sauce
1 Protein-Plus Pizza Crust (page 159)
1 cup shredded low-fat Cheddar cheese
1 teaspoon ground cumin
1/3 cup chopped scallions
1/2 cup frozen defrosted corn kernels
1 can (4 ounces) diced green chilies (hot chilies optional)
1/4 cup sliced black olives

Spread ¾ cup of the enchilada sauce over the dough, leaving a ½-inch rim around the edges. Sprinkle with cheese, cumin, and scallions. Bake in a preheated 450-degree oven for about 15 minutes. Remove the pizza from the oven and top with corn, green chilies, and olives. Drizzle with remaining enchilada sauce. Continue to bake 2 more minutes. *Makes 6 slices.*

GARLIC SHRIMP PIZZA

Per slice (including crust and sauce):
228 calories
15 grams protein
8 grams fat
24 grams
  carbohydrate

Complementary toppings:
Provolone cheese (instead of sauce), artichoke hearts, celery, black olives, green olives, fresh mushrooms, capers, thyme, tarragon.

Shortcut crust:
Puffed wheat or brown rice cakes.

1 cup Simple Pizza Sauce (recipe opposite)
1 Protein-Plus Pizza Crust (page 159)
1/3 cup freshly grated Parmesan cheese
9 large raw shrimp, peeled, deveined, and halved lengthwise
1 green bell pepper, julienned
4 to 6 freshly pressed garlic cloves
2 tablespoons extra-virgin olive oil
2 tablespoons snipped fresh parsley
Freshly ground pepper to taste

Spread sauce over the dough, leaving a ½-inch rim around the edges. Sprinkle with ¼ cup of the Parmesan cheese and bake in a preheated 450-degree oven for 12 minutes. Meanwhile, toss shrimp and green pepper in garlic and olive oil until well coated. Remove the pizza from the oven and arrange it decoratively with shrimp (3 halves per slice) and pepper strips. Sprinkle with remaining Parmesan cheese, parsley, and pepper to taste. Bake 5 minutes more. *Makes 6 slices.*

MEDITERRANEAN PIZZA

Per slice (including crust and sauce):
249 calories
13 grams protein
10 grams fat
27 grams
   carbohydrate

Complementary toppings:
Sliced hard-boiled eggs, Greek olives (pitted), sage, rosemary.

Shortcut crust:
Whole wheat pita bread.

1 cup Simple Pizza Sauce (page 160)
2 freshly pressed garlic cloves
¾ teaspoon dried oregano
1 Protein-Plus Pizza Crust (page 159)
1 small eggplant, peeled and thinly sliced
12 spinach leaves
2 tablespoons extra-virgin olive oil
3 ounces feta cheese, crumbled
¼ cup dry-packed sun-dried tomatoes (rehydrated in ½ cup hot water for 30
    minutes)
Freshly ground pepper to taste

Mix sauce with garlic and oregano. Spread half the sauce over the dough, leaving a ½-inch rim around the edges. Arrange with eggplant slices and top with remaining sauce. Bake in a preheated 450-degree oven for 12 minutes.

Remove the pizza from the oven and arrange the top decoratively with spinach leaves. Drizzle 1 tablespoon of oil over the top and scatter feta cheese over it. Bake 5 minutes more. Add sun-dried tomatoes, drizzle on the remaining oil, and season with pepper to taste. *Makes 6 slices.*

PIZZA FRESCA

Per slice (including crust and sauce):
229 calories
17 grams protein
7 grams fat
26 grams
   carbohydrate

Complementary toppings:
Just about any kind of vegetable, smoked turkey breast (see The Club Omelet, page 126), fresh garlic, basil, dill, celery seed, chervil, parsley.

1 cup Simple Pizza Sauce (page 160)
1 Protein-Plus Pizza Crust (page 159)
¾ teaspoon each dried marjoram and savory
1 cup shredded low-fat Monterey Jack cheese
½ cup thinly sliced leek
1 zucchini, thinly sliced
1 yellow crookneck squash, thinly sliced
1 small carrot, thinly sliced
½ pound Italian plum tomatoes, thinly sliced
1 tablespoon extra-virgin olive oil
Freshly ground pepper to taste

Spread sauce over dough, leaving a ½-inch rim around the edges. Sprinkle with half the marjoram, savory, and cheese. Top with leek slices. Bake in a preheated 450-degree oven for 12 minutes.

Shortcut crust:
Whole wheat
tortilla.

Remove the pizza from the oven and arrange with zucchini, squash, carrot, and tomatoes, and sprinkle on remaining herbs. Bake 5 minutes more. Drizzle olive oil over pizza and season with pepper to taste. *Makes 6 slices.*

FENNEL, PEPPER, AND PROSCIUTTO PIZZA

Per slice (including crust and sauce):
270 calories
14 grams protein
12 grams fat
26 grams
  carbohydrate

Complementary toppings:
Low-fat Gruyère cheese (instead of sauce), freshly grated Parmesan cheese, leek, smoked salmon, basil, rosemary.

Shortcut crust:
Thickly sliced whole wheat bread.

1 cup Simple Pizza Sauce (page 160)
1 Protein-Plus Pizza Crust (page 159)
½ small fennel bulb, thinly sliced
2 shallots, thinly sliced
2 tablespoons extra-virgin olive oil
½ teaspoon dried thyme
Vegetable salt and freshly ground pepper to taste
1 cup roasted red pepper strips (see Chicken Rouille, page 85, for roasting
    directions; or substitute prepacked roasted red peppers, rinsed and drained)
1 tablespoon Marsala wine
6 ounces sliced prosciutto

Spread sauce over dough, leaving a ½-inch rim around the edges. Arrange with slices of fennel and shallots. Drizzle 1 tablespoon oil over the top and sprinkle on thyme and salt and pepper to taste. Bake in a preheated 450-degree oven for 15 minutes.

Meanwhile, toss red pepper strips in remaining oil blended with Marsala wine, and season with more salt and pepper if desired. Remove the pizza from the oven, arrange with red pepper strips and bake 2 minutes more. Then top with prosciutto slices (1 ounce per slice) and serve. *Makes 6 slices.*

— 10 —
VEGETABLES

VITAL VEGETABLES

Calorie Cuts
Make low-cal spaghetti with spaghetti squash. Boil whole uncut squash in a large pot with enough water to cover for about 30 minutes. Cut the squash in half and scoop out the seeds. Using a fork, scrape out the spaghetti like pulp and drain in a colander. Serve topped with Wine Marrow Sauce (page 156) or "natural-style" marinara sauce and freshly grated Parmesan cheese. It will make about 4 servings.

Cooking vegetables right is an art, but overcooking them is a crime. It is a fact that heat destroys delicate living enzymes, nutrients, and fiber, so preserving these elements rather than pleasing the palate should be your primary goal. Most vegetables don't hold up well under high and lengthy heat, and all vegetables lose nutrients. The more heat, the more destruction, so you must cook them with care. Be aware that the over-cooking point sneaks up very rapidly. It's always best to undercook vegetables a bit and let them stand with the heat off, as they will continue to cook for a few minutes due to their residual heat retention. You can always cook them a little more if you need to, but there's no turning back once they are ruined. Greens should be just wilted when cooked, and for most purposes, vegetables should be tender-crisp. You may need to practice your cooking techniques, but practice makes a perfect vegetable.

Vegetables do well with most moist and dry methods of cooking, as long as the cooking time is kept in check. But never boil a vegetable unless you plan to consume the cooking liquid (as in a soup) or it is an unpeeled potato or root. Direct contact with the water will leach out vitamins and minerals. And be careful with pressure cooking. It saves time, but you'll have puree faster than you can flex your bicep. When-ever possible, cook plain vegetables whole or cut in half and unpeeled, as the skin is a protector of the nutrients and fiber inside. Cut or peel them after they have been cooked and allowed to stand.

These calorie-controlled recipes were designed for maximum nutri-tion with a minimum of preparation time. There is an emphasis on potatoes, since potatoes (particularly sweet potatoes and yams) are a wonderful source of vitamin A, fiber, and natural, unrefined complex carbohydrates for the bodybuilder. Although rarely eaten uncooked, they are extremely healthful when they are partially cooked to a tender-crunchy consistency or grated raw into a salad.

The cooking times for the following recipes are approximate, depending on the size of your vegetables and whether you are using gas or electric heat. Microwave ovens vary, too. To test their doneness, pierce the vegetables or potatoes with a fork two thirds of the way through cooking. That way you can be certain that you are preserving as much of their vitality and nutrients as possible for your good health.

Fast Tracks

● Make bistro onion soup by boiling slices of sweet Bermuda onions in Chicken Stock (page 96) with a dash of Worcestershire sauce until onion is soft. Serve with torn chunks of whole grain bread or even some low-fat Gruyère or Swiss cheese melted over the top.

● Microwave or steam vegetables with cloves of garlic and sprigs of fresh herbs for flavor without fuss.

● Create a miniature still life using tiny gourmet vegetables. It's elegant and easy because you don't have to cut up raw vegetables. Microwave until tender-crisp: whole baby carrots, baby artichokes, baby zucchini or scallop squash, tiny French beans or snow peas, tiny new potatoes —or anything tiny you can get your hands on. Serve them chilled and decoratively arranged with one of the six Skinny Dips (pages 188–190). Very impressive.

● Grill corn in their husks right on your barbecue. Cook them 15 to 20 minutes over hot coals, turning them every 4 to 5 minutes. A super-fast stove-top way to cook corn is to drop trimmed, unhusked ears into a pot of boiling water for only a minute or two. Drain and let them cool before husking. They will be healthfully crisp, with all their nutrients intact.

CRUNCHY VEGETABLE-NUT STIR-FRY

Per serving:
200 calories
2 grams protein
6 grams fat
33 grams
  carbohydrate

1 teaspoon peanut oil
1 freshly pressed garlic clove
¼ pound broccoli florets
¼ pound cauliflower florets
1 carrot, sliced ¼ inch thick
1 celery rib, sliced diagonally
¼ teaspoon minced fresh ginger
¼ cup Chicken Stock (page 96)
1 can (4½ ounces) water chestnuts, sliced
1 tablespoon chopped walnuts
1 tablespoon sherry
1 tablespoon low-sodium tamari

Heat oil over medium-low heat in a covered nonstick skillet or wok. Add garlic, broccoli, cauliflower, carrot, celery, and ginger. Cook slowly, stirring often. Use stock as needed for liquid, and cover if necessary. When vegetables are cooked but slightly crunchy, add water chestnuts and walnuts and toss until they are heated through. Combine sherry and tamari and add to stir-fry, cooking a few moments until most of the liquid has evaporated. *Serves 2.*

SESAME GREEN BEANS

Per serving:
57 calories
2 grams protein
4 grams fat
4 grams
  carbohydrate

1 pound fresh young green beans, ends trimmed
1½ teaspoons sesame oil
1 teaspoon freshly squeezed lemon juice
½ teaspoon grated lemon peel
1 tablespoon sesame seeds
1 tablespoon low-sodium tamari (optional)

Steam green beans for 15 to 20 minutes (checking them once after 15 minutes), until they are tender-crisp. Place them in a vegetable serving dish and stir in sesame oil, lemon juice and rind, and half the sesame seeds. Sprinkle the top with remaining sesame seeds and tamari, if desired. *Serves 4.*

ORANGE-BRAISED CHARD

Per serving:
125 calories
4 grams protein
8 grams fat
10 grams
 carbohydrate

1 orange
1 tablespoon extra-virgin olive oil
4 bay leaves
1 yellow onion, sliced
2 bunches red or green chard leaves, rinsed and cut crosswise into
 1-inch-wide strips
¼ cup pine nuts (pignoli)

Grate 1 tablespoon of colored peel from the orange and reserve. Cut the orange in half, squeeze one half, and reserve the juice. Peel the remaining half, slice crosswise, and cut the slices into small sections. Set them aside.

Heat oil in a large covered nonstick skillet. Add bay leaves and cook them over medium heat for about 30 seconds, until they begin to turn brown. Add reserved orange peel along with onion and continue to cook over medium heat for about 10 minutes, using the reserved orange juice now and then for braising until it is gone.

When done, remove bay leaves and add chard. Cover, lower heat, and simmer about 2 minutes, or until chard is just wilted. Uncover and stir in reserved orange sections along with pine nuts. Continue to cook, uncovered, 1 more minute, stirring several times until everything is well mixed. For a fuller flavor and more nutrients, retain pan liquid and serve with chard. *Serves 4.*

QUICK CREAMED CORN

Per serving:
131 calories
5 grams protein
2 grams fat
25 grams
 carbohydrate

8 ears fresh corn
4 tablespoons freshly grated Parmesan cheese
2 tablespoons finely minced white onion
Evaporated nonfat milk (optional)

With a sharp knife, slice off the kernels of corn from each cob into a 1-quart covered microwave-safe dish. With the dull side of the knife, scrape the excess milky liquid from each cob into the dish of corn. Stir in Parmesan cheese and onion. Cover and microwave on medium-high for 8 to 10 minutes, stirring once during cooking. Add a little evaporated milk if a creamier consistency is desired. *Serves 6.*

EGGPLANT-TOFU MANICOTTI

Eggplant replaces the traditional flour crepes in this version of an old favorite.

Per serving:
164 calories
11 grams protein
5 grams fat
20 grams
  carbohydrate

1 large eggplant, sliced ¼-inch-thick lengthwise
1 bunch (about ½ pound) chopped fresh spinach leaves
8 ounces soft tofu, drained and mashed
½ cup finely chopped white onion
2 freshly pressed garlic cloves
Vegetable salt and freshly ground pepper to taste
½ recipe Wine Marrow Sauce (page 156), or substitute equal amount of
    "natural-style" marinara sauce
½ cup shredded part-skim mozzarella cheese

To soften the eggplant, place 8 of the largest slices in a single layer on a large baking sheet and freeze. Then defrost them between several layers of paper towels, pressing them with the flat of your hand to squeeze out excess water.

Next place spinach in a colander and pour boiling water over it to wilt it. Let it drain. Mix spinach well with tofu, onion, garlic, and salt and pepper, if desired. Spoon equal amounts of the tofu-spinach filling onto each slice of eggplant. Fold ends over filling to overlap. Spread ½ cup of the sauce in the bottom of a 9 x 12-inch baking dish or pan and place the eggplant, overlapping side down, in the dish. Spoon the remaining sauce over the tops.

Cover loosely with foil and bake in a 375-degree oven for about 15 minutes. Remove foil, sprinkle the top with mozzarella, and bake, uncovered, for another 5 minutes. Remove eggplant carefully with a spatula to serve. *Serves 4 (2 crepes per serving).*

MIXED VEGETABLE-HERB SALAD

Nearly all frozen vegetables are parcooked for packaging. And the freezing process softens them further, so there's no need to cook them again. Here's something healthy you can do with frozen vegetables right from the package.

Per serving:
102 calories
4 grams protein
3 grams fat
16 grams
  carbohydrate

Cheesy option:
Mix freshly grated Parmesan or Romano cheese into the salad.

1 package (10 ounces) mixed frozen vegetables, defrosted, rinsed, and drained
⅓ cup plain nonfat yogurt
1 tablespoon reduced-calorie safflower oil mayonnaise
1 tablespoon minced fresh scallions
1 tablespoon minced fresh parsley
1 teaspoon minced fresh dill
Vegetable salt and freshly ground pepper to taste

Mix all ingredients together in a large covered container. Cover and chill at least several hours before serving. *Serves 2.*

HEALTHY POTATO AND CARROT FRIES

It's amazing how little oil these need to taste good!

Per serving:
228 calories
5 grams protein
7 grams fat
37 grams
  carbohydrate

Tangy option:
Serve fries sprinkled with a little malt vinegar.

2 russet potatoes
2 carrots
1 tablespoon extra-virgin olive oil
½ teaspoon dried basil
Vegetable salt and freshly ground pepper to taste

Rinse and cut unpeeled potatoes and carrots into sticks about ¼ inch wide and 4 inches long, and place them in a large bowl. Add olive oil and toss sticks until well coated. Arrange them, spread slightly apart, on a large baking sheet or piece of aluminum foil. Sprinkle them with basil and salt and pepper to taste. Bake them in a preheated 400-degree oven for 40 to 45 minutes, until crisp and golden. *Serves 2.*

Per serving:
212 calories
5 grams protein
6 grams fat
36 grams
  carbohydrate

Meal plan:
If you like meat and potatoes, why not have it Italian-style? This potato salad is wonderful mixed with slices of char-broiled steak (go for rare). Or, you can toss in chunks of chicken breast, or make a sea salad with fresh or canned tuna or salmon. Or mix it with other cooked vegetables such as asparagus, broccoli, zucchini, bell peppers, or wilted fresh spinach leaves.

ITALIAN POTATO SALAD

6 new white or red potatoes, rinsed and quartered
1½ tablespoons extra-virgin olive oil
1 tablespoon freshly squeezed lemon juice
2 shallots, finely minced
1 tablespoon chopped fresh Italian parsley
1 teaspoon minced fresh oregano
Vegetable salt and freshly ground pepper to taste

Arrange potato quarters evenly, skin side down, in a large covered microwave-safe dish. Add ¼ cup of water, cover, and microwave on high for 15 to 18 minutes, until potatoes are tender but slightly crunchy. Let them stand, covered, several minutes before preparation.

Drain the cooking water, add remaining ingredients, and toss well. Serve salad at room temperature. *Serves 4.*

Here are four simple, healthy, and delicious super spud recipes that call for no butter, oil, or dressing:

DUCHESS POTATOES

Per serving:
98 calories
2 grams protein
0 grams fat
23 grams
  carbohydrate

2 large Idaho potatoes (or substitute russet potatoes)
1 ripe banana
Freshly ground nutmeg to taste

Rinse whole potatoes and bake them in a 350-degree oven for about 45 minutes. Remove the potatoes from the oven, turn off the heat, and keep the oven door shut.

Cut the potatoes in half lengthwise and carefully scoop out the flesh from each half. In a medium-size bowl, mash potatoes well with banana and nutmeg to taste. Spoon equal portions of the potato mixture back into each potato skin and sprinkle on more nutmeg, if desired.

To reheat, place potatoes skin side down in the oven for several minutes and let the residual heat warm them. *Serves 4.*

SWEETHEART POTATOES

Per serving:
95 calories
1 gram protein
0 grams fat
22 grams
  carbohydrate

Pipe this:
Use a pastry tube to make "blossoms" around these or Duchess Potatoes (page 171). They're elegant and kids will love them too.

2 round, well-formed sweet potatoes
1 soft ripe pear, cored and peeled
2 tablespoons freshly squeezed orange juice

Rinse whole potatoes and bake them in a 350-degree oven for about 40 minutes. Remove the potatoes from the oven, turn the heat off, and keep the oven door shut.

Cut the potatoes in half lengthwise and carefully scoop out the flesh from each half. In a medium-size bowl, mash potatoes well with pear and orange juice. Spoon equal portions of the potato mixture back into each potato skin.

To reheat, place potatoes skin side down in the oven for several minutes and let the residual heat warm them. *Serves 4.*

BAKED YAMS WITH APPLES

Per serving:
99 calories
1 gram protein
0 grams fat
23 grams
  carbohydrate

Sweet tip:
When a yam is sweet, it's like candy. To pick one out, break a tiny piece off the tip when it is raw. The brighter orange it is inside (as opposed to pale yellow), the sweeter the yam.

2 medium-size fat, well-formed yams
½ teaspoon ground allspice
1 large apple, cored, peeled, and thinly sliced
Pure maple syrup to taste (optional)

Rinse whole potatoes and cut them in half lengthwise. Place each half on a large piece of aluminum foil. Sprinkle the top of each yam half with a pinch of allspice. Place one quarter of the apple slices across the top of each one and sprinkle with remaining allspice. Wrap them tightly in the foil so that apples are secure on top. Bake them in a 350-degree oven for about 30 minutes, or until centers are soft when pierced with a knife. Unwrap to serve. While they are still hot, drizzle on maple syrup (or raw honey), if desired. *Serves 4.*

PARSLEYED POTATOES AND ONIONS

Per serving:
127 calories
4 grams protein
0 grams fat
28 grams
   carbohydrate

2 large oval new red or white potatoes, whole
1 small red onion, thinly sliced and cut in half crosswise
2 tablespoons dried parsley, finely crumbled
Vegetable salt and freshly ground pepper to taste
¼ cup reduced Chicken Stock (page 96), or substitute nonfat milk

Rinse potatoes and place each one on a large piece of aluminum foil. Cut crosswise into ½-inch-thick slices, about three quarters of the way down, without cutting through the bottom of the potato. Sprinkle onion slices with half the dried parsley and salt and pepper to taste. Insert a half slice of onion into each slit of each potato. Drizzle 2 tablespoons of stock over each potato and top with remaining parsley and salt and pepper, if desired. Wrap each potato tightly in the foil and bake in a preheated 350-degree oven for about 40 minutes. *Serves 2.*

GREAT MASHED POTATOES

Per serving:
157 calories
4 grams protein
4 grams fat
27 grams
   carbohydrate

Low-calorie note:
If you want to cut way down on calories, replace the milk with warm potato cooking liquid or Chicken Stock (page 96), and omit the butter called for. Instead stir in a tablespoon or two of freshly grated Parmesan cheese for a real zippy flavor.

To make great rich-tasting mashed potatoes without a lot of fattening ingredients, use red or white new potatoes (if you want a slightly sweet and creamy consistency), or russet potatoes (if you want a coarser, grainier texture). Boil them whole to retain their nutrients. The smaller the potatoes you use, the better and faster they will cook. The next recipe adds only 44 calories to a plain serving of potatoes.

2 pounds potatoes, unpeeled
1 tablespoon butter, softened
⅔ cup evaporated nonfat milk, warmed
Vegetable salt and freshly ground pepper to taste

Boil potatoes, partially covered, in enough water to cover them, until they are fork-tender, about 20 to 30 minutes. Drain them. When they are cool enough to handle, peel and mash them by hand, or with an electric mixer, along with the remaining ingredients. Do not use a blender or food processor or it will dry them out too much. *Serves 6.*

POTATO POWER BOATS

Mashed potato relay: Got any leftover potatoes? Make potato puffs. Fold 2 egg whites, stiffly beaten, into 1 cup of very moist mashed potatoes. Add shredded cheese if you like, or your favorite herbs and seasonings. Spoon small mounds of the potato mixture onto a nonstick baking sheet and bake in a 350-degree oven for 15 to 20 minutes.

The potato is pure power food. Wrapped in that mineral-rich potato skin is one of nature's greatest sources of complex carbohydrates for raw energy. And because it's right from the earth, natural and unprocessed, the potato rates higher nutritionally than bread, pasta, and most grains, which all require more than one step of milling, processing, and cooking. When cooked right (either baked, steamed, or microwaved) the potato's nutrient and high fiber content remain highly intact. One medium-size potato (about 5 x 2½ inches) supplies 150 calories, 4 grams of protein, 33 grams of complex carbohydrate, nearly 1 gram of dietary fiber, and no fat. The potato is also high in potassium, a key bodybuilding nutrient. You've got to admit, one potato packs a wallop!

These recipes are designed for minimum preparation, so you don't have to be an ace in the kitchen to rev 'em up. Brown-skinned baking potatoes make the best Potato Power Boats. Wash the potato first under tap water by rubbing the skin lightly with a clean dishcloth or your hand. Scrubbing it with a brush removes too many minerals. For best results, these potatoes should be baked, not microwaved or steamed, in a 350-degree oven for about 45 minutes, or until you can just pierce the center firmly with a fork . Do not overbake. When the potato is done, remove it from the oven and let it stand for 5 minutes. Then slit the top lengthwise, leaving about ½ inch uncut on each end. Gently squeeze the potato open from end to end with your palms, being careful not to rip the skin. Scoop out the potato flesh, leaving about ⅛ inch of the potato intact with the skin. Place the scooped-out potato in a small bowl and reserve it for your recipe. Follow this procedure for each potato boat.

Be sure to eat the skin of your potato boat. It really is the best part. If you like your potato skin a little moister, you can wrap it in aluminum foil before baking it. Or you can rub the skin with a little safflower oil first to keep it from getting too dry and flaky while baking.

To reheat a Potato Power Boat, you may put it back in the oven for 5 minutes with the heat on. Or you can microwave it. Simply zap it for 30 seconds first, then at 15-second intervals if it's not hot enough. Remember, the potato is already cooked—you don't want to overdo it. Otherwise, follow any reheating instructions in the individual recipes.

Potato Power Boats are ideal for individual meals, and are as handy as a sandwich for transport. Make several at a time, wrap each one, and take one to work, to school, the gym, or on a picnic. If you plan to microwave it, pack it in microwave-safe plastic. They also make an excellent side dish for a buffet or dinner party.

SHRIMP BOAT

Per serving:
295 calories
22 grams protein
6 grams fat
40 grams
   carbohydrate

¼ cup plain nonfat yogurt
2 teaspoons reduced-calorie safflower oil mayonnaise
2 ounces cooked fresh or frozen defrosted tiny shrimp
1 tablespoon chopped pimientoes
1 teaspoon chopped fresh parsley
⅛ teaspoon celery seed
Vegetable salt and freshly ground pepper to taste
1 baked potato

Blend yogurt and mayonnaise together in a small bowl. Add shrimp, pimientoes, parsley, celery seed, and salt and pepper, if desired, and mix everything together well. Break reserved potato up into small chunks with a fork. Add to shrimp mixture and toss well to coat. Spoon filling into potato boat, chill if desired, and serve. *Serves 1.*

EGG SALAD BOAT

Per serving:
400 calories
24 grams protein
16 grams fat
38 grams
   carbohydrate

High-pro note:
Omit the egg yolks
and add 1 more
chopped egg white.

¼ cup 1 percent low-fat cottage cheese
2 teaspoons reduced-calorie safflower oil mayonnaise
1 teaspoon prepared yellow mustard
1 baked potato
2 hard-boiled eggs, coarsely chopped
1½ tablespoons finely chopped fresh chives
Vegetable salt and paprika to taste

In a small bowl, cream together cottage cheese, mayonnaise, and mustard. Finely mash in half of the reserved potato. Break remaining potato into small chunks and add, along with chopped eggs and chives, to cottage cheese mixture. Lightly toss everything together. Season with salt, if desired, and paprika to taste. Spoon filling back into potato boat, chill if desired, and serve. *Serves 1.*

BROCCOLI BOAT

Per serving:
326 calories
8 grams protein
16 grams fat
37 grams
  carbohydrate

1 baked potato
½ cup steamed broccoli florets (or substitute frozen defrosted broccoli, drained)
1 tablespoon extra-virgin olive oil
1 small freshly pressed garlic clove
1 teaspoon finely chopped fresh basil
1 tablespoon freshly grated Romano cheese
Vegetable salt and freshly ground pepper to taste

In a small bowl, break reserved potato into small chunks. Add broccoli, olive oil, garlic, basil, Romano cheese, and salt and pepper, if desired. Toss everything together lightly. Spoon filling into potato boat and heat if desired. *Serves 1.*

Vegetable tidbit: You can substitute your favorite fresh or frozen vegetables for broccoli. If you do use frozen vegetables, it's healthier not to precook them, as most vegetables are already parcooked and the freezing process softens them further.

TUNA BOAT

Per serving:
359 calories
34 grams protein
7 grams fat
39 grams
  carbohydrate

1 baked potato
2 ounces water-packed albacore, rinsed and drained
¼ cup plain nonfat yogurt
1 ounce low-fat Swiss cheese, shredded
1 tablespoon finely minced white onion
1 teaspoon chopped fresh dill
Vegetable salt and freshly ground pepper to taste

Coarsely mash reserved potato in a small bowl. Crumble in albacore. Add yogurt, half the shredded cheese, the onion, dill, and salt and pepper, if desired, and mix everything together well. Spoon filling into potato boat and sprinkle the top with the remaining shredded cheese. Place the potato on a piece of aluminum foil or in a small ovenproof dish and bake in a 350-degree oven for 8 to 10 minutes, until cheese has melted. Serve immediately. *Serves 1.*

MEAL-IN-A-BOAT

Per serving:
289 calories
16 grams protein
8 grams fat
38 grams
  carbohydrate

1 ounce soft tofu
2 teaspoons reduced-calorie safflower oil mayonnaise
¼ teaspoon prepared horseradish
2 teaspoons low-sodium tamari
1 small freshly pressed garlic clove
1 baked potato
¼ cup frozen defrosted chopped spinach, drained
1½ ounces diced smoked turkey (see The Club Omelet, page 126)
Freshly ground pepper to taste

In a small bowl, blend tofu, mayonnaise, horseradish, tamari, and garlic together. Add the reserved potato to the tofu mixture and mash it in coarsely with a fork. Add spinach and smoked turkey and toss everything together until well mixed. Season with pepper to taste. Spoon filling into potato boat, heat if desired, and serve. *Serves 1.*

PARTY BOAT
(Make a fleet of them!)

Per serving:
252 calories
17 grams protein
12 grams fat
20 grams
  carbohydrate

1 baked potato
2 ounces sharp or smoked low-fat Cheddar cheese, shredded
4 tablespoons plain nonfat yogurt
2 tablespoons chopped fresh chives
2 tablespoons "natural-style" soy bacon bits

Mash reserved potato with shredded cheese in a small bowl. Halve potato boat lengthwise and fill each half with the potato-cheese mixture. Place them on a piece of aluminum foil or in an ovenproof dish and bake in a 350-degree oven for 7 to 8 minutes. Top each half with 2 tablespoons of yogurt, 1 tablespoon of chives, and 1 tablespoon of bacon bits. Serve immediately. *Makes 2 party servings.*

BEAN PROTEIN

Beans and peas are a superbly satisfying, delicious, and economical source of food. When eaten with rice, corn, or other grains, the combination becomes a complete protein. Besides being extremely high in protein, beans are also a valuable source of fiber, iron, thiamin, riboflavin, and niacin. A 4-ounce serving has approximately 8 grams of protein

Fast Tracks
Make a quick and healthy express pea soup. Simply whir in a blender until smooth: one 10-ounce package frozen defrosted peas (rinsed and drained), 1 cup hot Chicken Stock (page 96), and your favorite low-sodium seasoning to taste. When done, stir in 1 more cup of hot stock and serve immediately. Makes 4 servings at 50 calories, with 4 grams protein, 1 gram fat, and 8 grams carbohydrate per serving.

and only about 130 calories, much less than most meats and poultry, with absolutely no fat.

To prepare dried beans for cooking (or sprouting), always pick out any misshapen or discolored ones, then rinse them to get the grit out. When you put them in water, remove any that float. Most dried beans need to be rehydrated with water before cooking. Cover them with water and store them in a cool place for 6 to 8 hours, or overnight. If it is warm, refrigerate them so they won't spoil. If they sprout, consider yourself talented. They come alive with nourishing vitamins and nutrients and are wonderful this way in salads. They also require less cooking, which helps preserve the fiber and nutrients. Before boiling, add enough water to cover them if the beans have soaked up most of it. When cooking, stir them carefully and as little as possible to keep the skins from breaking.

Here's a final refrain. If your musical talent is "for beans," you can throw away the soaking water and boil them in fresh water with a sprinkle of baking soda for 30 minutes. Drain them once more, replace with fresh water, and continue cooking them until they are done. A few more of the nutrients will be lost, but that's the price you'll have to pay for keeping your reputation. So if beans strike a high note with you, try some of these tasty lean bean dishes and discover yet another way to get more protein for your money and your calories.

SMOKED SPLIT PEA SOUP

Here is a delightful way to obtain the smoky flavor of ham bone in pea soup sans the ham—and the salt and the chemicals.

Per serving:
109 calories
7 grams protein
0 grams fat
19 grams
  carbohydrate

4 cups water
1 cup dried split peas
1 garlic clove, minced
1 white onion, sliced
2 carrots, diced
¼ teaspoon liquid smoke
Vegetable salt and freshly ground pepper to taste

Rinse and drain split peas. In a large covered kettle or stockpot, bring water, peas, garlic, onion, and carrots to a boil for 5 minutes. Lower heat and simmer, partially covered, for 40 to 45 minutes, until soup thickens. Add liquid smoke and salt and pepper to taste. *Serves 6.*

LANAI BAKED BEANS

Per serving:
169 calories
10 grams protein
1 gram fat
59 grams
  carbohydrate

Fast Tracks
A dash of vegetable oil added to boiling beans, pastas, or soups will keep them from frothing over.

2 cups dried navy beans
1 teaspoon minced fresh ginger
1 freshly minced garlic clove
1 can (20 ounces) crushed unsweetened pineapple (or substitute 2 cups
    coarsely pureed fresh pineapple)
1 tablespoon raw honey
2 teaspoons white wine vinegar
2 tablespoons low-sodium tamari
1 cup unsweetened pineapple juice
Freshly ground pepper to taste

Rinse and drain beans. Soak them overnight in enough water to cover. To cook, put them, along with soaking water and the ginger and garlic, into a medium-size covered kettle or stockpot. Bring to a boil, lower heat, and simmer, covered, for ½ hour, adding more water if necessary.

Drain beans, then combine with remaining ingredients. Turn into a 4-quart casserole dish and bake, covered, in a 350-degree oven for 2 hours. Uncover during the last 10 minutes of baking. *Serves 8.*

BARBECUED BEANS

Per serving:
208 calories
10 grams protein
1 gram fat
42 grams
  carbohydrate

1½ cups dried kidney beans
2 freshly minced garlic cloves
½ teaspoon celery seeds
4 black peppercorns
1 can (8 ounces) tomato sauce
½ cup blackstrap molasses
2 tablespoons red wine vinegar
1 teaspoon Worcestershire sauce
¾ teaspoon dry mustard
1 yellow onion, chopped
¼ teaspoon liquid smoke

Rinse and drain beans. Soak overnight in enough water to cover. To cook, put beans, along with soaking water and garlic, celery seeds, and peppercorns, into a large covered kettle or stockpot. Bring to a boil. Lower heat and simmer, covered, for 1 hour. Add remaining ingredients (and a little more water, if necessary) and continue to simmer, covered, for another 35 to 45 minutes. *Serves 6.*

HONEY-BAKED BEANS

Per serving:
180 calories
10 grams protein
1 gram fat
34 grams
  carbohydrate

2 cups dried white beans
½ teaspoon ground cardamom
2 ground cloves
⅔ cup plain nonfat yogurt
1 large white onion, finely chopped
3 tablespoons raw honey
1 cup Chicken Stock (page 96), or substitute water
Vegetable salt and freshly ground pepper to taste

Rinse and drain beans. Soak them for 2 hours in enough water to cover. Put beans and soaking water, along with the cardamom and cloves, into a medium-size covered kettle or stockpot. Bring to a boil, lower heat, and simmer, covered, for 45 to 50 minutes. Add a little water if beans become too dry.

Drain and pour beans into a 4-quart ovenproof covered casserole dish. Stir in remaining ingredients and bake, covered, in a 350-degree oven for 2 hours. *Serves 8.*

MEAN BEAN AND CHEESE BURRITO

Per serving:
184 calories
12 grams protein
2 grams fat
30 grams
  carbohydrate

Note:
Though burritos are traditionally made with flour tortillas, you can make this dish a more complete protein by substituting corn tortillas for the whole wheat tortillas.

1 cup dried pinto beans
1 small white onion, chopped
2 freshly chopped garlic cloves
Vegetable salt to taste
1 tablespoon chili powder (adjust amount to taste)
8 whole wheat tortillas
1 cup Chicken Stock (page 96), warmed
1 cup shredded low-fat Monterey Jack cheese
½ cup chopped scallions
1 ripe tomato, seeded and chopped (optional)

Rinse and drain beans. In a large covered saucepan, soak beans in enough water to cover overnight. When done, bring them to a boil in soaking water, along with the onion, garlic, and salt to taste, adding more water to cover them if necessary. Then lower the heat and simmer them, covered, for about 1½ hours, until tender.

Drain the beans, onion, and garlic and process them, along with the chili powder, in a food processor until smooth. Dip tortillas in warm chicken stock and spoon an equal amount of the pureed beans onto each tortilla. Sprinkle with 1 tablespoon of the shredded cheese and a few chopped scallions, leaving some of both for garnish. Overlap the sides of the burrito and secure the overlapping center with a dab of bean dip. Arrange each burrito carefully, seam side down, in a 10-inch round or square covered microwave-safe baking dish. Sprinkle the tops with the remaining cheese and scallions.

For a soft tortilla, cover and microwave on medium-high for 8 to 10 minutes, until hot. For a crispier tortilla, bake uncovered in a pre-heated 350-degree oven for 12 to 15 minutes, just until heated through. To serve, remove the burritos with a spatula and top with chopped tomatoes, if desired. *Makes 8 burritos or servings.*

ALL-PURPOSE BEAN DIP

This bean puree is a Mediterranean staple. Healthy and high in protein, it will provide you with complete protein when you put a dollop on cooked vegetables or brown rice. Use it as a condiment to serve along-side lean meat or chicken, or stir it into brothy soups and stocks. It's wonderful as a dip for assorted Super Veggies and spread on chunks of whole grain bread or crackers, and of course all by itself.

Per serving:
106 calories
4 grams protein
4 grams fat
13 grams
  carbohydrate

1 cup dried chick-peas (garbanzo beans)
3 tablespoons extra-virgin olive oil
3 garlic cloves
2 tablespoons freshly squeezed lemon juice
⅓ cup chopped fresh parsley
Vegetable salt to taste
Dash of hot red pepper sauce

Wash and drain beans. In a large covered saucepan, soak beans in enough water to cover overnight. To cook, bring them to a boil in soaking water for 5 minutes, adding more water to cover them if necessary. Then lower heat and simmer, covered, for 1½ to 2 hours until tender. Drain and transfer beans to a food processor along with remaining ingredients. Process until smooth. Store in a covered container and keep refrigerated, but serve at room temperature. *Makes about 3½ cups, or 12 dip-size servings.*

Photo: Bob Gardner

— 11 —
SALADS

VEGETABLE SUPERSALADS

Fast Tracks
If you have a lot of leftover fresh parsley (or any other herb) you're not going to use, rinse it and spread it out on paper towels in a warm dry place for a couple of days. When it is dry and crispy, discard the stems, crumble the leaves, and store them in an airtight jar for future use.

Salads are a great way to capitalize on nature's nutritional gifts. Not with just lettuce salads, but salads made from all kinds of fresh vegetables we normally eat cooked—or don't eat at all! To take advantage of their fresh-from-the-garden goodness is more than enjoying a casual dose of vitamins and minerals. It's lifesaving.

All fresh vegetables have a high biological value and contain many elements essential to good health. But certain vegetables contain anti-cancer producing properties as well. These include cruciferous vegetables such as cabbage, brussels sprouts, broccoli, cauliflower, rutabaga, and turnips. The dark green vegetables of the cruciferous family, along with other green and yellow vegetables—collards, kale, spinach, squash, sweet potatoes, yams, and carrots—all contain high amounts of beta-carotene, a building block of vitamin A that is believed to work in preventing cellular damage (cancer) by protecting cells against breakdown due to dangerous free radical movement. Two other key elements contained in cruciferous vegetables are vitamin C, an antioxidant that strengthens the immune system, and another protective element against cancer in the form of indoles, which fight toxins in the body. Not to be forgotten is the role fresh vegetables play in providing various types of cholesterol-fighting fiber, complex carbohydrates, and last but not least, the vital living enzymes that play host to a spectrum of other essential vitamins and minerals.

The following recipes offer a healthy array of cool, colorful, raw vegetables and salads with delicious low-calorie dressings. But don't limit yourself to only the vegetables called for in the recipes. Salads aren't just a matter of recipes—they are a matter of choices, important

Fast Tracks
The best way to get
the grit and sand out
of lettuce leaves and
greens is to immerse
them in a sinkful of
water with a splash
of vinegar, swish
them around a bit,
and drain them in a
colander.

ones. All raw vegetables have a specific value. Incorporate them into your diet and consume a variety of them every day for a long life of good health.

A word about salad dressings: Oil-free dressings are the rage, but most contain sugar, salt, imitation flavorings, inferior oils, gums, stabilizers, and chemicals. All that and most are lousy tasting, too! Make your own oil-free Italian dressing using a base of ⅔ cup vinegar (either wine, cider, or rice), ⅓ cup water, and 1 tablespoon arrowroot. In a small saucepan, heat the vinegar just to boiling. Moisten the arrowroot in the water and add to the hot vinegar. Stir for about 15 seconds until it thickens like salad dressing. To this you can add, while it is still hot, dried herbs, spices, freshly pressed garlic, finely minced bell peppers or onions, vegetable salt or freshly ground pepper, or any other condiment and seasoning needed to make your favorite salad dressing—except oil! Let it cool to room temperature to serve. It will stay thick. This dressing base yields 1 cup and is only about 3 calories per tablespoon!

As for store-bought low-calorie dressings, especially the vinaigrette kinds, you can give them zest by adding to the bottle 1 teaspoon to 1 tablespoon prepared horseradish, Dijon mustard, hot red pepper sauce, Worcestershire sauce, tomato paste, "natural-style" catsup, low-sodium tamari, miso, or sherry. Shake well before using.

ABC SUPERSALAD

This cruciferous vegetable salad provides a wealth of nutrients in the form of vitamin A, beta-carotene, and vitamin C. It's rounded off with a healthy buttermilk dressing.

The Salad:

Per serving:
53 calories
5 grams protein
0 grams fat
8 grams
  carbohydrate

1 cup coarsely shredded green cabbage
1 cup coarsely shredded red cabbage
1 cup small broccoli florets
1 cup small cauliflower florets

The Dressing:

Splurge a little!
You can make a richer ranch-style dressing by replacing the yogurt with an equal amount of reduced-calorie safflower oil mayonnaise.

⅔ cup buttermilk
⅓ cup plain nonfat yogurt
2 tablespoons freshly minced white onion
1 large garlic clove
1 teaspoon each dried parsley and dill weed
Vegetable salt and freshly ground pepper to taste

Whir all dressing ingredients in a blender until smooth. Store in an airtight jar and chill overnight. To make salad, mix all the vegetables together in a large serving bowl. Pour dressing over the salad and toss well. *Serves 4.*

Per serving:
224 calories
4 grams protein
21 grams fat
5 grams
  carbohydrate

Want a slimmer Caesar?
There's lots of iron in the egg yolk, but you may omit the yolk and substitute another egg white instead.

Want a richer Caesar?
Add ¼ cup of freshly grated Parmesan cheese to the dressing ingredients.

SPINACH SUPERSALAD

This salad is high in vitamin A, vitamin C, and iron, with each of these nutrients helping to boost the absorption of the other. It's tossed with a super Caesar dressing.

The Salad:

1 bunch spinach leaves (about ½ pound), torn
1 large carrot, julienned
1 red bell pepper, cut into thin strips
8 large mushrooms, thinly sliced

The Dressing:

1 raw egg
⅓ cup extra-virgin olive oil
¼ cup freshly squeezed lemon juice
2 garlic cloves
1 anchovy (or substitute 1 teaspoon Worcestershire sauce)
¼ teaspoon freshly ground pepper
Vegetable salt to taste

Whir all dressing ingredients in a blender until smooth but not thick. Store in an airtight jar and chill overnight. To make the salad, mix all salad ingredients together in a large serving bowl. Pour in Caesar dressing and toss well. *Serves 4.*

WALDORF SUPERSALAD

Here's a delightful variation of a Waldorf salad using two different kinds of summer squash, known for their high vitamin A and beta-carotene content. But "hold the mayo" with this light oil and vinegar dressing.

The Salad:

Per serving:
191 calories
12 grams protein
16 grams fat
12 grams
   carbohydrate

2 zucchini, coarsely shredded
2 yellow crookneck squash, coarsely shredded
2 red apples, cored and coarsely chopped
1 large celery rib, thinly sliced
1 scallion, thinly sliced
½ cup chopped walnuts

The Dressing:

¼ cup safflower oil
3 tablespoons cider vinegar
1 tablespoon unsweetened apple juice concentrate
¼ teaspoon dry mustard
Vegetable salt and freshly ground pepper to taste

Toss vegetables and walnuts in a large serving bowl. Whisk dressing ingredients together in a cup, pour over the salad, and toss well. Chill 1 hour before serving. *Serves 6.*

THREE-GREEN SUPERSALAD

The slight bitterness in this salad of vitamin A-rich greens is complemented by grapes, pine nuts, and a sweet mustardy dressing.

The Salad:

Per serving:
282 calories
4 grams protein
22 grams fat
17 grams
   carbohydrate

12 curly endive leaves
2 cups loosely packed dandelion greens, torn
1 head Bibb lettuce, torn
½ cup seedless red grapes, halved
⅓ cup pine nuts (pignoli)

The Dressing:

¼ cup safflower oil
1 tablespoon walnut oil
¼ cup white wine vinegar
1½ tablespoons raw honey
1 tablespoon prepared brown mustard
1 small shallot
½ teaspoon dried tarragon
Freshly ground pepper to taste

Whir all dressing ingredients in a blender until creamy. Chill at least 1 hour before serving. Line each of four chilled salad plates with 3 leaves of endive. Toss dandelion greens and Bibb lettuce together. Place equal portions of salad on each bed of endive. Drizzle equal portions of dressing over salads and serve. *Serves 4.*

SUPER VEGGIES WITH SKINNY DIPS

Salads aside, freshly cut raw vegetable snacks are the best way to get a variety of all the super veggies. And don't just keep it down to carrots and celery. Include things you would normally eat cooked to get the full benefit of their nutrients and fiber. Cut them in slices, sticks, stalks, and strips and munch them alone or with low-calorie dips and dressing. Here are six great Skinny Dips, all with just a few calories per tablespoon, along with a list of assorted Super Veggies to go with them. They are perfect for entertaining. Create a vegetable still life on a bed of ice and serve with several dips. Or, if you are just entertaining yourself, keep a bunch of cut vegetables around. They will last for a week in airtight storage containers. Freshen them by rinsing them in cold water, or better yet, keep crunchy vegetables crunchier by floating them in ice water. Even the dips taste better after a day or two. Honestly, you'll love having ready-made nutritional snacks around, especially when you are hungry and you don't want to fix things. And now let the fun begin.

Prepare and enjoy these freshly cut raw Super Veggies with or without any of the dips below and on the following pages.

Asparagus

Bell peppers

Broccoli

Brussels sprouts

Carrots

Cauliflower

Celery (hearts and roots)

Cherry tomatoes

Cucumber

Fennel

Jicama

Mushrooms

Potatoes (all kinds)

Radishes

Scallions

Snap beans

Snow peas

Summer squash (all kinds)

Turnips (all kinds)

CURRIED CUCUMBER DIP

Per 2 tablespoons:

12 calories

1 gram protein

0 grams fat

2 grams
  carbohydrate

1 cup plain nonfat yogurt

½ cucumber, peeled, seeded, and chunked

1 large garlic clove

1 tablespoon curry powder

Vegetable salt to taste

Mint leaves (optional)

Process all ingredients, except mint leaves, in a blender or food processor to a creamy but slightly chunky consistency. Refrigerate in an airtight container. To serve, sprinkle the top of the dip with snipped mint and garnish with whole leaves, if desired. *Makes about 1⅓ cups.*

SMOKED HORSERADISH DIP

Per 2 tablespoons:

55 calories

1 gram protein

4 grams fat

10 grams
  carbohydrate

1 cup Lowest-Calorie Mayonnaise (page 194)

2 tablespoons freshly grated Parmesan cheese

2 tablespoons prepared horseradish

2 freshly pressed garlic cloves

¼ teaspoon liquid smoke (adjust to taste)

"Natural-style" imitation bacon bits (optional)

Mix everything together well, except bacon bits, and refrigerate in an airtight container. To serve, sprinkle the top of the dip with imitation bits, if desired. *Makes about 1¼ cups.*

CHUNKY GUACAMOLE

Per 2 tablespoons:
26 calories
0 grams protein
2 grams fat
2 grams
  carbohydrate

1 large ripe avocado, coarsely mashed
½ cup plain nonfat yogurt
1 ripe tomato, seeded and finely chopped
2 ounces diced mild green chilies
1 freshly pressed garlic clove
Dash of Tabasco sauce
Vegetable salt to taste
Sprig of parsley, snipped

Mix everything together well, except parsley, and refrigerate in an airtight container. Sprinkle with parsley before serving. *Makes about 2 cups.*

POOR BOY PESTO DIP

Per 2 tablespoons:
17 calories
1 gram protein
1 gram fat
1 gram
  carbohydrate

1 package frozen defrosted chopped spinach (undrained)
½ cup 1 percent low-fat cottage cheese
1 egg white
1 tablespoon extra-virgin olive oil
2 garlic cloves
1 tablespoon dried basil
Vegetable salt and freshly ground pepper to taste
Freshly grated Parmesan cheese (optional)

Whir all ingredients, except Parmesan cheese, in a blender until almost smooth. Refrigerate in an airtight container. Before serving, stir in a tablespoon or two of Parmesan cheese, or sprinkle it over the top of the dip if a more robust pesto is desired. *Makes a little over 2 cups.*

HERB AND ONION DIP

Per 2 tablespoons:
45 calories
1 gram protein
4 grams fat
2 grams
  carbohydrate

1 cup Lowest-Calorie Mayonnaise (page 194)
¼ cup chopped fresh scallions (bulb only; finely chop green part and reserve)
¼ cup chopped fresh Italian parsley
2 teaspoons each chopped fresh tarragon and basil
1 large shallot
1 teaspoon prepared yellow mustard
Vegetable salt to taste

Whir all ingredients, except scallion greens, in a blender until tiny green flecks remain. Refrigerate in an airtight container. To serve, sprinkle the top of the dip with reserved scallion greens. *Makes about 1⅓ cups.*

DEVILED EGG AND SHRIMP DIP

Per 2 tablespoons:
42 calories
2 grams protein
3 grams fat
2 grams
  carbohydrate

1 cup Lowest-Calorie Mayonnaise (page 194)
1 large hard-boiled egg
½ cup cooked tiny fresh or frozen defrosted shrimp
2 tablespoons chopped green bell pepper
1½ teaspoons prepared yellow mustard
2 teaspoons chopped fresh dill
½ teaspoon capers
Freshly ground pepper to taste
Radishes, sliced (optional)

Process all ingredients, except radishes, in a blender or food processor to a chunky consistency. Refrigerate in an airtight container. To serve, garnish the top of the dip with radish slices, if desired. *Makes about 2 cups.*

NEW WAVE SEA SALADS

Oh boy, it's time for lunch. It's time to boost your blood sugar and it's time to get your strength back. It's . . . oh no . . . not another can of tuna. And . . . yahoo . . . a boiled potato, too! This isn't your lucky day. But hold on to your weightbelt. It *is* a lucky day if you take along one of these new totable sea salads. For the bodybuilder on the go, or anybody who wants to stay fit, they are a new wave in salad for a new wave in power lunch. They are packed with lean protein and complex carbohydrates—all you need to see you through the day, and in one carryall container. And they even taste better after they have set for a while, so you'll really enjoy them when the time comes to eat. Although they're plenty healthy sans salad greens, "lettuce" help you make a regular salad production out of these with some sensational serving suggestions, too. Yup, these New Wave Sea Salads are powerful, portable, and personal, and with or without the frills, they stand for style. Okay, you can bring your rice cakes!

Fast Tracks

● Gourmet vinegars are expensive to buy and take weeks to make. But you can make your own seasoned vinegar in just a few minutes. Use good naturally aged cider vinegar, wine vinegar (white is milder than red), or rice vinegar.

● For fruit vinegar, whir in a blender 1 cup vinegar, 2 tablespoons raw honey (optional), and about 2 tablespoons of the following fresh or unsweetened frozen fruits: pineapple, raspberries, blueberries, boysenberries, cranberries, nectarines, peaches, pears, plums, grapes, or a slice of orange, tangerine, lemon, or lime. You can also add a little pure vanilla extract, cinnamon, a few cloves, or cardamom seeds.

● For herb vinegar, whir in a blender 1 cup vinegar, a clove of garlic (optional) and a small sprig of one of the following herbs: basil, thyme, tarragon, rosemary, oregano, dill, mint, cilantro, parsley, or 1 tablespoon of chopped chives. Add a little wine, if desired.

● Strain the vinegars through a large sieve lined with cheesecloth or a wet paper towel. Now you have flavor! Drizzle the vinegars over a variety of foods and use them in place of rich salad dressings. They are best used within a day. Or if you feel like waiting a week, drop fresh herb sprigs (dried herbs are okay, too) or pieces of your favorite dried fruit into the vinegar bottle. Adding a few teaspoons of balsamic vinegar will give it an extra zing.

SALMON SALAD MEDLEY

Per serving:
223 calories
24 grams protein
12 grams fat
4 grams
  carbohydrate

Salad suggestion:
If available, add yellow bell peppers to the salad for a festive touch. Serve stuffed in a tomato or on a bed of red-leaf lettuce surrounded by slices of ripe avocado.

1 can (1 pound) red salmon, rinsed and drained
1 green bell pepper, diced
1 red bell pepper, diced
2 tablespoons chopped scallion
¼ cup reduced-calorie safflower oil mayonnaise
1 tablespoon freshly squeezed lemon juice
1 teaspoon Dijon mustard
2 tablespoons minced fresh chervil
Cayenne pepper to taste

In a large covered container, crumble in salmon (crushing fine edible bones), bell peppers, and scallion. Combine remaining ingredients in a small bowl, pour over salmon and vegetables, and lightly toss everything together. Cover and chill for 1 hour. *Serves 4.*

MARINATED SHRIMP AND CUCUMBER SALAD

Per serving:
182 calories
23 grams protein
1 gram fat
21 grams
  carbohydrate

Salad suggestion:
Add mung bean sprouts to the above ingredients. Serve the salad on a bed of watercress, Napa cabbage, or boiled Chinese rice noodles.

½ pound raw tiny fresh or frozen defrosted shrimp
1 small cucumber, peeled, seeded, and chopped
¼ cup finely diced red onion
1 tablespoon chopped fresh cilantro
1 teaspoon minced fresh ginger
½ cup rice vinegar
1½ tablespoons raw honey

In a large covered container, combine all ingredients together well. Cover and let them stand refrigerated for at least 4 hours, tossing several times during marinating. *Serves 2.*

BROWN RICE AND CALAMARI SALAD

Per serving:
238 calories
24 grams protein
9 grams fat
15 grams
  carbohydrate

1¼ pounds cleaned raw baby squid (calamari)
1 cup cooked brown rice
4 shallots, finely chopped
⅓ cup sliced pimiento-stuffed green olives
2 tablespoons minced fresh Italian parsley
2 tablespoons extra-virgin olive oil

Salad suggestion:
Serve on a bed of
spinach leaves or
green-leaf lettuce
accompanied by
roasted red pepper
strips.

1½ tablespoons white wine vinegar (or substitute 1½ tablespoons liquid from the stuffed olives)
Vegetable salt and freshly ground pepper to taste

Slice the main body of the squid into ¼-inch-thick rings and cut the tentacles into small pieces. In a large pot, bring 2 quarts of water to a boil. Drop in squid and drain immediately in a large colander. Rinse squid in cold water to cool and drain again. Toss the squid with remaining ingredients in a large covered container. Cover and let stand refrigerated for several hours before serving. *Serves 4.*

MARINATED ORANGE-SCALLOP SALAD

Per serving:
222 calories
19 grams protein
7 grams fat
21 grams
 carbohydrate

Salad suggestion:
Serve on a bed of
delicate radicchio
leaves or hearts of
romaine. Garnish
with thinly sliced
red radishes.

½ cup each freshly squeezed lime and orange juice
½ pound fresh raw bay scallops
2 oranges, peeled and cut into bite-size chunks
1 tablespoon extra-virgin olive oil
2 tablespoons chopped fresh parsley
⅛ teaspoon sea salt
Freshly ground pepper to taste

Mix lime and orange juice in a large covered container. Toss scallops in with the juice, cover, and let them stand refrigerated for 4 to 6 hours, stirring several times during the marinating. When done, drain scallops and discard the juice. Toss marinated scallops together with remaining ingredients and serve chilled. *Serves 2.*

CRAB COLESLAW

Per serving:
155 calories
12 grams protein
8 grams fat
9 grams
 carbohydrate

Salad suggestion:
For a wave of color,
serve on a bed of
red and green
cabbage leaves.

2 cups finely shredded cabbage
½ cup shredded carrots
1 tablespoon finely minced white onion
⅓ cup reduced-calorie safflower oil mayonnaise
2 tablespoons plain nonfat yogurt
1 tablespoon cider vinegar
2 teaspoons raw honey
¼ teaspoon dry mustard
½ pound cooked fresh or frozen defrosted crabmeat
1 parsley sprig, snipped

In a large bowl, toss all ingredients together well, adding the crab last. Cover and let coleslaw stand refrigerated for at least several hours before serving, sprinkled with parsley. *Serves 4.*

TUNA PICNIC SALAD

No utensils are needed here. Cut the celery ribs in half and store them in a container along with the tuna.

Per serving:
237 calories
23 grams protein
8 grams fat
18 grams
 carbohydrate

Salad suggestion:
Serve on a bed of alfalfa sprouts or butter lettuce with carrots, cucumber, and jicama rounds. Sprinkle with shredded unsweetened dried coconut.

> *1 can (6½ ounces) water-packed albacore, rinsed and drained*
> *¼ cup Lowest-Calorie Mayonnaise (recipe follows)*
> *1 small red apple, cored and finely chopped*
> *1 tablespoon seedless raisins*
> *1 tablespoon raw sunflower seeds*
> *⅛ teaspoon curry powder*
> *4 celery ribs*

Mix all ingredients together, except celery, in a covered container and chill. When ready to eat, fill each celery rib by scooping it into the tuna mixture. *Serves 2.*

LOWEST-CALORIE MAYONNAISE

Per tablespoon:
29 calories
0 grams protein
3 grams fat
1 gram
 carbohydrate

Here's a super low-calorie mayonnaise blend that's ideal for use in cold meat, fish, and salad dishes. It contains only slightly more than a quarter of the calories of regular mayonnaise! Use it in place of the reduced-calorie safflower mayonnaise called for in these recipes if you wish.

Blend together well equal parts reduced-calorie safflower oil mayonnaise and plain nonfat yogurt.

FRUIT SALADS FOR ALL SEASONS

Fruit is a gift of nature. There is nothing else like it that is so abundant, so sweet, so nutritious, and so alive. Fresh fruit is probably your best source of obtaining the essential living enzymes that you can get only from raw food. Fresh fruit, especially the yellow and orange variety, is high in vitamin A in the form of the blockbusters carotene and beta-carotene. All fruits, particularly citrus and tropical fruits, are abundant in vitamin C and its helper, the bioflavonoids. It is by far the most complete and effective source of complex carbohydrates, providing long-lasting energy and vital nourishment at the same time. And fresh fruit is fiber plus, especially the water-soluble kind that is made up of pectins and gums. This type of fiber is known to help regulate glucose metabolism, and to lower blood pressure and harmful cholesterol. In fact, just two pieces of fresh fruit such as apples, bananas, oranges, and pears per day will give you approximately the same amount of the same type of fiber found in ⅓ cup of the highly touted oat bran, the difference being that oat bran is a processed starch, largely devoid of its original nutrients. Fruit is the real thing, and a lot more delicious.

Really, you can't eat too much fresh fruit, especially when you get a bumper crop of your favorite kind. But when you're just ready to try something other than "au naturel," cut up one of these bountiful fruit salads made with seasonal fresh fruits. You'll find fruit salads for all seasons and for all reasons, because they are created to capture the goodness of nature year-round with your good health in mind. Now, what could be more "ap-peeling?"

Healthful Hints

• Cheese and fruit have paired well for centuries and are an intelligent combination in nutrition. Cheese is rich and flavorful and packed with protein and calcium and should not be eliminated from the normal diet. Sweet and juicy fruit is a refreshing complement and is high in vitamins and minerals as well as complex carbohydrates and fiber. One provides what the other doesn't and together they cover the nutritional spectrum. Select your cheeses wisely, choosing either vitally superior, aged raw cheeses or low-fat, low-sodium cheeses. Here are some ideal cheese and fruit compositions for all occasions.
• Gorgonzola cheese, ripe bosc pears, and walnuts
• Wedges of dewy Cranshaw or casaba melons topped with low-fat farmer's cheese and fresh blueberries
• Aged sharp Cheddar cheese and crisp apples
• Low-fat cottage cheese topped with fresh pineapple, bananas, and raw sunflower seeds
• Low-fat Muenster cheese, champagne or muscat grapes, and black walnuts
• Dried figs stuffed with part-skim ricotta cheese alongside wedges of juicy oranges (also try them stuffed with raw almond or cashew butter)
• Low-fat Gruyère cheese, ripe juicy cherries, and almonds
• Low-fat Swiss cheese with red ripe raspberries and hazelnuts
• Wedges of honeydew melon crumbled with feta cheese and pistachios
• Low-fat Monterey Jack cheese with ripe peaches (or dried apricots) and pecans

SUMMER NECTAR SALAD

The complementary nectars and colors of summer are in this cool fruit salad, splashed with a warm poppy seed dressing.

Per serving:
69 calories
1 gram protein
0 grams fat
16 grams
  carbohydrate

¼ *ripe casaba melon, seeded, peeled, and cut into chunks*
2 *large ripe peaches, pitted and sliced*
3 *ripe plums, pitted and chunked*
¾ *cup green seedless grapes, halved*
6 *leaf lettuce leaves*
½ *cup freshly squeezed orange juice, strained*
2 *teaspoons arrowroot (moistened in 2 tablespoons water)*
1 *tablespoon freshly squeezed lemon juice, strained*
1 *tablespoon raw honey*
¼ *teaspoon pure vanilla extract*
1 *teaspoon poppy seeds*

Toss all the fruits together and place them in a large serving bowl lined with lettuce leaves. Chill.

In a small saucepan, heat orange juice just to boiling. Add moistened arrowroot and stir for 10 to 15 seconds until thick. Remove saucepan from heat and stir in lemon juice, honey, vanilla, and poppy seeds until blended. Pour warm dressing over cold fruits. *Serves 6.*

STRAWBERRIES ON THE GREEN

Spring is another word for strawberry, and strawberry is another word for vitamin C. For something refreshing, try this light minty brunch salad tossed with strawberries and a basil dressing.

Per serving:
76 calories
1 gram protein
5 grams fat
7 grams
  carbohydrate

1 *head butter lettuce, torn*
½ *cup loosely packed fresh mint leaves*
1 *pint ripe strawberries, hulled and sliced*
2 *tablespoons safflower oil*
1 *tablespoon freshly squeezed lime juice*
1 *tablespoon white wine vinegar*
1 *tablespoon raw honey*
1 *teaspoon dried basil*

Mix lettuce, mint, and strawberries in a large serving bowl. Combine dressing ingredients, pour over salad, and toss well. *Serves 6.*

HI-PO FRUIT SALAD

Made with fruits containing the highest amount of potassium, this succulent fruit salad gets a boost with high-potassium dressing of yogurt and blackstrap molasses. All these fruits are available in the summer.

Per serving:
136 calories
4 grams protein
0 grams fat
31 grams
  carbohydrate

2 oranges, cut into bite-size sections
2 ripe nectarines, pitted and sliced
2 bananas, sliced
1 ripe papaya, seeded, peeled, and cut into bite-size chunks
1 cup plain nonfat yogurt
¼ cup blackstrap molasses
½ teaspoon ground ginger

Combine fruits in a large serving bowl. In a smaller bowl, blend yogurt, molasses, and ginger together. Cover both bowls and refrigerate until ready to use. Just before serving, gently toss the fruit with the dressing. *Serves 6.*

AUTUMN APPLE SLAW

Autumn stands for apples, and this nutty crunchy fruit salad is perfect for fall.

Per serving:
125 calories
2 grams protein
6 grams fat
17 grams
  carbohydrate

2 cups coarsely chopped apples (your favorite kind)
1½ cups coarsely shredded cabbage
½ cup finely chopped fresh pineapple (or substitute one 8-ounce can
    crushed unsweetened pineapple, drained)
⅓ cup chopped pecans
¼ cup seedless golden raisins
½ cup Lowest-Calorie Mayonnaise (page 194)
¼ cup sweetened pineapple juice concentrate

Mix salad ingredients in a large bowl. Blend mayonnaise and pineapple juice concentrate together and add to the salad ingredients until well combined. Cover and chill 1 hour to 1 day before serving. *Serves 8.*

ISLAND FRUIT SALAD

Here's a tropical "high-C" salad made with fragrant, passionate mango and papaya. It's topped with an unusual papaya seed dressing.

Per serving:
116 calories
1 gram protein
5 grams fat
17 grams
   carbohydrate

1 bunch watercress
1 large ripe papaya, peeled and sliced (reserve 1 teaspoon of papaya seeds)
1 ripe mango, pitted, peeled, and cut into chunks
½ cup fresh pineapple chunks
2 ripe kiwi, peeled and sliced
¼ cup freshly squeezed orange juice
2 tablespoons freshly squeezed lime juice
2 tablespoons safflower oil
1 teaspoon prepared yellow mustard
½ teaspoon raw honey

Arrange watercress in a bed on a round platter. Fan the slices of papaya over the watercress in pinwheel fashion. Combine mango and pineapple chunks in the center. Decorate with kiwi slices and chill.

Add to a blender the orange and lime juice, oil, mustard, honey, and reserved papaya seeds and whir just until tiny black flecks remain. Drizzle dressing over salad. *Serves 6.*

CALYPSO COMPOTE

In the dead of winter you can enjoy the Caribbean with the sweetest and heartiest fruits available in this yummy, rummy fruit cup.

Per serving:
95 calories
1 gram protein
1 gram fat
21 grams
   carbohydrate

Nutty note:
Serve fruit cups topped with freshly grated nutmeg or chopped macadamia nuts.

¼ cup pitted and chopped dates
2 tablespoons shredded fresh or unsweetened dried coconut
¼ cup light rum
1 large pink grapefruit
2 ripe bananas, sliced
⅔ cup fresh pineapple chunks

In a large covered container, mix dates with coconut and rum. Cover and let stand for 1 to 2 hours. Cut grapefruit in half. Remove sections with a grapefruit knife and add to date-coconut mix, along with bananas and pineapple. Toss everything together lightly. Spoon into individual compote cups and chill. *Serves 6.*

SUPER-C FRUIT SALAD

This beautiful and citrusy fruit palette is made with a pink guava dressing. Guavas are the highest in vitamin C of all the fruits, bar none. Kiwi is next, with oranges and grapefruits running a close third. All are available in the winter or year-round.

Per serving:
126 calories
2 grams protein
0 grams fat
30 grams
  carbohydrate

2 small grapefruit, peeled and sliced crosswise
2 large oranges, peeled and sliced crosswise
3 ripe kiwi, peeled and sliced crosswise
4 large ripe guavas
Juice of 1 lime
2 tablespoons raw honey (or to taste)
Mint sprigs

Arrange grapefruit, orange, and kiwi slices decoratively on a large platter. Cut guavas in half, scoop out the seeds, and discard them. Or scoop out very ripe guava flesh and press it through a sieve to remove the seeds. Spoon the pulp into a blender, add lime juice and honey, and whir everything until smooth. Drizzle guava dressing over salad and garnish with mint sprigs. *Serves 6.*

Photo: Bob Gardner

— 12 —
DESSERTS

DESSERTS TO DIET FOR

Fast Tracks
If you have too many pears, nectarines, peaches, or bananas that ripen at once, puree them with a couple of ice cubes and a flavoring extract and use them as a topping over cottage cheese, yogurt, or frozen yogurt. Freeze what you don't use.

Can you remember the last time you ate a sinful dessert? You just couldn't say no, then you just couldn't wait until you got to the gym to work it off. You swore up and down you'd never do it again . . . until the next time. If that sounds familiar, then listen to this: meringue toppings, coconut crusts, fresh fruit fillings, and fruit juice glazes in tantalizing tortes, tarts, puddings, and parfaits—they're totally tempting yet entirely healthy, all unrefined and designed to keep your blood sugar stable while satisfying that reckless urge. So why go and do something to die for (again!) when you can diet on these dazzling desserts without an ounce of remorse? Now, if that doesn't knock your gym socks off, nothing will.

FRESH BANANA PUDDING

Per serving:
104 calories
3 grams protein
0 grams fat
23 grams
  carbohydrate

1 cup nonfat milk
1 cup evaporated nonfat milk
2 tablespoons arrowroot
3 tablespoons raw honey
1 teaspoon pure vanilla extract
Pinch of sea salt
2 ripe bananas, mashed

Heat 1½ cups of the milk, just to boiling, in a small nonstick saucepan. Dissolve arrowroot and remaining milk and add to the saucepan. Stir constantly for 10 to 15 seconds, until mixture begins to thicken. Reduce

201

FRESH BANANA PUDDING *(continued)*

heat to low and add honey, vanilla, and a pinch of sea salt, if desired. Stir constantly for 1 minute more. Remove the saucepan of thickened milk from the heat and stir in bananas until well blended. Serve warm or chilled. *Serves 6.*

Rich banana pudding: Add 1 or 2 egg yolks (along with honey) to the thickened milk mixture after you have reduced the heat. Stir constantly for 1 minute as directed.

Banana rice pudding: Stir in 1 to 2 cups of plain cooked brown rice to finished pudding mixture.

Banana coconut pudding: Substitute 1 cup of Coconut Milk (page 103) for 1 cup of nonfat milk. Add shredded unsweetened dried coconut, if desired.

Banana rum pudding: Add ¼ teaspoon of rum extract along with the vanilla.

APRICOT-ALMOND TORTE

The crust is pure egg whites!

Per serving:
137 calories
4 grams protein
3 grams fat
24 grams
    carbohydrate

4 egg whites, warmed to room temperature
1 tablespoon raw honey
½ teaspoon freshly squeezed lemon juice
Safflower oil
½ cup unsweetened filtered pear or apple juice concentrate
½ cup water
2 teaspoons arrowroot
1 teaspoon almond extract
½ teaspoon pure vanilla extract
12 fresh soft ripe apricots, pitted, peeled, and halved
¼ cup sliced almonds

Helpful hint:
Sometimes soft apricots are hard to find. If they are not quite ripe enough to peel, roll them around on a hard surface with the

In a large bowl, beat egg whites with an electric mixer until foamy. Drizzle in honey and lemon juice and continue beating until stiff but moist peaks form.

Lightly oil a large nonstick baking sheet, torte, or pizza pan and wipe off the excess with a paper towel. With a large wet spoon, spread meringue evenly into a large circle about ¾ inch thick, shaping it with a slight rise around the rim. Bake in a preheated 250-degree oven for about 1 hour. Then turn the oven off and let the meringue shell stand

palm of your hand to "bruise" them. This will loosen the skin and help make them juicier as well. Or you can use dried apricot halves for this recipe by rehydrating them in enough hot water to cover for 30 minutes before using.

another 1½ to 2 hours in the oven, until dried out completely. When this is done, run a spatula under and around the shell and carefully slide it off onto a large round cake or serving plate.

In a medium-size saucepan, combine juice concentrate plus ¼ cup of the water. Bring it to a slow boil. Dissolve arrowroot in remaining ¼ cup of water along with almond and vanilla extracts and pour into saucepan. Lower heat to a simmer and stir 10 to 15 seconds, or just until mixture begins to thicken. Remove saucepan from heat and immediately spread half the glaze mixture over the meringue crust. Arrange apricot halves on the top of the glazed shell in a decorative fashion. Spoon remaining glaze over the fruit and sprinkle with sliced almonds. Cut the torte with a sharp pointed knife. *Serves 6.*

Per serving:
70 calories
4 grams protein
0 grams fat
13 grams
 carbohydrate

If you must:
For a more traditional zabaglione, use egg yolks, omitting 1 beaten egg white for every egg yolk you use. Whisk together egg yolk(s), port, and fructose in a small double boiler. Cook over boiling water, whisking constantly until mixture is thick and frothy. Then fold it into any amount of egg white you are using.

STRAWBERRIES WITH ZABAGLIONE

Zabaglione is a rich and famous Italian dessert topping made with egg yolks and sometimes whipping cream. Here is an excellent fat-free rendition.

4 egg whites, warmed to room temperature
3 tablespoons port wine
2 tablespoons granulated fructose
1 pint large ripe strawberries, rinsed and hulled
1½ teaspoons finely grated orange peel

In a large bowl, beat egg whites with an electric mixer until foamy. In a very small saucepan, bring port to a boil and immediately remove it from the heat. Add fructose and stir for 10 seconds, until dissolved. Stir port and fructose into egg white foam until well combined. Pour half the port foam into four large stemmed dessert glasses. Add strawberries and top with equal amounts of remaining port foam. Sprinkle the tops with grated orange peel. Serve at once. *Serves 4.*

Per ounce:
20 calories
1 gram protein
0 grams fat
4 grams
  carbohydrate

Super low-calorie option:
Omit honey and water and substitute 6 packets of NutraSweet along with an additional ⅓ cup of cold water. This brings the frozen yogurt down to 13 calories per ounce with 2 grams of carbohydrate. If you want a richer frozen yogurt, use nonfat milk instead of water.

Per serving:
220 calories
3 grams protein
5 grams fat
43 grams
  carbohydrate

CHERRY VANILLA FROZEN YOGURT

1 cup plain nonfat yogurt
2 egg whites
⅔ cup ice water
3 tablespoons raw honey (diluted in 3 tablespoons hot water)
1 teaspoon pure vanilla extract
1 cup fresh pitted sweet cherries, frozen (or substitute unsweetened
    frozen cherries)

Add all ingredients, except cherries, to a food processor and process at a low speed until smooth and foamy. Gradually add frozen cherries and pulse-blend until small fruit flecks remain. Cover container and freeze about 3 hours. When frozen, remove the container from the freezer and pulse-blend again until smooth. Freeze again for another 1 to 2 hours. Pulse-blend once more to desired consistency just before serving. *Makes about 24 ounces.*

CARAMEL-PECAN FILLED APPLES

4 golden apples
1 cup unsweetened apple juice (or substitute water)
⅔ cup pure maple syrup
⅓ cup evaporated nonfat milk
¼ cup chopped pecans

Peel and core apples, being careful not to cut through the bottoms. Place them in an 8- or 9-inch-square covered baking dish along with the apple juice. Cover tightly and bake in a 350-degree oven for about 45 minutes, or until apples are tender.

Fifteen minutes before apples are done, bring maple syrup and evaporated milk to a boil in a medium-size nonstick saucepan. Cook and stir constantly for 7 to 8 minutes, until mixture is reduced to a little less than half. Remove saucepan from heat, stir in pecans, and keep sauce warm.

When apples are cooked, baste them once with the apple juice. Remove them from the baking dish and place each one in an individual dessert bowl. Fill each apple center with just enough caramel-pecan filling to let it overflow the top a bit. *Serves 4.*

PEACH PARFAIT WITH HONEY-NUT TOPPING

The Parfait:

1 cup plain nonfat yogurt
4 large ripe peaches, pitted, peeled, and sliced
3 tablespoons raw honey
1 teaspoon pure vanilla extract
1 packet unflavored gelatin
¼ cup cold water

The Topping:

⅓ cup raw wheat germ
3 tablespoons chopped walnuts
1½ tablespoons raw honey

Per serving:
233 calories
9 grams protein
5 grams fat
41 grams
    carbohydrate

Sweet note:
Unsweetened frozen
fruits generally can
be found in
supermarket or
health food stores
that have a frozen
food section. The
sweetness and
consistency of
raspberries (and
other fruits as well)
may vary when
bought frozen. If
they taste flat, add 1
tablespoon freshly
squeezed lemon
juice for water, plus
1 tablespoon of
granulated fructose
(or to taste) before
blending. Then,
depending on
thickness, add more
or less water as
needed.

Combine half the yogurt, peach slices, honey, and vanilla in a food processor or blender and process until smooth. In a very small saucepan, soften gelatin in the cold water for 5 minutes, then stir over low heat until completely dissolved. Add gelatin to yogurt mixture and process about 10 seconds more. Arrange half the remaining peach slices on the bottom of four large stemmed dessert glasses. Top equally with half the yogurt mixture. Add another layer of the remaining peach slices and top with remaining yogurt mixture. Chill.

In a small bowl, mix 3 tablespoons of the wheat germ, walnuts, and honey together until well combined and crumbs form. Sprinkle with remaining wheat germ and toss until crumbs are dry-coated, not sticky. Sprinkle the top of each parfait with equal amounts of the nut topping. *Serves 4.*

LEMON MERINGUE TARTS WITH
COCONUT CRUST

The Crust:

Per tart:
268 calories
4 grams protein
11 grams fat
31 grams
   carbohydrate

1 cup finely shredded unsweetened dried coconut
²/₃ cup whole wheat pastry flour
3 tablespoons safflower oil
2 tablespoons granulated fructose

The Lemon Filling:

²/₃ cup granulated fructose
4 tablespoons arrowroot
Pinch of sea salt
2 tablespoons whole wheat pastry flour
1¹/₄ cups hot water
3 egg yolks, lightly beaten
¹/₃ cup freshly squeezed lemon juice
1¹/₂ teaspoons grated lemon peel

The Meringue Topping:

4 tablespoons granulated fructose
1 tablespoon arrowroot
¹/₂ cup cold water
4 egg whites, warmed to room temperature
³/₄ teaspoon pure vanilla extract

For the crust, mix everything together in a large bowl with fingers until well combined. Using your finger or the back of a wet teaspoon, press equal amounts of the crust mix onto the bottom and sides of 8 tart tins. Bake them in a 350-degree oven for about 15 minutes, until crusts are golden. Remove them from the oven and let them cool.

For the filling, combine fructose, arrowroot, and salt in a large nonstick saucepan. Moisten flour in ¹/₃ cup of the hot water and stir it into the remaining hot water until it is smooth. Slowly stir the hot water and flour into saucepan of fructose and arrowroot. Bring mixture to a boil over medium-high heat, then reduce to low heat, stirring constantly for about 8 minutes. Remove saucepan from the heat and stir in egg yolks. Bring mixture to a second boil over medium-high heat, then reduce to low heat, stirring constantly for about 4 minutes. Remove the saucepan from the heat once more and slowly stir in lemon juice along with lemon peel. Turn filling into cooled tart crusts.

For the topping, combine fructose, arrowroot, and water in a small saucepan and stir until mixture dissolves. Bring to a boil over medium-high heat, stirring constantly for 10 to 15 seconds, until mixture thickens. Remove the saucepan from the heat and let it cool. In a large bowl, beat egg whites and vanilla with an electric mixer until stiff, but not dry, peaks form. Stir fructose and arrowroot mixture into egg whites just until blended. Spread an equal amount of the meringue mixture over the top of each tart. Bake in a preheated 350-degree oven for 10 to 12 minutes, until meringue tops are golden brown. Remove them from the oven and let them cool to room temperature before serving. *Makes 8 tarts.*

PEARS WITH RASPBERRY PUREE IN SWEET "CRÈME FRAÎCHE"

Per serving:
160 calories
8 grams protein
3 grams fat
27 grams carbohydrate

Too rich or too thick: For a richer "crème fraîche," use half ricotta and half buttermilk. If you want it thicker but not richer, substitute plain nonfat yogurt for the buttermilk.

1 cup buttermilk
½ cup part-skim ricotta cheese
2 tablespoons granulated fructose
¾ teaspoon pure vanilla extract
2 large ripe pears, halved, peeled, and cored
8 ounces fresh or unsweetened frozen defrosted raspberries
1 to 2 tablespoons water
Mint sprigs

In a blender, whir buttermilk, ricotta, fructose, and vanilla together at low speed. Pour equal amounts of the mixture into four shallow individual dessert bowls. Place 1 pear half, flat side down, in each bowl of the crème mixture. Then puree undrained raspberries in a blender until slushy. Add water, if needed. Pour equal amounts of the puree over each pear half and garnish with a sprig of mint. *Serves 4.*

CHEESECAKE FANTASIES

Come to Cheesecake Fantasies, where calories *are* a fantasy but richness and taste are the real thing. These cheesecakes are so creamy and delicious you won't even know you're eating cheesecake with half the calories of the blowout stuff. And that's not all. Made with high quality, low-fat dairy products, calorie for calorie their protein and calcium value is higher than most other dairy, grain, or bean dishes, making these cheesecakes the ultimate bodybuilding dessert. So come and revel in Cheesecake Fantasies and discover that you can now have your cheesecake and eat it too!

Baking Note: If a cheesecake becomes too brown on top before it's done, cover the pan or tin loosely with foil, but do not let it touch the cheesecake. Remove the foil immediately when it's done baking. If there is doubt whether the cheesecake is done, it should be slightly quivery, but not liquidy, when jiggled. Before placing a cheesecake in the refrigerator, cool it to room temperature, otherwise it will collect moisture and you will end up with a cheesecake that is mushy on top and soggy on the bottom. When storing a cheesecake in the refrigerator for more than a day, keep it tightly covered to prevent it from taking on the flavor and odor of other items in the refrigerator. This will also keep it moist.

CHEESECAKE CRUST

To make a great cheesecake, a good cookie-like crust is a must. If you use the proper ingredients, it should have a praline flavor and crunchiness. Here's how. Start with a 9-inch springform or regular pie tin. For a fancier cheesecake, you can use a deep torte pan with a removable bottom so that the cheesecake can be lifted out and placed on a serving platter. With the right crust, a free-standing cheesecake holds up very elegantly.

Per slice:
143 calories
2 grams protein
7 grams fat
20 grams
   carbohydrate

8 ounces ''natural-style'' whole wheat honey wheat graham crackers, crushed
4 tablespoons butter, softened
2 tablespoons raw honey (or maple syrup)
½ teaspoon pure vanilla extract

Using a blender or food processor, grind crushed graham crackers to a fine but not powdery consistency. Then mix in well the softened butter, raw honey (or maple syrup), and vanilla extract.

Using your fingers, press the mixture tightly and evenly in the pie tin to form a crust on the bottom and along the sides. Bake crust in a preheated 400-degree oven for 10 minutes, or until slightly browned. Remove it from the oven and let it cool completely before adding the cheesecake filling. This is very important so that you do not trap any heat that will turn to moisture and cause the crust to become soggy. *Makes 1 pie crust, enough for 10 slices.*

Cheesecake crust fantasies: For a variation you can add ¼ cup very finely chopped nuts to the crust mixture. Suggestions are macadamia nuts for the Double-Rich Pineapple Cheesecake, pecans for the Maple-Carob Cheesecake, almonds for the Strawberry-Amaretto Cheesecake, and walnuts for the Fluffy Orange Cheesecake. For a tropical touch, spice up the crust by adding ½ teaspoon ground cinnamon, ginger, or cardamom. Or you can make a nut-only crust without any flour. Mix together 1½ cups finely ground nuts and 1½ tablespoons softened butter, blended with 2 tablespoons raw honey and ½ teaspoon pure vanilla extract.

MAPLE-CAROB CHEESECAKE

Chocolate lovers must try this rich but light cheesecake made with part-skim ricotta cheese. It has the delicately nutty flavor of natural carob (a healthy substitute for chocolate) and is accented with the sweetness of pure maple syrup.

Per slice (including crust):
318 calories
11 grams protein
12 grams fat
38 grams carbohydrate

4 eggs, separated and warmed to room temperature
⅔ cup pure maple syrup
1 pint part-skim ricotta cheese
2 tablespoons whole wheat pastry flour
1 cup plain nonfat yogurt
2 tablespoons Carob Syrup (recipe follows)
1 teaspoon pure vanilla extract
1 Cheesecake Crust (recipe opposite)

In a large bowl, beat egg whites with an electric mixer until soft peaks form. In another bowl, beat maple syrup, ricotta, flour, yogurt, carob syrup, and vanilla until soft and creamy. Add egg yolks, one at a time, and continue beating until well blended. Gently fold in egg whites and pour into prepared crust. Bake in a preheated 350-degree oven for 1¼ hours. Turn off oven and let cheesecake stand for 30 minutes before removing. Cool to room temperature and chill. *Makes 10 slices.*

CAROB SYRUP

Mix equal parts of sifted roasted carob powder and water in a small nonstick saucepan. Bring to a boil over low heat and stir constantly for about 5 minutes, or until syrup is smooth and lump-free. Sweeten it with your favorite natural sweetener if you want to use it on other desserts that call for chocolate syrup.

STRAWBERRY-AMARETTO CHEESECAKE

Here it is—a no-bake cheesecake! Amaretto-soaked strawberries make this easy recipe an impressive dessert.

Per slice (including crust):
255 calories
7 grams protein
8 grams fat
42 grams
 carbohydrate

Another berry good option:
In place of strawberries, any seasonal berries or nectary fruits— nectarines, peaches, plums—soaked in your favorite liqueur can be substituted without otherwise changing the recipe.

1 pint fresh strawberries, washed and hulled (or substitute one 12-ounce package unsweetened frozen defrosted strawberries)
½ cup amaretto liqueur
Raw honey to taste
2 tablespoons freshly squeezed lemon juice
1½ tablespoons arrowroot
1 Cheesecake Crust (page 208)
1 packet unflavored gelatin
2 tablespoons boiling water
1 cup nonfat milk
1 cup 1 percent low-fat cottage cheese
¼ cup raw honey
¼ teaspoon almond extract

Soak strawberries in amaretto (and honey to taste, depending on sweetness of strawberries) and chill for several hours. Drain and reserve 2 tablespoons of the amaretto. Combine it with the lemon juice in a small nonstick saucepan. Dissolve arrowroot in the reserved amaretto and bring it to a boil, stirring constantly for about 1 minute, or until very thick. Remove it from the heat, let cool until just warm, and stir in strawberries. Spread mixture over the bottom of the crust and chill.

In a small bowl, dissolve gelatin in boiling water. Combine milk, cottage cheese, honey, and almond extract in a blender or food processor and blend until creamy. Add gelatin mixture to the cheese mixture and continue to blend until smooth. Carefully spread cheesecake mixture over the strawberry mixture and chill for 1 hour before serving. *Makes 10 slices.*

FLUFFY ORANGE CHEESECAKE

Similar to the popular New York–style cheesecake, this one is a slimmer, healthier version with just a hint of orange.

Per slice (including crust):
269 calories
12 grams protein
9 grams fat
36 grams
   carbohydrate

1 pint 1 percent low-fat cottage cheese
1 cup buttermilk
½ cup raw honey
3 tablespoons freshly squeezed orange juice
1 tablespoon grated orange rind
1 teaspoon pure vanilla extract
4 eggs, separated and warmed to room temperature
½ teaspoon cream of tartar
1 Cheesecake Crust (page 208)

Blend cottage cheese, buttermilk, honey, orange juice, orange rind, and vanilla in a blender or food processor until smooth. Add egg yolks and process once more, just until blended. In a large bowl, beat egg whites with an electric mixer until foamy. Add cream of tartar and continue beating until stiff, but not dry, peaks form. Carefully fold cheese mixture into egg whites until blended. Turn into prepared crust.

Bake in a preheated 350-degree oven for 1¼ hours. Turn off oven and let cheesecake stand for 1 hour more before removing. Cool thoroughly and chill. *Makes 10 slices.*

TROPICAL TOFU CHEESECAKE

Here's a unique recipe for people with a special diet who may want to try something different. It contains no eggs or dairy products, and if you prefer, you may omit the honey since it is quite sweet on its own. Surprisingly delicious, this rich treat is truly tofu in paradise.

Per slice (including crust):
308 calories
8 grams protein
15 grams fat
41 grams
   carbohydrate

1 cup unsweetened pineapple juice
½ cup shredded unsweetened dried coconut
1 packet unflavored gelatin
2 tablespoons boiling water
½ cup pitted, chopped dates
½ cup chopped unsweetened dried papaya
½ cup Cashew Milk (recipe follows)
1 tablespoon raw honey

TROPICAL TOFU CHEESECAKE *(continued)*

16 ounces firm tofu, crumbled
1 ripe banana
2 tablespoons safflower oil
1 tablespoon freshly squeezed lemon juice
1 teaspoon pure vanilla extract
1 Cheesecake Crust (page 208; omit butter and use ¼ cup safflower oil,
*   if desired)*

In a small nonstick saucepan, bring pineapple juice and shredded coconut to a boil. Reduce heat and simmer for 5 minutes. Then pour mixture into a blender or food processor and blend for 30 seconds. Strain mixture through a fine sieve and back into the saucepan.

Dissolve gelatin in boiling water and add to the pineapple-coconut milk. Bring mixture back to a boil and stir until blended. Remove saucepan from the heat and stir in dried fruits, cashew milk, and honey.

In a large bowl, coarsely mash tofu and banana along with oil, lemon juice, and vanilla. Add pineapple-coconut milk and dried fruit back into the blender with the banana-tofu mixture. Blend entire mixture together just until smooth. Pour into prepared crust and chill overnight. *Makes 10 slices.*

CASHEW MILK

Whir 1 part chopped raw cashew (or substitute dry-roasted unsalted) nuts along with 2 parts water in a blender until creamy.

DOUBLE-RICH PINEAPPLE CHEESECAKE

For the cheesecake fantasizer, here is the cheesecake "nonpareil." Naughty, but not so naughty, this two-layer confection originally made with cream cheese and sour cream is deliciously re-created with healthier, lower-calorie ingredients.

The Filling:

Per slice (including crust):
318 calories
10 grams protein
17 grams fat
32 grams
  carbohydrate

12 ounces Neufchâtel cheese, softened
2 eggs
¼ cup granulated fructose
1 teaspoon pure vanilla extract
1 can (20 ounces) crushed unsweetened pineapple, drained
1 Cheesecake Crust (page 208)

The Topping:

1 pint plain nonfat yogurt
1½ tablespoons granulated fructose
1 teaspoon pure vanilla extract

In a large bowl, blend Neufchâtel, eggs, fructose, and vanilla together with an electric mixer until creamy. Stir in pineapple. Pour into prepared crust. Bake in a preheated 375-degree oven for 20 minutes. Remove from oven and let cool for 30 minutes before adding topping.

In a medium-size bowl, whisk topping ingredients together until fructose has dissolved. Spread it evenly over the cooled filling. Bake once more in a preheated 375-degree oven for 5 minutes. Remove from oven and let cool. Chill before serving. *Makes 10 slices.*

CRUSTLESS COTTAGE CHEESECAKE

Here's just what you've been waiting for—a simple cheesecake that's light, luscious, and crustless!

Per piece:
98 calories
9 grams protein
2 grams fat
11 grams
  carbohydrate

2 eggs
2½ cups 1 percent low-fat cottage cheese
⅓ cup raw honey
1 teaspoon each pure vanilla and almond extract
2 tablespoons freshly squeezed lemon juice
Fresh fruit (optional)

Combine all ingredients, except fruit, in a blender and whir until creamy. Place a pan of water on the bottom of the oven, preheated to 350 degrees. Pour cottage cheese mixture into a 9-inch nonstick square baking pan or dish and bake on the top rack of the oven for 45 minutes, until top is golden brown. Remove it from the oven to cool, then chill. Garnish with fresh fruit, if desired. *Makes 9 pieces.*

SMART COOKIES

Spaced-out note:
All cookies should
be spaced about 2
inches apart before
cooking to allow for
expansion.

What's better than one Smart Cookie? One dozen! And that's what you can have if you bake 'em right. These cookies are heaped with more healthy goodies per square inch than any other dumb cookies you've ever had. Each and every cookie recipe is made without either flour, oil, butter, eggs, or sweetener. We call 'em, you pick 'em. Oat bran is featured in one of them (great for the heart), and protein powder in another, so there's no excuse not to eat them—they're all natural. Now, what could be more brilliant than whipping up a batch of these Smart Cookies? I dunno, amino acid Popsicles maybe? Oh well, I can't think of everything.

ALMOND BUTTER COOKIES
(Contain no oil or butter)

Here's a nutty new twist on traditional peanut butter cookies.

Per cookie:
57 calories
2 grams protein
3 grams fat
7 grams
   carbohydrate

1 cup almond butter
⅔ cup raw honey
1 egg
¼ teaspoon each pure vanilla and almond extract
1½ cups whole wheat pastry flour
¾ teaspoon baking soda
4 dozen almond halves for garnish

Nutty fact:
Almond butter is
available in health
food stores. (Go for
raw if you can get
it.) Also try this
recipe using other
nut butters such as
cashew or
macadamia nut,
omitting the almond
extract, if desired.

In a large bowl, combine almond butter, honey, egg, and vanilla and almond extract and mix well. In a medium-size bowl, sift together flour and baking soda and add to almond butter mixture. Stir just enough to blend everything together.

Roll the dough into small balls and form patties about 1½ inches in diameter. Place them on a nonstick baking sheet and gently press an almond half onto the top of each cookie. Bake in a preheated 350-degree oven for 10 to 12 minutes, until lightly browned. Remove the cookies from the baking sheet and place them on a wire rack to cool. *Makes about 4 dozen.*

FRUIT 'N NUT COOKIES
(Contain no eggs or butter)

These scaled-down fruitcake cookies are made with good-for-the-heart monounsaturated peanut oil and are an ideal holiday treat.

Per cookie:
63 calories
1 gram protein
3 grams fat
8 grams
  carbohydrate

½ cup peanut oil
½ cup pure maple syrup
1 teaspoon pure vanilla extract
2¼ cups whole wheat pastry flour
½ cup finely chopped dried apricots
½ cup seedless golden raisins
½ cup chopped pecans

Such a good idea:
Omit 2 tablespoons of oil plus ½ cup flour and replace them with 1 cup shredded carrots for a sweet, moist, lower-calorie cookie.

In a large bowl, blend oil, maple syrup, and vanilla. Stir in flour. Add fruit and nuts and mix everything thoroughly. Form dough into 1-inch balls and place them on a nonstick baking sheet. Press them down lightly to flatten. Bake in a preheated 325-degree oven for 15 to 18 minutes, until golden brown. Remove cookies from baking sheet and place them on a wire rack to cool. *Makes about 4 dozen.*

MACADAMIA-COCONUT MACAROONS
(Contain no flour, oil, butter, or egg yolks)

What more—or less—could you ask for?

Per macaroon:
79 calories
2 grams protein
5 grams fat
7 grams
  carbohydrate

3 egg whites, warmed to room temperature
½ cup raw honey
¼ teaspoon almond extract
2 cups shredded unsweetened dried coconut
½ cup chopped unsalted macadamia nuts

In a large bowl, beat egg whites with an electric mixer until soft peaks form. Then add honey, together with almond extract, in a fine stream and continue beating for several more minutes until meringue is stiff but not dry. Gently fold in coconut and macadamia nuts. Drop teaspoonfuls of the macaroon mixture onto a large nonstick baking sheet. Bake in a 350-degree oven for 18 to 20 minutes. Remove macaroons immediately from the baking sheet and place them on a wire rack to cool. *Makes about 2 dozen.*

SUNSHINE COOKIES
(Contain no butter or egg yolks)

These delicious, delicate tasting cookies will make your heart smile with cholesterol-lowering oat bran.

Per cookie:
36 calories
1 gram protein
2 grams fat
5 grams
  carbohydrate

Oat note:
Use oat bran cereal flakes that contain oats and nothing else.

¼ cup safflower oil
⅓ cup raw honey
1 egg white
3 tablespoons freshly squeezed orange juice
2 teaspoons grated orange rind
½ teaspoon pure vanilla extract
1 cup oat bran flakes, finely crushed
½ cup whole wheat pastry flour
½ teaspoon baking soda
¼ cup sesame seeds

In a medium-size bowl, beat oil, honey, egg white, orange juice, orange rind, and vanilla together with an electric mixer until well blended. In a smaller bowl, combine oat bran flakes, flour, and baking soda.

Add dry mixture to liquid mixture and blend thoroughly. Drop dough in even-shaped teaspoonfuls onto a nonstick baking sheet. Sprinkle cookie tops with sesame seeds.

Bake in a preheated 350-degree oven for 8 to 10 minutes, until edges turn golden. Remove cookies from baking sheet and place them on a wire rack to cool. *Makes about 3 dozen.*

GINGERBREAD MUSCLEMAN COOKIES

(Contain no egg yolks)

This old-fashioned favorite is boosted with protein powder to give it more goodness per calorie. Cut out cookie shapes or make "gingerbread musclemen" using a stencil.

Per cookie:
39 calories
1 gram protein
1 gram fat
6 grams
  carbohydrate

4 tablespoons butter, softened (or substitute ¼ cup safflower oil)
⅔ cup blackstrap molasses
2 egg whites
2 cups whole wheat pastry flour
1 teaspoon baking soda
1½ teaspoons ground ginger
1 teaspoon each ground cloves and cinnamon
½ cup unflavored milk and egg protein powder

In a large bowl, combine butter, molasses, and egg whites and beat with an electric mixer until frothy. In a medium-size bowl, mix together flour, baking soda, spices, and protein powder. Add dry mixture to liquid mixture, stirring just enough to blend. Cover dough and chill for several hours or overnight.

Roll dough out on a lightly floured surface to about a ⅛-inch thickness. Cut into shapes using cookie cutters or stencils. Carefully place cookies on a large nonstick baking sheet. Bake in a preheated 350-degree oven for 8 to 10 minutes, until cookies are firm to the touch. Let stand for several minutes, then move them with a spatula to a wire rack to cool. *Makes about 4 dozen regular-size cookies.*

SUGGESTED READINGS

Carper, Jean. *Total Nutrition Guide*. New York: Bantam Books, 1987.

DeVries, Arnold. *The Elixir of Life*. Chicago: Chandler Book Co., 1958.

———. *Primitive Man and His Food*. Chicago: Chandler Book Co., 1952.

Dunne, Lavon J. *Nutrition Almanac* (third edition). New York: McGraw-Hill Publishing Co., 1990.

Fox, Edward L. *Nutrient Utilization During Exercise*. Columbus, OH: Ross Laboratories, 1983.

Gerras, Charles. *Feasting on Raw Foods*. Emmaus, PA: Rodale Press, 1980.

Harris, Marvin. *Good to Eat*. New York: Simon & Schuster, 1985.

Haskell, William L., James Scala, and James H. Whittam. *Nutrition and Athletic Performance*. Palo Alto, CA: Bull Publishing Co., 1982.

Hatfield, Frederick C. *Ultimate Sports Nutrition*. Chicago: Contemporary Books, 1987.

———, Martin Zucker, and David A. Lopez. *Joe Weider Resource Library* (18 volumes). Woodland Hills, CA: Weider Health & Fitness, 1990.

Howell, Edward. *Enzyme Nutrition*. Wayne, NJ: Avery Publishing Group, 1985.

Kennedy, Robert. *Rock Hard!* New York: Warner Books, 1987.

Kenton, Leslie, and Susannah Kenton. *Raw Energy*. London: Century Publishing Co., Ltd., 1984.

Kimber, Tim, et al. *Gold's Gym Nutrition Bible*. Chicago: Contemporary Books, 1986.

Mindell, Earl. *Vitamin Bible*. New York: Warner Books, 1985.

Price, Weston A. *Nutrition and Physical Degeneration*. La Mesa, CA: Price-Pottenger Nutritional Foundation, Inc., 1982.

Reynolds, Bill, and Joyce Vedral. *Supercut: Nutrition for the Ultimate Physique*. Chicago: Contemporary Books, 1985.

Wade, Carlson. *Amino Acid Book*. New Canaan, CT: Keats Publishing, Inc., 1985.

Watt, Bernice L., and Annabel L. Merrill. *Composition of Foods*. Washington, DC: U.S. Department of Agriculture, October 1975.

Weider, Joe. *Bodybuilding Nutrition and Training Programs*. Chicago: Contemporary Books, 1981.

————. *More Bodybuilding Nutrition and Training Programs*. Chicago: Contemporary Books, 1982.

Zane, Frank, and Christine Zane. *Zane Nutrition*. New York: Simon & Schuster, 1986.

INDEX